Rethinking Peace and Conflict Studies

Series Editor: Oliver Richmond, Reader, School of International Relations, University of St. Andrews

Titles include:

Rethinking Peace and Conflict Studies
Series Standing Order ISBN 1–4039–9575-3 (hardback) and 1–4039–9576–1 (paperback)

You can receive future titles in this series as they are published by placing a standing order. Please contact your bookseller or, in case of difficulty, write to us at the address below with your name and address, the title of the series and one of the ISBNs quoted above.

Customer Services Department, Macmillan Distribution Ltd, Houndmills, Basingstoke, Hampshire RG21 6XS, England

Books by the Same Author

John Darby and Roger Mac Ginty eds.
The Management of Peace Processes

Roger Mac Ginty and John Darby
Guns and Government: The Management of the Northern Ireland Peace Process

John Darby and Roger Mac Ginty eds.
Contemporary Peacemaking: Conflict, Violence and Peace Processes

No War, No Peace

The Rejuvenation of Stalled
Peace Processes and Peace Accords

Roger Mac Ginty

First published in 2006 by
PALGRAVE MACMILLAN
Houndmills, Basingstoke, Hampshire RG21 6XS and
175 Fifth Avenue, New York, N.Y. 10010
Companies and representatives throughout the world.

PALGRAVE MACMILLAN is the global academic imprint of the Palgrave
Macmillan division of St. Martin's Press, LLC and of Palgrave Macmillan Ltd.
Macmillan® is a registered trademark in the United States, United Kingdom
and other countries. Palgrave is a registered trademark in the European
Union and other countries.

ISBN-13: 978–1–4039–4661–4 hardback
ISBN-10: 1–4039–4661–2 hardback

This book is printed on paper suitable for recycling and made from fully
managed and sustained forest sources. Logging, pulping and manufacturing
processes are expected to conform to the environmental regulations of the
country of origin.

A catalogue record for this book is available from the British Library.

A catalog record for this book is available from the Library of Congress.

Printed and bound in Great Britain by
CPI Antony Rowe, Chippenham and Eastbourne

*For my father
and the memory of my mother*

Contents

List of Tables and Figures

Tables

Figures

Abbreviations

CTA	Conflict Transformation Agency
DDR	Disarmament, Demobilisation and Reintegration
DFID	Department for International Development
DUP	Democratic Unionist Party
FARC	Revolutionary Armed Forces of Colombia
GDP	Gross Domestic Product
GOL	Government of Liberia
IFI	International Financial Institution
IGAD	Inter-governmental Authority on Development
IMF	International Monetary Fund
IPKF	Indian Peace Keeping Force
IRA	Irish Republican Army
JVP	Janata Vimukthi Peramuna/People's Liberation Front
KLA	Kosovo Liberation Army
LRA	Lord's Resistance Army
LTTE	Liberation Tigers of Tamil Eelam
LURD	Liberians United for Reconciliation and Democracy
MILF	Moro Islamic Liberation Front
MODEL	Movement for Democracy in Liberia
NATO	North Atlantic Treaty Organisation
NCP(M)	Communist Party of Nepal (Maoist)
NGO	Non Governmental Organisation
OSCE	Organization for Security and Co-operation in Europe
PCIA	Peace and Conflict Impact Assessments
PIOOM	Interdisciplinary Research Programme on Root Causes of Human Rights Violations
PLO	Palestine Liberation Organisation
SSR	Security Sector Reform
TNG	Transitional National Government
UNDP	United Nations Development Programme
UNTAC	United Nations Transitional Authority in Cambodia
USAID	United States Agency for International Aid
UUP	Ulster Unionist Party
WTO	World Trade Organisation

About the Author

Roger Mac Ginty is a lecturer at the Department of Politics and the Post-war Reconstruction and Development Unit (PRDU) at the University of York. His previous books include *Contemporary Peacemaking: Conflict, Violence and Peace Processes* and *The Management of Peace Processes* (both edited with John Darby).

Acknowledgements

Two incidents contributed to the approach adopted in this work. The first occurred during a research interview I conducted with the Ambassador from a Middle Eastern state. He showed enormous patience as I repeatedly pressed him to expand upon his meaning of the word 'peace'. A bomb had exploded in the capital city of his home country that morning and he was more than generous with his time. Finally he snapped in the face of my tiresome interview technique. 'Peace!' he barked. 'Why do you Europeans always talk about peace? You don't want peace for us. You want peace for yourselves – so you can feel good about yourselves.' A similar thought-provoking moment occurred during a taxi journey to an airport following a conference. My conference paper, which questioned the western obsession with state-building during peacemaking processes, had gone down poorly among an audience of academics and policymakers who took state-building as their starting point and who were largely committed to econometric methodologies. A fellow conference participant who was sharing the taxi journey turned to me and asked with genuine puzzlement 'So what are you ... some sort of theorist?' For her, and for many other academics and policymakers interested in peacemaking, critical perspectives were of absolutely no relevance to the task of making peace. These incidents, and many more in war-torn societies, have had an enormous influence on my approach to conceptualising peace and peacemaking.

I am indebted to many individuals for their support and help during the writing of this book: Kris Brown, Alan Bullion, Feargal Cochrane, Mick Cox, Cathy Gormley-Heenan, Tim Jacoby, Gráinne Kelly, Jim McAuley, Indika Perera, Tim Shaw, Mark Stuart, Gareth Wardell, Wanda Wigfall-Williams and Andy Williams all deserve my sincere thanks. At York, my colleagues Neil Carter, Sally Carter, Mark Evans, Anna O'Connell, Simon Parker, Jon Parkin and Alp Özerdem have provided support and distraction. Past and present PhD students (Veronique Barbelet, Christine Hamieh, Sarah Holt, Fernando Medina, David Russell and Chrissie Steenkamp) have been sources of inspiration, as have successive classes in the MA in Post-war Recovery Studies. Sultan Barakat, at the Post-War Reconstruction and Development Unit at York, has provided inspiration as well as encyclopaedic knowledge of conflict and reconstruction. The School of Maori and Pacific Development at the

University of Waikato were generous hosts at the beginning of this project. Oliver Richmond kindly provided constructive comments on an earlier draft of this manuscript. I am immensely grateful to John Darby for his sage advice and friendship. I acknowledge the support of Alison Howson at Palgrave and am grateful to the anonymous referee from Palgrave for useful feedback. Countless individuals in societies emerging from civil war have shown immense courtesy and patience in the face of my questions. My niece Niamh Doyle contributed nothing to this work but asked to be mentioned here. Finally, my wife Rosemary deserves the greatest thanks of all: she will be delighted that with the completion of this book, my excuse for delaying redecoration of the bedroom has disappeared.

Introduction

Using the name of peace as a deception,
[they] teach us this manner of feigned
friendship and of destruction by peace.

Hugh O Neill

No war, no peace

In March 2005, 12-year-old Tamil schoolgirl Nagendiram Dushika was knocked down and killed by a speeding military vehicle in Jaffna in the northeast of Sri Lanka. Despite the existence of a ceasefire between the Tamil Tigers and the Government of Sri Lanka, the Jaffna peninsula resembled an armed camp with government troops deployed in large numbers. Friction between local people and the mainly Sinhalese military was common. Frequent road accidents involving military vehicles and allegations of sexual assault against soldiers meant that Jaffna's 'peace' offered only a limited respite from the war. In October 1994, just over a year after the signing of the Declaration of Principles between the Palestine Liberation Organisation (PLO) and the Israeli government, a Hamas suicide bomb killed 22 on a bus in Tel Aviv. During the next 18 months, over one hundred Israelis were killed in suicide attacks, prompting Israel to launch ferocious responses. Such was the 'peace' of Oslo. In July 2005, seven years after Northern Ireland's Belfast Agreement, a Protestant family's north Belfast home came under attack from a rioting Catholic mob. 'It's just because we're Protestants', the head of the household said. In 2004, 447 households living in publicly owned property were intimidated from their homes. In 2003, the figure was 685. Such attacks, many of them casual and opportune, provided a

1

backdrop to Northern Ireland's peace process and peace accord. In 2000, Paulo do Carmo returned to his East Timor home, following displacement amidst earlier fighting. 'We returned from exile to an empty place', he said. 'We did not even have water or food. There were no houses left. Everything had gone.' The prospects for post-war recovery were poor. In the year following Paulo's return, East Timor's Gross Domestic Product fell by 2 per cent, and two years on from independence 41 per cent of the population lived below the poverty line of 55 US cents per day.[1]

All of these examples occurred *after* a peace accord had been reached in a deeply divided society or in the context of a long-standing peace process with established ceasefires. In many cases, the peace accords were comprehensive documents that went far beyond the mere cessation of hostilities between armed groups. Many contemporary peace accords provide for minority protection, the recognition of cultural rights, the redistribution of resources, reconstruction programmes, healing and truth recovery as well as the more traditional issues of constitutional, territorial and security reform. An increasing array of international actors has become involved in supporting the implementation of peace accords, with the United Nations and regional organisations developing sophisticated peace intervention mechanisms. The development agencies of third party states (often highly capable industrialised states) and non-governmental organizations (NGOs) have also been heavily involved in peace-support operations, striving to ensure that disarmament timetables are met, refugees are repatriated, transparent electoral processes are instituted and shattered infrastructure is reconstructed. The enormous hope and moral energy invested by the international community into societies emerging from civil war suggests something close to a universal ideology in favour of peace. The international community's faith and hope has been reinforced by hard cash, in the form of massive development and reconstruction assistance, and by blood through the lives of UN personnel and NGO workers. In many ways, peace accords have never enjoyed such a propitious implementation environment.

Yet as the opening examples illustrate, many contemporary peace accords have failed to deliver durable, high-quality peace. Instead, the peace that prevails is often prefixed with terms attesting to its compromised quality: 'brittle', 'fragile', 'turbulent', 'armed', 'nervous' and so on. Many of the characteristics of the 'prefix peace' resemble those of the war that preceded it: inter-group tension and systematic discrimination against out-groups, widespread insecurity arising from the presence of armed groups, grinding poverty with few prospects for economic advancement, militarism, poor provision of public goods and a profound disconnection between government and people. Rather than peace, many post-peace accord societies experience a 'no war, no peace' situation: a grudging hiatus in violent conflict crowned with an internationally supported peace accord that finds little approval at home after initial enthusiasm has worn off. The accord may have more support in Washington, New York and Geneva than in the post-civil war society. While most direct violence between the main armed groups may cease, other types of violence may persist: spoiling, inter-communal rioting and crime and so on. The indirect violence of inter-group antipathy and intimidation may remain untouched by the peace accord. Public optimism that may have attended the signing of the peace accord may be quickly punctured as the reality of the 'prefix peace' dawns, particularly its failure to effect real quality-of-life changes and the perception that the out-group is the chief beneficiary of the accord. These disappointments may stand in sharp contrast to the national and international hubris that attended the signing of the peace accord, the protections promised by the new constitutional or political dispensation, or the scale of international support for the implementation of the peace accord.

A number of post-peace accord societies have slipped into situations of a grudging acceptance of the need for a co-existence with traditional enemies, but little enthusiasm for a truly transformative peace (for example, Northern Ireland, Lebanon, Bosnia-Herzegovina, Moldova, Ivory Coast, Abkhazia). The enthusiasm that local actors may have shown during the early stages of a peace process or first months following a peace accord becomes difficult to sustain in the midst of intra-party tensions and apparent bad faith by 'the other side'. Organs of the international community, rather than local actors, become the main initiators and implementers of the peace accord. Certainly they are often the actors with the greatest capacity and resources, and local actors may experience difficulty in achieving a sense of ownership of the peace accord: its implementation becomes something that is done to them rather than a process in which they are full participants. In effect, the peace accord becomes stalled. International peace-support programmes and projects (government reform, disarmament, democracy training etc.) may continue apace, rigidly fulfilling the donor's timetable but oblivious to the profound disconnection between local people and the peace accord. The implementation of the peace accord becomes a technocratic exercise of ticking boxes, counting heads and weapons, amending constitutions, and reconstructing housing units, while the more thorny affective and perceptual issues of reconciliation, exclusion, and the restoration of dignity are left unaddressed. Amidst the hubbub of technocratic and neo-institutional peace accord implementation it may be difficult to notice that the peace is not working or that the main parties to the conflict have not actually addressed the core grievances that have caused and maintained the conflict.

No war, no peace situations also prevail in cases of stalled peace processes, wherein the antagonists have failed to reach a comprehensive peace accord but the peace process and its ceasefire assume semi-permanence. The peace process is more comfortable than war, but this comfort brings with it little urgency to push for a far-reaching peace settlement. Sri Lanka, Nepal, Colombia and Israel–Palestine have all witnessed such peace processes at one stage or another, whereby the language of a peace process is used, a routine of inter-group meetings is established and elements of the international community deploy their peace-support machinery and rhetoric. In all four cases, the peace process tottered along making significant advances here and avoiding cataclysmic collapse there. On meeting impasse, the parties – for some-time at least – demurred a resumption of full-scale conflict but failed to seriously re-engage with the peace process. In a sense, the peace process became a comfort zone. The parties could gain international kudos from their involvement in the peace process (however hollow that involve-ment may have become) and could enjoy the advantages of respite that accompany a ceasefire. For all intents and purposes though, the peace process was no longer a vehicle capable of enabling effective conflict transformation.

Outline of the book

This book is concerned with the quality of peace in post-peace accord and stalled peace process societies. Its focus is on civil or intra-state war. Crucially, the book takes a *critical* stance on the nature of contemporary peacemaking. It moves beyond the 'problem-solving' approach that characterises much research and literature on the implementation of peace accords and fulfilment of peace processes. As Herman Schmid's seminal critique of peace studies reminds us, 'problem-solving' approaches are prone to too readily accept the bases of conflict and its management, and to accept contemporary methods of peacemaking as normatively good regardless of the actual impact of the peacemaking.[3] Much research on post-peace accord societies concentrates on recommending how peace accords can be better implemented – in a sense, 'fixing' broken accords. A basic premise of such work is that the peace accord is a blueprint for peace and that the problems of the post-accord society stem from the failure to properly implement the accord. The ubiquity of the problem-solving approach in peace and conflict studies reflects the co-option of many researchers into orthodox peacemaking schemes through the strictures of funding, employment and access to information. By adopting a critical stance, this book identifies many peace accords and peacemaking schemes as part of the problem rather than the 'solution'. To recommend the full implementation of a peace accord without critically examining the nature of the accord and its implementation process may compound the problems of a post-peace accord society. Many contemporary peace accords minister to conflict manifestations rather than causes, reinforce rather than challenge inter-group division, attend to armed groups but neglect less vocal but more vulnerable constituencies and fail to deliver appreciable quality-of-life changes to many inhabitants. In short, they deliver poor quality peace.

This work also adopts an unashamedly normative approach. This may rest uneasily with the increasingly technocratic, positivistic and econometric basis of the social sciences and policymaking. Yet it is entirely legitimate to comment on the *quality* of contemporary peace and peacemaking. Many of the insights and arguments in the book are inspired by first hand observations of shocking and iniquitous conditions in societies 'blessed' by a peace process or accord. In a socially constructed world, it is disingenuous to pretend that there can be a science of peace or peacemaking that is ignorant of affective and human factors.

The key to understanding the nature, successes and failures of contemporary peacemaking is the conceptualisation of peace and peacemaking. This book argues that a distinctive version of peace and peacemaking, called here 'the liberal democratic peace', is gaining increasing hegemony through its promotion by key international actors involved in peace-support interventions. The select group of international organisations, international financial institutions and leading states who initiate, fund and shape many peace accord implementation programmes are sponsoring an increasingly standardised model of peacemaking that is applied in various locations regardless of local circumstances. There is much laudable about the liberal democratic peace model, though its over-rigid application and its dependence on peculiar and western variants of liberalism and democracy explain many of the problems experienced in contemporary post-peace accord societies. Thus it is crucial that any investigation into contemporary peacemaking unpacks the core concepts behind attempts to make peace. Important here are the assumptions that underlie the liberal democratic peace: its apparent universality, its supposed superiority over alternative (often traditional) approaches to peacemaking and its tendency to concentrate on the ending of direct violence rather than addressing the structural factors underlying the conflict.

This work adopts a comparative approach. It is mindful of Stedman's warning against 'glib generalizations', which assume that 'actions and strategies that work in a more benign conflict environment such as Guatemala or Namibia will work in a more demanding environment such as Bosnia or Sierra Leone'.[4] The sheer variety in peacemaking processes (coerced or voluntary; initiated internally or externally; involving two or multiple groups) and peace accords (comprehensive or interim; publicly endorsed or an elite-level compact) presents considerable obstacles to any comparative project. Yet the regularity with which peace accords face the same problems and the increasing standardisation of peace implementation schemes invite comparison. Seemingly disparate examples can help illustrate common experiences facing post-peace accord societies.

Although concentrating on the failings of contemporary peace accords and stalled peace processes, this work is anxious not to be a counsel of doom that chronicles the problems of peace without offering directions towards the attainment of widely enjoyed peace capable of making quality-of-life differences. The aim is not to offer recommendations on how to 'fix' a malfunctioning peace accord or a becalmed peace process. Instead, it is to offer comparative insights into peace-enhancing schemes that worked in one location and may have applicability in another. Caution is required in this endeavour since local exigencies preclude the wholesale transfer of unmodified peace-support methodologies. Yet the mass of peacemaking processes and accords over the past two decades represents a significant repository of experience capable of recommending what works and what doesn't.

The first three chapters of the book conceptualise and unpack key terms central to this work: peace, liberal democratic peace and conflict. In some respects, the proliferation of dysfunctional peace processes and stalled peace accords, and the manner in which they are serviced by NGOs and elements of the international community, reflects a failure to conceptualise and critically interrogate key notions at the heart of peacemaking processes. The term 'peace' in particular has been neglected by peace and conflict studies. It has been blithely accepted as being normatively good regardless of the actions pursued in its name. Since peace is the ultimate aim of the peace journey, it seems sensible, if not essential, that we have some idea of our destination before we start on a journey. Given the regularity with which 'peace' results in compromised 'no war, no peace' situations, it seems appropriate that we conceptualise peace in light of observed evidence. Unlike many studies of peace and peacemaking, a definition of peace is reached and is used to inform the rest of the work. The second chapter conceptualises the variant of peace sponsored by most internationally supported peace interventions: the liberal democratic peace. While acknowledging that the liberal democratic peace has not been rigidly applied in all locations, the chapter notes its tendency towards template-style peace implementation and how the quality of peace it delivers is often far-removed from notions of positive and sustainable peace. To a large extent, the liberal democratic peace provides the intellectual and practical framework for contemporary international peace-support interventions. Its component parts of marketisation, good governance and democratisation shape the experiences of millions in post-peace accord societies.

The third chapter interrogates the notion of conflict. It notes the tendency in much literature to regard violence as a mere manifestation of wider conflict and argues instead that violence is often the shop window of conflict and can contain important evidential clues on the dynamics and intensity of conflict and its propensity to react positively to peace initiatives. Moreover, since peace processes and stalled peace accords often witness more indirect rather than direct violence, it is prudent that we adopt a holistic understanding of violence in order to understand more fully the dysfunction of peace accords. While much academic literature concentrates on conflict escalation, or the trajectory from political tension to overt violence, this chapter argues that we must not overlook conflict maintenance. Most civil wars are, to twist Hobbes' famous quotation, 'nasty, brutish and long' and attention must be paid to the chronic nature of conflicts that enables them to continue over many generations and withstand moderating pressure.[5]

The fourth chapter proposes an experimental peace assessment methodology or diagnostic tool to identify the failings of stalled peace accords and processes. The insights offered by existing conflict assessment models are useful but may lack the critical perspective required to move investigations of stalled peace accords beyond a recipe for 'fixing' a broken implementation mechanism, while ignoring the basic failure of the accord to address core conflict causation and maintenance factors. The proposed critical peace assessment model does not take the partially implemented peace accord as its starting point. Instead, it begins its diagnostic task by encouraging the inhabitants and stakeholders in post-peace accord societies to imagine peace and then analyse their current situation to illustrate the 'peace gap' between their actual experiences of 'peace' and their expectations of peace. Such an approach may seem hopelessly naïve and inadequate in the face of the acute difficulties faced by societies emerging from protracted civil war. Yet critical approaches are required to break the cycle whereby peace-support interventions are restricted to implementing a peace accord regardless of the utility of that accord.

The final three chapters concentrate on key recurring factors that have thwarted peace in many societies that have experienced peace processes and accords over the past two decades: violence, poverty and external intervention. Other peace thwarting issues not covered here (for example, judicial and police reform, reconciliation and remembrance, and the marginalisation of women and other groups) could also illustrate how peace processes and peace accords have failed to deliver sustainable peace, though all studies require boundaries. Many analyses of violence in the context of peace processes and peace accords have dwelt on spoiler violence or deliberate attempts by armed groups to derail peace initiatives. Chapter 5 advances the spoiler debate by distinguishing between deliberate and accidental spoiling, with the latter category having the potential to spoil peace initiatives as a by-product of its original aim. While crime, intra-group feuding and low-level street violence may not harbour the conscious political aim of undermining a peace accord or process, they are still capable of spoiling peace, mainly by puncturing the optimism of the pro-peace constituency required to sustain a peace-making process.

Chapter 6 examines the recurring failure of peace dividends to materialise following peace accords. If peace accord environments are unable to deliver appreciable changes to standards of living, to provide alternative employment to former combatants and sustain reconstruction programmes then it will become irrational for many constituencies to continue to support the peace accord. Many of the economic problems facing societies emerging from civil war are structural in nature and are immune to national-level remedies. Yet some reconstruction processes have shown more success than others. The chapter finds that it was an early case of post-war reconstruction (the Marshall Plan following the Second World War) that offers some of the most valuable lessons for sustainable post-war reconstruction. While the contexts of post-Second World War Europe and contemporary civil wars are vastly different, elements of the processes and ethos behind the Marshall Plan continue to offer valuable – and neglected – insights. The final chapter examines external factors with the potential to thwart the implementation of sustainable peace. In many respects, external actors are often the key to successful peace implementation. They alone may possess the capability to provide basic public security in a post-peace accord territory, to disarm antagonists, finance reconstruction and organise development interventions. Yet peace-support interventions can be counter-productive, thwarting the fulfilment of peace initiatives through inconclusive interventions that freeze rather than transform a conflict. In a significant number of cases, peace processes and peace accords were essentially creatures of the international community, with external third parties showing a good deal more enthusiasm for the peace than the sullen population of the war-torn region. In addition, in some cases 'bad neighbours' have deliberately sought to undermine efforts to reach peace.

The concluding chapter asks 'what works?' The past two decades have witnessed a mass of peacemaking efforts. All of them have had a trial and error quality and there have been many costly failures. Yet, some peace processes, and especially elements within peace processes, have delivered (partial) success. While caution is shown in advocating unrestricted 'lending and borrowing' between peace processes, the conclusion seeks to identify transferable lessons on the management of peace processes and fulfilment of peace beyond the limitation of peace accords. It takes the form of a series of propositions for the rejuvenation or 'kick-starting' of failed peace processes and peace accords. These propositions constitute a radical challenge to the dominance of the liberal democratic peace.

Concluding Discussion

The term 'peace' and the projects initiated in its name are capable of generating tremendous moral energy. Peace processes and peace accords are also frequently the scene of immense political, security and economic activity, much of it supported by the international community, highly visible and of symbolic importance. To criticise peace processes and peace accords risks castigation as an opponent of peace and as a rejectionist of the only serious attempt to rid a state of the scourge of civil war. Cicero's observation that 'an unjust peace is better than a just war' cautions against minimising the benefits that any respite from violence can bring. Yet the mere deployment of the word 'peace' should offer no insulation against critical scrutiny. While many peace processes and peace accords have brought real benefits to the inhabitants and neighbours of societies emerging from civil war, others have limited or even counter-productive impacts.

Perhaps the most common deficiency found in contemporary peace-making processes is their limited ambition. In many ways, this criticism is easy to make and risks minimising the pressures faced by peacemakers. Yet, with remarkable frequency, peace processes are constructed and peace accords signed that reveal an essential conservatism and deliver a peace with questionable durability and equity. Thus, many peace processes and accords deal with conflict manifestations rather than causes, their negotiation and implementation are restricted to local elites and external third parties and exclude whole sections of society in civil war society and the essentially interim measures of ceasefires and armistices are accepted in place of more comprehensive peace settlements. This work is motivated by the need to conceptualise and explain stalled peace processes and accords. At one level, a 'stalled' peace accord is to be welcomed: it offers relief from warfare and promises that the peace process can be rejuvenated and deliver a more effective peace. Yet, the danger of conflict recidivism is ever present with stalled peace processes and accords, thus awarding urgency to the study of mired peace processes.

Six factors set this work apart from much other literature on peace and conflict. First, the book adopts a critical perspective that separates it from many orthodox, policy-oriented studies. As such, it can be read as a challenge to the substantial literature that offers guidance on how to fix 'broken' peace processes and accords. An essential aim of this work is to recommend, where appropriate, a fundamental revision of how to conceptualise and approach peace and peacemaking. Second, and related to the adoption of a critical perspective, this work maintains a normative approach. Such a viewpoint may be unfashionable in policy and social scientific publications. Yet peacemaking has a persistent moral dimension that requires space alongside more technocratic approaches. The pervasive neo-institutional perspective that concentrates on rebuilding state capacity as part of post-war reconstruction risks overlooking the human factor.

A third point of differentiation between this and many other works is that it takes peace as its point of departure. The conceptualisation and definition of peace has been a significant absentee from many studies of peace and conflict. In this work, peace is defined as the facilitation of non-exploitative, sustainable and inclusive relationships free from direct and indirect violence and the threat of such violence. In other words, a holistic view of peace is adopted that stands in contrast with the compromised version of peace prevailing in many post-peace accord societies. The notion of imagining peace and contrasting that with the reality or observed evidence of peace in post-war societies awards the book its fourth point of originality. The book contains an innovative proposal for a diagnostic tool to help identify the shortcomings of stalled peace processes and peace accords. The critical peace assessment methodology proposed and explained in this book rests on the idea of incorporating idealised views of peace into any audit of a becalmed peace accord. Profound thinking on the essential meanings and outcomes of peace has been largely absent from much contemporary literature and policy on peacemaking, and the implementation of a critical peace assessment methodology may help redress this shortcoming. Blue-skies thinking on the nature and meaning of peace has been dismissed in many ages and contexts as the work of the 'woolly-minded' or 'hopelessly naive'. Instead, those interested in peace and conflict studies have been encouraged to employ 'more sensible' (and usually less critical) approaches. This book suggests that such orthodox thinking about peace has been partially responsible for the poor quality peace that prevails in many post-peace accord societies.

Fifth, this work identifies the liberal democratic peace as the central concept around which contemporary internationally supported peacemaking can be explained. The use of the 'liberal democratic peace' formulation is deliberate and marks a departure from the more commonly used 'liberal peace'. This denotes the importance of democracy in the rhetoric and operationalisation of contemporary peacemaking. The use of the liberal democratic peace as an explanatory model allows us to identify and explicate the key proponents, components, strategies and ideas behind contemporary peacemaking. Finally, this book is inspired by primary research undertaken by the author in societies experiencing peace processes and peace accords. It attempts to reflect the dissatisfaction that many people in such circumstances have with 'peace'. Personal observations from Sri Lanka to Bosnia and Croatia, from Northern Ireland to Mindanao and beyond have shown that for many people, 'peace' is poverty, insecurity and excludes true reconciliation with former antagonists. No war, no peace situations demand urgent academic and policy attention.

1
Peace

> The Romans brought devastation, but they called it peace.
>
> Tacitus

Introduction

Peace: virtually everyone supports it. Statesmen and women solemnly pledge themselves and their followers to the pursuit of it. Millions join rallies and demonstrations to publicly identify with the concept. Peace has inspired great works of art, music and literature and it is difficult to keep up with the ever-growing list of books, scholarly journals, theories and conferences concerned with peace. The multiplicity of peace research and advocacy institutes, as well as practical NGOs working in conflict zones, has led some to identify a 'peace industry'.[1] Yet, for all this ubiquity, the term 'peace' is grossly under-conceptualised, with many commentators invoking and prescribing peace but sidestepping the tricky task of unpacking and defining it (a definition of peace is reached later in this chapter).[2] The vast majority of books with the word 'peace' in their title are actually concerned with war or conflict.

As a labelling device, 'peace' is generous in the extreme. Consider, for example, the tremendous organising, rhetorical and moral power of the word 'peace' in the Israeli–Palestinian peace process.[3] The antagonists, and the international community, recognised the immense value of the terms 'peace' and 'peace process' and competed over the appropriation and usage of the terms. However, despite the common vocabulary of peace, it was clear that the antagonists and others held very different conceptualisations of peace. For many Israelis, peace was primarily conceived in terms of security, while for many Palestinians peace was primarily a matter of dignity and the territorial and repatriation rights that would accompany the achievement of dignity. The term 'peace' became something of a weapon with which the antagonists browbeat each other. Both sides transgressed the spirit and letter of even the most lax definition of peace. Each side sought to claim the moral high ground by appealing for the other to re-engage with the 'peace process' when there was little evidence of the existence of peace or a peace-making process. Herein lies the problem: what does the term 'peace' actually mean?

Clearly, the term is capable of meaning different things to different people and of changing its meaning over time and across contexts. Sartori reminds us of the costs 'conceptual stretching': 'we can cover more ... by saying less, and by saying less in a far less precise manner.'[4] Table 1.1 presents a by no means exhaustive selection of possible peace aims and possible methods of attaining these aims. This bewildering diversity of aims and methods illustrates the vast territory covered by the single word 'peace', with the peace aim ranging from personal well-being to international order, and the peace means ranging from personal lifestyle choices to regime change by force. Attempts to unpack the notion of peace are often bedevilled by more questions than answers. Moreover, much of the literature on peacemaking concentrates on the mechanics of managing the de-escalation of violent conflict rather than conceptualisations of the ultimate objective or goal of the conflict management process, however illusionary and unobtainable the goal may be. A concentration on the practicalities of staunching

Table 1.1   Possible peace aims and means

Peace aim	Possible peace achieving methods
Personal well-being	Personal journey of enlightenment and lifestyle choices
Shared pacific ideal	Education, spread of communitarian ideas
Ordered society	Social contract or control by an authority
International stability	International legislation, balance of power, benign hegemony
Social justice	Social transformation, participatory polity
Equity	Class solidarity, revolution
Democracy	Democratisation programme, regime change
Cessation of hostilities	Peace treaty, subordination/exhaustion of one protagonist

violent conflict is understandable, but if we fail to pause to consider the direction and destination of the journey, then we run the risk of becoming lost. Indeed, ill-conceived attempts at the pacific management of conflict could exacerbate conflict. Thus, the need to understand peace is not an academic luxury, only posed by those removed from the immediacy of violent conflict. Instead, the urgency of violent conflict demands that we take seriously the conceptualisation of peace.

It is the contention of this book that the peace that follows the cessation of large-scale violence in contemporary ethnonational wars is often deficient. As illustrated in the introductory chapter, contemporary peace is often broken, fragile or tense. However, despite the poor quality of the peace on offer, the term peace is still employed with unabashed frequency. This dissonance between the unsatisfactory reality of peace on the ground and theoretical notions of peace is by no means novel. Peace scholars and others have traditionally imbued peace with a semi-spiritual aura and privileged status that bore little relation to the 'make-do' nature of peace that was typical of various post-war areas. This trend of the disjuncture between the moral and ideological aspirations of peace on the one hand and the often grim reality of peace on the other is a key feature of contemporary peacemaking. Enormous energy and resources, both international and local, are devoted to 'peace' making, keeping and building in the knowledge that the 'peace' that follows often leaves much to be desired. In many cases, this investment is based on hope and optimism rather than the observed evidence of conflict management techniques with a track record of success. The consistency with which peace is frustrated and unsatisfactory, and with which practical peace implementation policies fail to deliver anything but minimal versions of peace, raises profound questions over the conceptualisation of peace. Fundamentally, given the quality of peace on offer to most people in areas emerging from sustained intra-state war, should we revise downwards our expectations of peace? Similarly, should we redefine the meanings and value we attach to peace?

This chapter discusses peace in the light of the foregoing chapter on the contested and often unsatisfactory nature of war termination in post-Cold War ethnonational conflicts. It reviews some of the persistent questions regarding peace, such as whether it possesses intrinsic values, is universal or has an identifiable endpoint? Before reaching a definition of 'peace', the chapter identifies and discusses three meta-ideas that have underpinned much thinking on peace: religious and spiritual, appeals to humanity, and sustainability. It then asks the deliberately arresting question: why do we want peace? The chapter then reviews the principal strategies (Just War, pacifism and utopian restructuring of society to address the causes of conflict) whereby peace has traditionally been pursued. In its conclusion, the chapter revisits Schmid's 1968 attack on the conservatism of peace research and its tendency to accept conflict rather than investigate and challenge its deeper causes.[5] Many of Schmid's insights have more relevance today than when they were originally aired and underline the importance of maintaining a critical perspective in peace and conflict studies.

A core argument running through this book is the increasing dominance of a particular version of peace supported by leading states, international organisations and international financial institutions (IFIs): the liberal democratic peace. Such is the dominance of the liberal democratic peace that it is shaping how peace is made, received and defined. This peace is very much a social construct, reflecting prevailing political, economic and social power relations, and therefore, in order to understand the concept of peace it is essential that we investigate how peace is made.

The concept of peace

An initial question is to ascertain if peace contains intrinsic or inherent values regardless of context or application. Some values (social harmony and sustainability) are associated with peace with greater regularity than others so that it may be possible to regard them as core peace values. Yet, a constructivist approach – recognising that ideas of peace originate, are sustained and modified in a socially constructed world – may be more prudent. Thus, it is useful to see peace as not possessing hard and fixed values that are immutable across time and context. Skinner's warning that there are 'no perennial problems in philosophy' alerts us to the danger of presenting a history of the concept of peace as a seamless and coherent set of ideas that can be traced through antiquity.[6] Instead, he stresses the importance of the context in which ideas are received and interpreted:

> [O]ur own society is no different from any other in having its own local beliefs and arrangements of social and political life ... [T]hose features of our own arrangements which we may be disposed to accept as traditional or even 'timeless' truths may in fact be the merest contingencies of our peculiar history or social structure.[7]

The key point for our purposes is that ideas of peace are located in specific circumstances and contexts with the result that it is difficult to ascribe precise and constant values to what is essentially an amorphous concept.

Ideas of peace are likely to vary according to historical period, the nature and intensity of the violent conflict and crucially the socio-political and ideological position of the individual, group or entity interpreting the peace. Despite the constancy of the use of the word 'peace', the peace that followed the medieval wars between European warrior princes was a very different animal to the peace that followed the nineteenth century wars between the Maori and European settlers or the peace that was imagined in the depths of the nuclear arms race. Even the outcome of a single conflict is open to multiple interpretations, with parties to the same peace accord often using different criteria to calculate their attitude to the peace.

The foregoing paragraphs are not meant to promote despair at the futility of seeking to define peace across different contexts and time periods. Instead they are to flag an awareness of contextual factors in seeking to pin down the nature of peace and other meta-ideas in philosophy and politics. Many of the circumstances and contexts of peace and conflict share striking similarities and invite comparison. For example, responses and resistance by local communities to the pernicious effects of resource extraction by multinational companies may have similar traits in Bougainville, the Niger delta in Nigeria or Madagascar. At the same time though, all three cases will also be informed by local cultural factors and exigencies.

Complicating the inquiry into whether or not peace has intrinsic values is the tendency to view peace as the absence of war or violence; in effect 'nonwar'.[8] In other words, rather than a phenomenon in its own right, peace is often only conceptualised or imagined from a position that takes conflict as its point of departure. This negative starting point is understandable, particularly in the midst of war, but it is also likely to encourage context-specific conceptualisations of peace and discourage abstractions across cases which may aid our task of conceptualising peace.

Just as caution is required in associating peace with intrinsic values that stretch across time and context, circumspection is necessary in regarding peace as a universal concept. Ideas of peace are common to all religions, communities and forms of social and political organisation, but these conceptualisations of peace vary markedly. Meanings of peace are stretched beyond the tolerance of elasticity to the extent that it is worth asking if the same concept of peace can be applied in all cases. For example, Al-Qaeda and the United States both invoke peace in public statements but their versions of peace are very different. Indeed, Al-Qaeda pointed to this contradiction by noting: 'If [President] Bush and [Prime Minister] Sharon are men of peace, we are also men of peace.'[9]

So peace is universal in the sense that virtually all social communities profess a notion of peace, but these notions of peace do not comprise a discrete and coherent set of ideas that can claim unanimous allegiance. Yet, the view that there is one universal peace is persistent, particularly among hegemonic states and organisations. Leading western states, international organisations and civil society organisations have come to dominate the international system to such an extent that their notions of peace often prevail over more variegated and locally interpreted versions. This liberal democratic peace (the focus of the next chapter) brings with it a series of expectations, assumptions and peace-support activities that shape the nature of peace in many contemporary post-peace accord societies. The hegemonic states, institutions and organisations who back the liberal democratic peace possess what sociologists call 'naming power' whereby their version of peace is accepted as the norm while other versions are regarded as less appropriate. As Bourdieu notes:

> By structuring the perception which social agents have of the social world, the act of naming helps to establish the structure of this world, and does so all the more significantly the more widely recognised, i.e. authorized. There is no social agent who does not aspire as far as his circumstances permit, to have the power to name and create the world through naming.[10]

This naming power is most obviously political and economic, but it also has a cultural and moral aspect in shaping conceptualisations of peace. Crucially, the version of peace assumed by leading states and international organisations to have universal applicability is a western peculiarity. The implication of the liberal democratic peace is that peace is increasingly regarded as 'true peace' only if it conforms to western notions. The liberal democratic peace has been introduced and enforced with varying degrees of rigour, with locations deemed inaccessible, strategically unimportant or unlikely to be responsive to international intervention, receiving only liberal democratic peace-lite, if at all. In other locations, however, and especially those receiving extensive international peace-support operations, the liberal democratic peace has become the 'industry standard' and has been tremendously powerful in shaping the nature and quality of peace as experienced by the inhabitants of post-peace accord societies. The extent to which this variant of peace has managed to achieve universality is based more on the preponderance of its advocates rather than a widespread acceptance of its philosophy, components and methods.

A further issue germane to the conceptualisation of peace is that peace has no endpoint. Peace is a 'process' or a 'practice' rather than an event, such as the signing of a peace accord, or a commodity that can be objectified into a neat unit.[11] This point has profound implications for how we attempt to deal with violent conflict. Attempts to 'solve' conflict fundamentally misunderstand the fluid nature of both peace and conflict, and the need for conflict to be managed or transformed as part of a long-term endeavour that concentrates on the relationships between (former) combatants. The old riposte that 'only chemists have solutions' guards against technocratic notions that conflict can be solved if only pacific-minded alchemists mix the correct peace ingredients. Instead, at best, conflict can be managed or transformed with combatants gradually reappraising the basis of the conflict and adopting more pacific modes of interaction.[12] But the view that peace is a commodity has gained increasing purchase among major states and international organisations through their promotion of the increasingly homogenised liberal democratic model. Elements of the liberal democratic peace have undergone a process of commodification into pre-packaged templates delivered as part of internationally supported peace accord implementation plans. Component parts of this preferred model of peace are standardised into peace-support programmes and projects that differ little whether the implementation location is Bosnia or Rwanda. Peace, under the liberal democratic peace model, becomes formulaic and is reduced to time-limited events (two or three year projects on refugee repatriation, livelihood generation and democracy training). Aside from the issue of the quality of peace such standardised approaches deliver, the commodification of peace in internationally supported peace interventions is an antithesis to the view that peace is a process.

Peace advocacy

The difficulties associated with conceptualising peace (the combined absence of intrinsic values, universal meaning and an endpoint) have not diminished attempts to define or promote a preferred vision of peace. Different eras and contexts have witnessed the championing of different versions of peace and of elements within peace. Contemporary thinking on peace is by no means more sophisticated than earlier efforts. Thus, over the centuries, different types and subcategories of peace have been identified, as have special categories of people to be regarded as non-combatants. Importantly, many notions of peace have been guided by meta-ideas that attempt, intellectually and practically, to provide an all-encompassing argument in favour of a particular version of peace. Three meta-ideas have dominated peace advocacy: religious and spiritual, appeals to humanity, and sustainability. All three ideas are capable of borrowing from and supporting each other with the result that it is difficult to completely disaggregate the essential philosophical underpinnings of peace. For example, while religious and spiritual appeals to a higher authority may employ a faith discourse, they can also invoke a humane abhorrence at warfare and have a self-interest in sustaining a current system of government or social organisation.

Religious and spiritual appeals

Virtually all religions or sects within religions venerate some form of pacific intent and action (righteous deeds), and emphasise humanity or community. This is by no means universal (religious nationalism and fundamentalism have been prominent in the promotion of armed conflict and sectarianism) but the idea that human life is sacred or in some way divinely ordained has played an enormous role in the conceptualisation and definition of peace. Although many of the core elements of a contemporary peace-support operation may have modern or technical labels (refugee repatriation, minority protection etc.) they essentially rest on notions of empathy, charity and goodwill that would find approval among many religious communities.[13] The 'spiritual–moral formation' of many religions emphasise passivity, humanitarianism or identification with vulnerable groups.[14] Thus, historically, religious and spiritual faith has provided a key motivating factor behind peace advocacy and articulation. Many religious groups, especially in the post-Second World War era, have gone beyond advocacy and embraced peace activism, with the Society of Friends and the Mennonites in particular having long traditions of conflict transformation work, particularly 'track two' or behind the scenes peace support.[15] Religious and spiritual starting points for the advocacy and definition of peace have lost much of their popularity (especially in the global north where religion and spiritualism are regarded as properly located in the private rather than public realms). Yet, religion still retains purchase in traditional societies and informs much thinking on ideas of reconciliation. Sectarianism in deeply divided societies (e.g., Gujarat) and the apparent identification of 'Islamic fundamentalism' as a contributing factor in anti-western political violence have also placed greater emphasis on inter-faith dialogue and the need to reconcile faith communities.

Appeals to humanity

Appeals to humanity emphasise revulsion at violence towards other humans. This is particularly amplified if those under threat are non-combatants or in some way vulnerable.[16] Stress is placed on bearing witness, or the recording and dissemination of instances of inhumanity in the hope that they mobilise powerful affective responses and, in turn, action. Despite the regularity with which societies have been confronted with violence and inhumanity, it is difficult to become completely inured to the suffering of others.[17] Of course the 'packaging' of accounts of inhumanity is important. Allegations of the mistreatment of detainees at Baghdad's Abu Ghraib prison had been circulating for months, but were propelled centre-stage when photographic evidence was produced in April 2004. Similarly, the videotaping of prisoners and kidnap victims during the Iraq war caused particular outrage.[18] Central to the promotion of peace via appeals to humanity is an emphasis on the uniqueness of humans among other species. The very idea of 'humankind' is predicated on the recognition of the universal possession of human qualities that transcend socially constructed boundaries such as political or ideological categorisations. Thus, all humans have sentience and a higher consciousness by virtue of being human.

A significant development in the appeals to humanity discourse was its recognition of the individual as a sub-unit of humanity. Linked to this recognition of individuals as a discrete political and moral unit was the granting of rights to individuals. For much of recorded human history, the only individuals with significant rights were sovereigns or specialist professional categories such as clerics or warriors.[19] Thirteenth century theologian Thomas Acquinas (influenced by the works of Aristotle) played a key role in justifying the attribution of rights and responsibilities to the individual.[20] Debates over the unit of humanity to be prioritised in peacemaking – the individual or the group – are still very much alive. The unit chosen will have implications for the type of peace to be pursued and the method of its pursuit. A prioritisation of the individual, increasingly supported by a human rights discourse, can make uncomfortable demands on the group or state. For example, a state based on assumptions and legal strictures related to monotheism may have to reform as part of a peace accord to accommodate multiple faiths. It also raises questions of the universality of ideas, in that the bulk of human rights discourse has originated from the west and travels poorly to societies in which kinship and family groups are often regarded as the principal unit in society.

The appeals to humanity approach to peace has been criticised for its 'mere repetition of the horrors of war' or the chronicling of inhumanity in order to condemn it.[21] This strand of peace advocacy has also been criticised for its failure to move beyond hand-wringing in order to recommend schemes for securing peace. But these criticisms overlook its significant contribution in the broadening of conceptualisations of peace beyond the mere cessation of hostilities (negative peace).[22] By encouraging questions on the quality of life once peace has been declared, the appeals to humanity discourse plays a central role in the development of more holistic notions of peace that address the deep-rooted causes of conflict. The idea of positive peace moves beyond a focus on direct violence to address indirect violence or those underlying factors that contributed to conflict causation and – crucially – inhibited human potential. Thus, by using the lens of humanity, structural issues of social and economic development become central to conceptualisations of peace.

In short, the concept of peace was revolutionised by its inclusion of ideas of social progress and the development potential of individuals and societies. Peace in this view was no longer merely restricted to the regulation of armed combatants or securing ceasefires and attempting to make them permanent. Under the new formulation, not only was peace concerned with the context in which war was caused, maintained and ended, it was also concerned with a more holistic context of human development. Thus, issues of public health, education and opportunities for social and economic advancement came under the remit of peace. Under the rubric of negative peace, the task facing peacemakers in the civil war in the Democratic Republic of Congo from 1997 onwards was to staunch a conflict that had claimed approximately 300,000 lives as a result of direct violence. But a positive peace lens, with the concept of humanity at its centre, also includes the further 2.5 million that died as a result of public health emergencies and attempts to address a range of social and economic development issues beyond direct violence.[23]

Appeals to humanity have met stiff resistance though. A constant challenge to empathy on the basis of a common humanity has been the objectification of the enemy as less than human. In this view, the enemy (either an organised enemy force or a wider population) are stripped of the human characteristics that may provide points of human empathy. Nazi attempts to portray Slavs, Jews and others as sub-human provide a prominent example in which the dehumanisation was applied to entire races and social categories. Similar processes are often at work informally in conflict locations and are deeply embedded in social and political behaviour. Thus, Catholics and Protestants in Northern Ireland tell the same jokes about each other but with 'the other' as the butt of the humour. The effect of the dehumanisation process is to paint a picture of the out-group as an undifferentiated monolith bereft of individuals and possessing a homogenous (usually extreme and unflattering) worldview.[24] A further challenge facing appeals to humanity as an idea underpinning conceptualisations of peace, is the increasing technological sophistication of warfare, particularly as practised by those states with the economic wherewithal to engage in electronic technowar. The growing distance between the perpetrator and victim means that wars waged by the first world increasingly resemble 'first-person shooter' computer games and mark another step in this process of the dehumanisation of the enemy.[25] Recent US wars have been directed from the Central Command Headquarters in Tampa, Florida where targets are rendered into pixelated images and technology mediates the immediacy of battle. In such circumstances the common bonds of humanity erode.

Sustainability

Sustainability has been the third meta-idea that has underpinned thinking about peace. The basic principle has been to seek to arrest violent conflict before it reaches a stage where it risks destabilising a system of political or social organisation. The motive is often one of self-preservation and thus may be directed at staunching conflict spillover or the escalation of a localised conflict into a system-wide conflagration. Peace advocacy rationalised through notions of sustainability might involve the creation or perfection of mechanisms to ensure balance and reciprocity. Key to ideas of sustainability has been the limitation and regulation of warfare and violence rather than its extinction.

To a large extent, ideas of sustainability have been deeply conservative, often concerned with protecting or minimally reforming an existing order rather than advocating a fundamental revision of societal and political organisation. Therefore they have traditionally coincided with realist theories, such as balance of power, and can be categorised as promoting negative peace. The nuclear era, and the prospect of complete human annihilation, added urgency to peace advocacy based upon sustainability. As US Secretary of State Robert McNamara observed, 'There's no learning curve with nuclear weapons.'[26] But ideas of sustainability have been recast from negative to positive peace from the twentieth century onwards. By taking account of ecological and developmental perspectives, they have sought to adopt more holistic explanations of conflict and peace. Such ideas are not entirely novel, having been central to the understanding of peace in many traditional societies in which a delicate ecological balance had to be maintained to ensure the long-term exploitation of natural resources.[27] Nevertheless, increasing evidence of environmental degradation, and of the linkages between development processes and conflict, have encouraged many states and international organisations to extend their thinking on political sustainability to encompass environmental and developmental sustainability.

Championed by academics, NGOs and elements within international organisations and some governments, this broader view of peace has gradually been gaining wider acceptance. It has had a profound impact on conceptualisations of peace, particularly in extending the idea of peace beyond the securing of an armistice between combatants. Peace and conflict were now interconnected with a range of other process. The linkage of peace with development resulted in a more sophisticated understanding of the structural causes of conflict that went far beyond the more obvious and proximate causes and manifestations that attracted most attention. The peace-development synthesis also prompted more sophisticated peacemaking strategies. Often termed 'peacebuilding', these development-conscious peacemaking strategies attempted to bridge the gap between elite-level peace accords and the needs of all sectors of society. The key, of course, was the need to make peace, and the development processes that would underpin it, sustainable. Under this conceptualisation, peace was a long-term process rather than an event, required as much popular participation as possible and went far beyond the traditional security, constitutional and political issues that had defined peacemaking in earlier centuries. Sustainable peace was concerned with the condition of people in the war-affected area and attempted to address their development needs.

Critics of positive peace say that it approximates to a never-ending utopian wish-list that can never be fulfilled in those social democratic states unencumbered with violent conflict let alone societies emerging from violent conflict. They also argue that it is a recipe for destabilisation since any readjustments of social systems will necessarily create losers and generate grievances.

So having discussed the problems of conceptualising peace and outlining the meta-ideas that have underpinned thinking on peace, are we any closer to defining peace? It is worth re-stressing that consensus on a definition of peace remains illusive, not least because many authors write *about* peace but avoid defining it. The persistent problem of the gap between aspirational notions of peace on the one hand, and their practical operationalisation on the other, means that utopian definitions are tempered by the knowledge of what is feasible and practical. Notwithstanding the problems of implementation, peace demands utopian and lateral thinking. As a result the following definition of peace is proposed: the facilitation of non-exploitative, sustainable and inclusive social relationships free from direct and indirect violence and the threat of such violence.

An initial point to be made in relation to this definition, and in keeping with the overall theme of this book, is how far removed it is from the situation pertaining in many societies that have emerged from violent conflict in the post-Cold War era. The peace on offer to many inhabitants of post-war societies falls far short of this ideal, even when that peace is guaranteed by international organisations. A further point to make is that the definition is deliberately general. For example, it does not prescribe the nature of the facilitator, and is open to the idea that the facilitator of any peace may view western political organisation and behaviour as inappropriate or deviant. Also important is the emphasis on relationships, denoting the importance of sustainability. It also guards against 'peace by separation', whereby antagonists and their support populations regulate hostilities by maintaining a division between themselves as in the case of Israel's security barrier. Although such a strategy may staunch direct violence it does not encourage the development of relationships between antagonists. Peace under this conceptualisation is a process rather than an event and is not necessarily reactive to a particular conflict. A final point to make in relation to the definition is the emphasis on indirect violence and the threat of violence. Our conceptualisation of peace extends beyond actual physical violence to encompass the threats and intimidation that shape so much of daily life in deeply divided societies. The inclusion of indirect violence recognises that human development lies at the heart of peace. If people are free from direct violence but subsist in conditions of extreme poverty without opportunities for advancement then we cannot call that situation peace.

Why do we want peace?

At first this may seem an odd question, akin to asking why a child likes chocolate. Yet the question is legitimate for at least two reasons. First, the observed evidence of 'peace' in action is rarely inspiring. The peace that follows many contemporary violent conflicts is often unsatisfactory and is marked by the perpetuation of many of the features that characterised violent conflict such as social and economic dislocation, violence or inter-ethnic tension. In other words, if peace brings little material benefit to people in a war zone, then why are so many practical and moral resources dedicated to its attainment? A second reason for asking the 'why do we want peace?' question is that it allows us to investigate the value humans attach to peace and helps explain the investment of energy devoted to securing peace.

An obvious objection to the question of why do so many humans want peace is that many groups and individuals do not want peace. A human history littered by organised violence and warfare attests to the desire on the part of many to pursue war over peace. War can be the most rational means to deliver ends, particularly if calculations of a swift victory are made. As O'Connor notes, 'the emotional appeal of victory and the repugnance of defeat are endemic.'[28] War can also be popular, with the manipulation of public opinion in favour of group aggression often playing a central role in the assumption and retention of power in many political systems. War may also be deemed culturally appropriate if, for example, group honour has been offended. Maori warrior culture, for example, placed immense emphasis on *utu* or honour, with the result that war was pursued for the restoration of *utu* rather than the seizure of physical resources.[29] The positive cultural representation of warfare is common across many societies and allows militarism to be updated to suit the prevailing context.[30] Of course, for many people there is no choice in the matter of prioritising war over peace: war comes to them.

Despite the prevalence of war, and of societies based on the iniquitous regulation of human opportunity, the idea of peace remains popular. One reason why so many of us want peace is that we attach a higher expected utility to peace than to war, or the condition we identify as not peace.[31] The human suffering associated with war means that many will happily trade it for an alternative. The alternative is often flawed, and although given the label 'peace', falls far short of utopian notions of peace. Yet the immediacy of the horror of wars and violence mean that the contested and flawed peace is vastly more preferable than war itself. In such a situation it is possible to explain the human desire for peace in terms of rational self-interest: under certain circumstances humans will calculate that they will derive a higher marginal utility from a situation of non-war than war. Indeed for frontline combatants the calculation may be basic: they will have a much higher chance of avoiding death or injury in a situation of non-war. Those who at first supported war to bring benefits may recalculate their position and favour peace if the war is not progressing as expected.

But if we can explain why individuals and groups in the midst of violent conflict may opt for peace, then what explains the desire for peace on behalf of others? The already mentioned meta-ideas of religion and spirituality and common humanity can go some way towards explaining why humans would wish for peace on behalf of others. But stand-alone ideas of complete human altruism demand caution. There can be an element of self-interest in wishing for peace for others; third parties may be aware of the spillover dangers of a conflict and hope that a conflict involving others comes to an end before it destabilises their own environment. It is also possible that third parties will receive a psychological or esteem-related boost from the knowledge that far away conflicts reach a pacific conclusion. The pleasure of peace by proxy may be related to a sense of humanity in which one act of violence is a stain on all humankind and, conversely, peace in one area improves the whole.

How do we achieve peace?

Three western traditions have dominated theoretical and practical peacemaking: Just War, pacifism and the restructuring of society in order to address the causes of conflict.[32] The approaches to peacemaking draw on the already discussed meta-ideas that inform thinking on peace and mark the point at which peace advocacy and justification becomes peace action. Like the meta-ideas, they are capable of synthesis and change. Fundamentally though, the peace that they have secured is often contested and unsatisfactory.

Just War

Just War is taken in this instance to mean the establishment of moral and practical standards that inform war causation and conduct. Although its origins lie in a distinct western philosophical tradition associated with Augustine, Thomas Acquinas and Hugo Grotius, Just War-type conventions are alive and well in the contemporary era.[33] They may not always use the term 'Just War', instead preferring expressions such as humane war, pre-emptive war, or humanitarian intervention. The tradition is not anti-war. Instead, it accepts that wars are a feature of human life, and seeks to rationalise their causation and conduct. The Just War tradition has sought to identify the conditions under which war might be legitimate or illegitimate. It also has much to say on combatant behaviour during war, seeking to distinguish between lawful and unlawful practices, and categorise groups as legitimate or illegitimate targets.

In essence, the Just War tradition has provided a rubric for the classification and justification of war and behaviour during war. The basis of the rubric has changed with time and circumstance. It has always represented a collision of the moral and the political spheres, with the moral sphere providing rhetoric that can cloak more political interests. All combatants stress the righteousness of their cause (whether in moral or political terms), but some combatants are favoured in promoting their justifications. For example, the moral language they employ may rhyme with dominant ethical notions of the era or a protagonist's ability to disseminate their version of the war cause may be vastly superior to that of their opponent. Thus, Just War thinking in the medieval period has been routinely criticised as the manipulation of moral strictures and interpretations of divine will to protect the privileges of the clerisy and justify Christian war. As Michael Howard notes:

> The Church accepted and blessed the warrior class from the very beginning: since they were fighting to defend Christendom against incursions of heathen Moslems, Magyars, and Norsemen, it would hardly do otherwise ... in war against the pagan no holds were barred, and knights indeed could gain remission for their sins by waging it.[34]

Wars within Christendom were more tricky, 'But Christian theologians agreed that certain wars were "just"; broadly speaking those waged on the authority of a lawful superior in a righteous cause.'[35]

Contemporary attempts to justify and limit war owe much to the Just War tradition, though they have been suitably updated to reflect modern moral preoccupations and political interests. Thus, justifications for the United States and United Kingdom invasion of Iraq in 2003 were able to point to the due process and warnings issued via the United Nations and diplomatic channels, the aim of relieving human suffering and the pre-emption of greater harm. Just War theory has also been subject to immense debate in the wake of 9/11 and in the context of humanitarian intervention.[36]

Despite the cynicism associated with the Just War tradition (or whatever label its modern reincarnation may prefer) and its use of moral claims to support the pursuit of war, it is worth recognising the impact of the tradition in limiting war. Ultimately the tradition has helped restrain the outbreak of war and injected discipline into how war has been waged. Clearly, human history is marked by the very many instances in which the outbreak of war was unrestrained and conduct in war was undisciplined, but the tradition has had a positive impact. By providing the philosophical basis for the legal rationalisation of war, it has prescribed the conditions under which states can legitimately enjoin war and has endowed a specialist language on war causation. Although not always respected, these 'ground rules' for engagement in war are visible in the corpus of international law that has developed over the past two centuries and the codification of concepts such as sovereignty, neutrality and combatant. Related to this has been states' creation of international organisations expressly mandated to secure peace. The Just War tradition has also helped regulate activities during war. Whether formally instituted or informally accepted, most violent conflicts have 'a vestigial taboo line'[37] or behaviour deemed so outrageous as to be unacceptable. These informal rules of war are not always due to the western Just War tradition and may be described as the customary rules of war with roots in cultural practice.

The dominant modern derivative of the Just War tradition is the preserve of leading states and international organisations and can be described as a moral–political guide for war-making and activity during war. As such it is a double-edged sword, capable of providing both a restraint on and a justification for war. Its influence on peacemaking and conceptualisations of peace has been profound. Fundamentally, it has lowered the bar of optimism in conceptualisations of peace. Consequently, many notions of peace are grounded amid the restrictions of the political world. This has the advantage of limiting much discourse and action on peace to the realms of the feasible. But it has the disadvantage of discouraging the imagination, lateral thinking and optimism that is crucial to peace. The dominant moral–political paradigm is concerned with the minimum standards of peace.

Pacifism

Pacifism has provided the basis for the second major approach to peacemaking. Centred on the principle of non-violent resistance, pacifism is the antithesis of the pursuit of political goals by war or coercion. The fact that pacifism is often labelled as an 'alternative' approach to peacemaking denotes the dominance of other approaches. Its basic tenet is that violence is unjustifiable, though there are many variants of pacifism, ranging from pragmatic or conditional pacifism that can envisage the use of violence under extreme circumstances to more absolutist variants. Pacifism should not be equated with passivity, in that many of its adherents are activists and adopt pacifism as a means of protest and disruption, often against a specific war or regime. The power of non-violence relies in the contrast it sets with the aggressor, and thus it requires that the aggressor possesses some level of self-awareness and can be 'embarrassed' into moderating their behaviour.

A significant trend in pacifist approaches to managing social and political conflict has been an attempt to establish and maintain a space between themselves and other actors. This often manifests itself in the physical withdrawal of pacifists from an area of violent conflict or tension, with Gandhi in India and Te Whiti in New Zealand displaying 'other worldly' characteristics that at once confounded opponents and were capable of demonstrating powerful symbolism. The latter's actions had an almost absurdist quality: serving food to government road builders as they encroached on Maori land, ploughing and cultivating land the government had seized and living in an open village rather than a bush fortress.[38]

Restructuring of political and economic systems

The utopian restructuring of society and political systems in order to address the causes of conflict has the potential to deliver positive peace. It suggests a holistic approach ready to transcend the manifestations of violent conflict and address the structural factors that cause and maintain conflict and inhibit human development. A key priority in this approach to peacemaking is the establishment, alteration or regulation of political and social institutions. It is predicated on a broad interpretation of peace and focuses on underlying and structural tensions and inequalities. It also pays attention to lines of communication within and between societies.

As the term 'restructuring' suggests, it is based on a recognition that existing systems of social and political organisation require *fundamental* change. Inertia and resistance from existing systems of organisation and a lack of capacity often limits just how fundamental this change can be. By its nature, it is an interventionist strategy believing in the regulation and perfectability of political mechanisms and institutions in order to mould political behaviour. In a sense, it is unashamed social and political engineering and many peace processes and accords take the form of attempts to reconfigure institutions in an attempt to accommodate more pacific inter-group relations.

Perhaps the most significant example of the utopian restructuring of political and social organisation to address the underlying causes of conflict was the creation of the United Nations. Although ideas of a pacific union had been circulating for centuries, the twentieth century was the first to realise the goal.[39] In one respect the United Nations is concerned with securing negative peace; traditional peacekeeping aims to separate warring parties rather than address the underlying causes of conflict. But the UN Charter, and the establishment of a series of UN agencies dedicated to human development, were significant in attaching importance to social development and the quality of human life. The UN Charter amounted to a revolutionary document in its mention – on behalf of member states – of women, the idea of human dignity and social progress. While the establishment of the United Nations was the macrolevel manifestation of an attempt to restructure political organisation, peacebuilding schemes represented micro-level approaches.

While the restructuring of political and social systems has the potential to effect significant pacific change, such restructuring is tempered by political and economic constraints. Key constraints include the observance of state sovereignty, an inertia in favour of power-holders and the western cultural bias found in many states, international organisations and NGOs involved in restructuring initiatives. The tendency of many contemporary peace processes and accords to deal with conflict manifestations and contain technocratic approaches to peace implementation places severe limitations on the ability of restructuring attempts to deal with underlying conflict causes. Moreover, there are few guarantees that the restructuring of mechanisms and institutions can effect changes in attitudes and behaviour. Many post-peace accord societies boast elaborate human rights and equality monitoring institutions but also host widely held unreconstructed inter-group attitudes.

Concluding discussion

Herman Schmid's extraordinarily clear-sighted (but neglected) critique of the emerging sub-discipline of peace studies has as much relevance today as it did when first published in 1968. Schmid was critical of the 'problem-oriented nature of peace research' or its willingness to accept conflicts and their contexts as given facts and attempt to 'fix' them within conservative parameters.[40] Rather than challenge and examine the basis of conflict, Schmid observed that peace research was content to adopt the terminology and conceptualisations preferred by international and supranational organisations. He noted that:

> the universalist ethos of peace research becomes operationalized into identification with the interests of the existing international system,

that is the interests of those who have power in the international system. So peace research becomes a factor supporting the status quo of the international power structure, providing the decision-makers of the system with knowledge for control, manipulation and integration of the system.[41]

Schmid's essential criticism was that peace research had been co-opted into reforming rather than challenging an exploitative international system. Its concentration on perfecting the mechanisms of managing negative peace camouflaged an unwillingness or inability to champion positive peace.

Over thirty years later, Schmid's arguments retain remarkable appeal. Post-Cold War civil wars have prompted an upsurge in peace-support interventionism by international organisations, third party states and NGOs. The complexity, sophistication and cost of interventions have multiplied with successive interventions. The range of components included in peace processes, peace accords and post-war reconstruction schemes has grown enormously, and a specialist language has developed to describe these components. Yet, these developments have continued in the absence of critical appraisal of the meaning of the term 'peace' and scrutiny of the quality of the peace on offer in the aftermath of contemporary civil wars. These failings are related and strike at the heart of the inability of many contemporary peace processes and peace accords to deal with the core conflict-contributing problems in deeply divided societies. Scrutiny of the meaning of the term peace is an essential, and often overlooked, part of peacemaking and building. The need to stop violence, the increasing standardisation of international peace-support interventions and the failure of many peace processes and accords to address core conflict issues all militate against critical examination of the meaning of the term peace.

The regularity with which poor quality peace is achieved (a ceasefire, an elite-level peace accord, continuing indirect violence etc.) has profound implications for the meaning of the term peace. If post-civil war peace must always be prefaced with terms that indicate its compromised nature (fragile, contested, violent, brittle, turbulent, nervous etc.) then there may be case for arguing that we should revise our definitions of peace to take account of the reality and ubiquity of negative peace. There is a danger that both the proponents and recipients of contemporary peace processes and accords become so acculturated to compromised notions of peace that their conceptualisations of peace will reflect this. Thus, the optimism, energy and healing potential of peace may be crushed by the deadening reality of negative peace. It should be stressed that this appeal for the critical scrutiny of contemporary peacemaking is not based on a naive notion that a celestial and uncompromised peace can materialise from the wreckage of complex social emergencies. Instead, the purpose is to caution against the blithe acceptance as 'good' of social processes graced with the label 'peace' and to encourage a raising of the threshold of optimism of what can be achieved and demanded under the banner of peace.

The liberal democratic peace (the subject of the next chapter), or the particular variety of peace promoted by leading elements of the international community, poses a major barrier to positive peace. As will be explained, inertia and structural factors combine to award the liberal democratic peace with an increasing monopoly in internationally supported peace interventions. Little space is left for alternative means of peacemaking and concepts of peace, including methods that may be considered positive or holistic peace. The near monopoly of the liberal democratic peace in internationally supported peace accords means that the critical scrutiny of the quality of peace on offer, and a critical stance on the idea of peace, can be considered subversive. Contemporary peace and conflict studies has largely failed to take up Schmid's challenge. The sub-discipline largely adopts a problem-solving approach and accepts conflicts, their contexts, peacemaking methods and the resultant peace. Much of it regards its essential task as one of fixing or 'putting back together again' national and regional systems that suffer the disequilibrium of war. Immense energy is invested into what can be described as technical tasks: understanding and designing systems that will sustain order in war-torn societies; engineering power-sharing accommodations between antagonists and disarming militants or repatriating refugees. Amid this myriad of activity (much of it laudable and making significant quality of life differences to millions of people) the task of imagining and conceptualising peace is often overlooked. Without such a starting point, there is a danger that the journey towards peace will be especially difficult.

2

Liberal Democratic Peace

> The human voice can never reach the
> distance covered by the still small voice
> of conscience.
>
> Gandhi

Introduction

It is difficult to mount and sustain arguments against liberalism,
democracy or peace, either as individual concepts or as a triumvirate.
Each has distinguished histories and merits, and is associated with
noble causes, groups and individuals. Yet, this chapter contends that
peculiar types of liberalism, democracy and peace have been awarded
primacy by leading states, international organisations and IFIs in their
peace-support interventions. The near hegemony achieved by this version of peace has had a profound impact on the management of contemporary violent ethnonational conflict in standardising the core
elements of peace initiatives and accords and reducing the space available
for alternative (non-western) approaches to peacemaking. Fundamentally,
the liberal democratic peace model often delivers a deeply flawed peace
that is deficient in the quality of the peace, democracy and liberty that
it offers to the inhabitants of societies emerging from civil war.

The dominance of the liberal democratic peace paradigm has important consequences for the manner in which states, international organisations, NGOs and others conceptualise, articulate and deal with
intra-state war and its aftermath.[1] First, the ascendancy of this approach
to peacemaking reduces the space for creative thinking on alternative
means of approaching the problem of managing ethnonational conflict.

The liberal democratic peace model is supported by such a powerful combination of actors and structures that other options, perhaps indigenous or traditional, find it difficult to gain acceptance. Such is the dominance of the liberal democratic peace that it affects both how we think about peace and the practical policies constructed in the pursuit of peace. Fundamentally, it narrows the range of peace-supporting responses to those considered appropriate under the liberal democratic peace rubric. A liberal democratic peace is imagined as superior to rival notions of peace. Second, and related to the last point, the dominance of this model of peacemaking encourages the use of a template approach to peacemaking on behalf of international organisations, IFIs and leading states. Broadly, the same type of peace and prescriptions are recommended for all conflicts and contexts, regardless of local circumstances, exigencies and structural factors. Consequently, there has been a tendency to extend the same peace-supporting policies from conflict area to conflict area with inadequate concern for local needs. Muggah notes that:

> A number of formulaic security and development oriented interventions are now regularly advanced by multilateral donors to secure the transition for war to peace ... these activities are generally subsumed under the mantle of 'reconstruction and development'.[2]

Many peacebuilding strategies have a familiar quality despite their application to very different geographical regions and in the aftermath of different types of conflict. The single-transferable peace-support package often includes disarmament, demobilisation and reintegration (DDR); civil society enhancement; democratisation programmes and marketisation. The lending and borrowing of good practice between peace processes is to be encouraged and has been a laudable engine of innovation in contemporary peacemaking, but what works in El Salvador or Somalia may not necessarily be applicable in Yemen or Nepal.[3]

The third and most serious charge to place at the door of the dominance of the liberal democratic peace paradigm is simply that it has a sustained record of producing bad peace. Bad peace is better than no peace and this chapter must not be mistaken for an exercise in hand-wringing and a cavilling rejection of all internationally supported peacemaking efforts. Millions of lives have been saved and improved by peace initiatives and accords underpinned by the ideas of liberty and democracy. The negative peace of ending organised violence often provides the foundation stone for many other developments that support a broader peace. But the constancy of peace accords that fail to deliver social justice and positive peace is a serious issue that demands an examination of the philosophical and conceptual bases of contemporary peacemaking. To that end, this chapter has four parts. First, it continues the last chapter's focus on the social construction of peace by examining the 'invention' of the liberal democratic peace.[4] This version of peace was not simply invented from scratch at the end of the Cold War or at another key moment in international history. Instead, it has been able to draw on powerful agents, structures and intellectual resources that have contributed to the dominant version of peace in earlier eras. The modern version of the liberal democratic peace is perhaps more sophisticated than its predecessors in the level of integration of its key elements and its ability to modify in order to keep pace with the interests of its sponsors.

In its second part, the chapter outlines democratic peace theory – an incredibly influential proposition based on the association between the democratic organisation of a state and pacific relations between states. Democratic peace theory has been internalised as a truism by leading states, international organisations and policymakers and is used as an intellectual foundation for the promotion of liberal democratic peace. From the perspective of the ending of civil wars, the chief failing of the democratic peace proposition is that it applies to inter-state, rather than intra-state, war. In other words, the proposition which has been used to justify the promotion of liberalism and democracy as integral parts of peacemaking in civil wars has little relevance to civil wars.

The third section of the chapter outlines how peculiar notions of liberalism and democracy award the liberal democratic peace its distinctive character. It finds that the types of liberalism and democracy promoted often form barriers to elements of a holistic or positive peace outlined in the last chapter. Finally, the chapter notes how the liberal democratic peace notion has been adopted and promoted by international organisations, leading states, IFIs and NGOs to the extent that it has become the hegemonic notion of peace in international peace-support interventions. In short, it is the version of peace preferred by the international community, however 'fictitious' the communal character of the international community may be.[5] The champions of the liberal democratic peace have the power to invest sufficient legitimacy in this model of peacemaking to the extent that they not only dominate peace-support activity but also how peace is conceptualised. Crucially, the peace delivered on behalf of the liberal democratic peace is often illiberal and undemocratic and far-removed from the holistic notions of positive peace outlined in the last chapter.

A note on terminology

The use of the term 'liberal democratic peace' is deliberate. Possible alternatives to the term are liberal peace, western peace, internationally supported peace or simply 'peace'. An essential part of this book is the identification and description of the dominant version of peace sponsored by powerful international actors. To simply label as 'peace' those situations, practices and aspirations effected by proponents of this dominant version of peace risks reinforcing the hegemony of that version while simultaneously undermining alternatives. Using the term 'liberal democratic peace' (rather than 'peace') serves as a statement that there can be no monopoly on the use of the term 'peace'. The term 'liberal peace' is common coinage in many historical and contemporary accounts of peacemaking, but it seems appropriate that we identify by name a core tenet of the dominant western version of peace: democratisation.[6] Thus the term 'liberal democratic peace' is used in this work. It is worth noting that the term 'liberal' may be problematic for some, particularly in the United States where it has acquired pejorative connotations in certain quarters, yet it is retained here to underline the substantial ideological underpinning internationally supported approaches to peacemaking. While the term 'western peace' is attractive because it captures the essential ethnocentricity of dominant versions of peace and peacemaking, 'liberal democratic peace' is preferred because it identifies by name the core components of this version of peace.

The invention of peace

The currently dominant version of the liberal democratic peace was invented in 1989. More precisely it was reinvented in 1989 because it had been 'invented' in 1945 and before that again in 1918 and at other interregnum moments when major international wars came to an end. Each occasion marked the beginning of a new era in which a particular type of peace gained ascendancy. On each occasion the essential elements of the peace were influenced by a mixture of realpolitik and prevailing ideologies. In the modern era, the versions of liberalism and democracy that were championed as part of the liberal democratic peace were western in origin and articulation and often insensitive to local circumstances and traditions. They also tended to reinforce the advantages of the victors and powerholders and shied away from a fundamental revision of social and political relationships within and between states. Liberty and democracy were to be extended only selectively and often in highly specific and compromised forms.[7] The version of liberalism reflected the competing demands of the individual, the market and the powerholders, with the individual the regular loser in these contests. Where extended, democracy also faced limitations and was as much an agent of conformity and replication of power relations as an agent of change. In most cases, democracy contained considerable conservative components that acted as barrier to, rather than facilitators of, positive peace. In each case, the peace of 1918, 1945 and 1989 saw the inclusion of open and free markets in the peace equation.

While the liberal democratic peace of 1918 and 1945 became skewed by unfavourable political, economic and cultural factors that left the peace with decidedly illiberal and undemocratic aspects, the liberal democratic peace of 1989 is still a work in progress. Thus far, four points can be made about it: first, its dominance as a peacemaking model is largely unchallenged, reaching levels of acceptance not accorded to the earlier versions of the liberal democratic peace. This dominance and acceptance should not be mistaken with popularity. Instead, it reflects the absence of alternatives and the disciplining effect that stems from the sponsorship of the liberal democratic peace by powerful states and institutions with the potential to disburse resources. Second, earlier versions of the liberal democratic peace were primarily focused on international peace or peace between states. While the post-1989 liberal democratic peace retains this focus, circumstances have demanded that it also pays attention to peace within states.[8] Third, the divergence of the post-1989 version of peace from the key ideas of democracy and liberalism has been startling. In some cases, the operationalisation of the liberal democratic peace has entailed the suppression of democracy and the denial of rights, for example, the overriding of nationalist preferences in post-Dayton Bosnia-Herzegovina.[9] In the post-9/11 period in particular, the notion of 'stabilisation' (more precisely security) has crept into the conceptualisation and promotion of the liberal democratic peace with profound consequences for liberty. Fourth, the liberal democratic peace is not simply a labelling device for the post-Cold War international political system. Instead, it is a functioning peacemaking model. It provides an intellectual and practical framework around which its architects can justify and promote a particular version of peace. As a model of peacemaking, it is replicable and – as will be discussed later – has led to the standardisation of peace-support interventions.

The invention of peace (both as a concept and as a set of practical policies) can be illustrated through history. Repeatedly, the notion of peace was constructed to conform to prevailing power relations and values. Thus the versions of peace 'invented' in medieval Europe as a response to the pervasiveness of private wars sought to reinforce the supremacy of the existing sources of power and wealth: sovereigns and their proto-states, and the church.[10] The period was one of widespread lawlessness in which:

> Institutionalised vengeance, through feud and vendetta, festered without respite, while gangs of bandits struck from the fringes of settled regions and bands of beggars, thieves and cutthroats roamed countryside and towns. A strong central government, backed by powerful magnates, would generally keep these elements at bay; but where the authorities faltered, anarchy quickly spread.[11]

Over time, the church and state campaigns for peace and order converged to the extent that there was a 'successful symbiosis between the ruling warrior class that provided order and the clerisy that legitimised it.'[12] Like subsequent inventions of peace, the medieval peace of the 'City of God and the City of Man' was essentially conservative and lacked the radicalism demanded by notions of positive peace.[13] Although the pattern of the invention of peace by elites continued, the preferred notion of peace underwent transformation. In particular, the moral authority of the church was replaced by that of the open market and, much more recently, the language (and at times action) of democracy, democratisation and good governance. One constant factor, despite the continual reinvention of the notion of peace, has been the primacy of the state or, more precisely, the primacy attached to the sovereignty of leading states.

The liberal democratic peace adopted a recognisably modern form in response to the First World War, with US President Woodrow Wilson cast in the role of the grandfather of the liberal democratic peace model.[14] Traumatised by the First World War and the inability of diplomacy to halt the slide into war, Wilson proposed a radical package of ideas and policies that he hoped would form the basis of a peaceful postwar world. In his famous January 1918 'Fourteen Points' speech, he proposed a new world order characterised by explicit peace agreements, open and accountable diplomatic relations between states, and arms control.[15] He also advocated the creation of a permanent international institution for the arbitration of inter-state disputes and the guarantee of 'political independence and territorial integrity to great and small states alike'.[16] Although his primary concern was peace among states, the underlying principle in his peace programme had relevance to relationships within states: 'justice to all peoples and nationalities, and their right to live on equal terms of liberty and safety with one another, whether they be strong or weak'.[17]

The inclusion of free trade in the notion of peace was evident in Wilson's worldview, with a call for 'the removal, so far as possible, of all economic barriers and the establishment of an equality of trade conditions among all the nations consenting to the peace and associating themselves for its maintenance'.[18] Wilson had justified the entry of the United States into the First World War on the grounds that 'The world must be made safe for democracy'[19] and believed that the spread of democracy and associated restraining values would act as an antidote to competition between states.[20] But Wilson's vision was too radical for its time and his idealism failed to rhyme with the intentions of other statesmen. While the post-First World War peace involved many innovative features, including coordinated post-war reconstruction efforts and the extension of suffrage in the United States, Britain and elsewhere, it also involved a punitive regime against the vanquished and the negative peace of arms control.[21] Ultimately, states failed to transfer sufficient legitimacy to the League of Nations, to enable it to thwart the rise of fascism.[22] The 1920s, and especially the 1930s, presented an 'illusion of peace' during which statesmen still referred to the democratic and liberal elements of the post-First World War peace as absolutism gathered pace.[23] This system collapsed into the Second World War which again prompted the search for a 'new' model of peace. Not only did the conclusion of the Second World War witness the establishment of the United Nations and the assumption of the United States to the position of superpower, it also saw the establishment of the international financial institutions that did much to guide development within and between states. Again, there was the setting out of a brave new agenda for the pacific management of disputes based on liberal ideas. The 1941 Atlantic Charter which formed the basis for Anglo-American cooperation during the war was a precursor for what was to come. The Allied campaign was pursued in the name of '[T]he right of all peoples to choose the form of government under which they will live' and to restore to all states 'access, on equal terms, to the trade and to the raw materials of the world which are needed for their economic prosperity'.[24] Again, the notion of the free market was internalised as a key component of the international order and the peace it would champion.

The ideals of the Atlantic Charter were enhanced after the war through the United Nations and its Charter. Despite the universalist ambitions of the United Nations, the ideas of liberalism and democracy that were central to the post-war peace reflected the biases and interests of leading western states. In principle, the aims of the United Nations were entirely laudable:

> to unite our strength to maintain international peace and security ... to ensure, by the acceptance of principles and the institution of methods, that armed force shall not be used, save in the common interest, and to employ international machinery for the promotion of the economic and social advancement of all peoples.[25]

Despite the new international machinery and the noble principles underpinning the new common security organisation, the long, cold peace of the Cold War was extremely dysfunctional. Superpower rivalries meant that the United Nations operated with something of a handicap for the duration of the Cold War, especially in relation to peace and conflict issues. The Cold War was a classic negative peace in that the nuclear arms race was met with marathon arms control talks but not a serious attempt to review the need for nuclear weapons and the deeper issues that lay behind their possession and proliferation. Europe was spared a major violent conflagration during the Cold War (neither NATO nor the Warsaw Pact fired a shot in anger), but the continent experienced the militarism of arms industries, conscription and the mobilisation of politics and populations against the enemy. Meanwhile, states in the developing world experienced a contagion of violent civil wars or wars of national liberation (often lubricated by the superpowers).

The democracy and liberal values championed by the West were to be shared selectively.[26] In many circumstances, pursuit of the Cold War was to be given priority over democracy and individual liberty. The rhetoric employed in western capitals to justify the Cold War was often faithful to the triumvirate of liberty, democracy and peace. Thus, one of the first Cold Warriors, US President Harry Truman, promised assistance to 'free peoples to work out their own destinies in their own way',[27] while one of the last Cold Warriors, President Reagan, advocated preparation 'for peace not only by reducing weapons but by bolstering prosperity, liberty, and democracy however and wherever we can'.[28] Yet, the on-the-ground manifestation of these ideals was often disastrous. Support for coups against democratically elected governments (Chile), death squads (Peru), the propping up of wicked regimes (South Africa) and the curtailment of individual liberty (the United States in the McCarthy period) were the lifeblood of the liberal democratic peace in the Cold

War era. In the West, the costs of the Cold War peace fell unevenly; boxer Mohammed Ali's query of why the burden of the Vietnam War fell more heavily on African Americans than on his paler skinned compatriots seems to sum up the point: 'Ain't no Vietcong ever called me "nigger".'[29]

The end of the Cold War facilitated the ascendance of the latest version of the liberal democratic peace. The Soviet Union collapsed as a superpower, as a patron to other states and as an alternative idea of social and political organisation to democratic capitalism.[30] The implications of the end of the Cold War were profound: client states lost patrons, borders were redrawn and the United Nations and multilateral interventionism were reinvigorated. The United States was transformed from the status of superpower to that of hegemon. Given our interest in the invention of the liberal democratic peace, two consequences of the end of the Cold War are particularly important. The first was the opening up of markets previously protected by state barriers. The Cold War had allowed some states (often aligned with the Soviet bloc) and some industries (in the US and Soviet blocs) to shield themselves from open trade. With the end of the Cold War, the free market became 'as close to a universally accepted institution as had ever existed in human history.'[31] This acceptance was often resigned in nature and reflected the lack of alternatives. The second consequence of the end of the Cold War for the liberal democratic peace was the intellectual fillip received by the ideas of liberalism and democracy. The immediate post-Cold War years were the apogee of democracy and liberalism as concepts for the organisation of society and relations between states and groups. Evidence of the intellectual triumph of liberalism and democracy came in commentary that stressed time and again that the ideas faced no credible alternative.[32] Francis Fukuyama's celebrated 'The end of history' essay summed up the liberal democratic triumph: 'the endpoint of mankind's ideological evolution and the universalization of Western liberal democracy as the final form of human government'.[33]

The chief point of this section is that peace has been invented and reinvented throughout history, with each reinvention reflecting the dominant values and power that dominate that particular era. The post-Cold War version of the liberal democratic peace draws heavily on structural components, values and modes of behaviour that were established in earlier attempts to construct a liberal democratic peace. Its reach is by no means universal and it is not without challenges and detractors. Importantly, the liberal democratic peace was not uniformly applied, with, for example, some post-war societies experiencing significant marketisation but cursory democratisation. For many societies, the liberal democratic peace presented opportunities for social progress and human emancipation. As will be illustrated later in the chapter though, the quality of the peace that was delivered by the liberal democratic peace has often been wanting.

Democratic peace theory

According to the democratic peace proposition, states with democratic governments do not go to war against one another.[34] The proposition has been the recipient of enormous academic attention, much of it repetitive and unenlightening. Quantitative research has tested the veracity of the proposition and attempted to measure the association between democracy and other variables apparently linked with pacific inter-state relations.[35] Qualitative research has attempted to unpack those components of the democratic state (for example, types of institutions or behaviour) thought to be responsible for their warlessness. The democratic peace proposition has spawned an academic debate of an extent far beyond the actual significance of the proposition. By itself, the academic attention is unimportant, but the democratic peace proposition has been enormously influential at the policy and decision-making levels in leading governments, international organisations and IFIs. The internalisation of democratic peace theory among elites is crucial to the prevalence of the liberal democratic peace paradigm that dominates interventionist thinking and policy in contemporary deeply divided and war-torn societies. As one commentator noted: 'Clinton converted the democratic peace proposition into a security policy manifesto by making it the center-piece of his post-Cold War democratic enlargement strategy.'[36] Democracy and democratisation (both often as rhetorical as real) lay at the heart of the post-Cold War foreign policy strategy that had been constructed by the United States, its allies and client international organisations by the mid-1990s. The democratic peace proposition was able to play a key role in providing the intellectual justification for the emphasis on democratisation in this strategy.

The linkage between democracy and peace has become a truism oft repeated in the mission statements of international organisations and foreign policy objectives of leading states. The sentiment was summarised in Boutros-Ghali's 1992 *Agenda for Peace* document thus:

> There is an obvious connection between democratic practices – such as the rule of law and transparency in decision-making – and the achievement of true peace and security in any new and stable

political order. These elements of good governance need to be promoted at all levels of international and national political communities.[37]

The implications of the democratic peace proposition are far-reaching. First, it is essentially a liberal concept that refutes realist notions that humankind is condemned to perpetual suspicion and anarchy.[38] Owen argues that it is 'liberal ideas that cause liberal democracies to tend away from war with one another'[39] with the self-preservation instincts of citizens restraining politicians from foreign policy adventurism. Humans, in this view, are capable of rational calculation. 'Liberal democracies are believed reasonable, predictable and trustworthy, because they are governed by their citizens' true interests, which harmonise with all individuals' true interests around the world.'[40] Rawls refers to this as 'The Law of Peoples' in which 'the interests which move peoples … are reasonable interests guided by and congruent with a fair equality and a due respect for all peoples'.[41] So the democratic peace proposition is steeped in liberal optimism and regards it as logical that an extension of liberal values among states would make the outbreak of inter-state war less likely. Second, the proposition is based on an association between political organisation within the state and the external behaviour of that state. As such, it invites scrutiny of the nature of the regime within the state and thus crosses the sovereignty taboo line. Traditional notions of sovereignty which had regarded politics within the state as off-limits to external actors now faced a challenge. In other words, the logic of the democratic peace proposition is interventionist. A third implication of the democratic peace proposition is that it immediately recommends a remedy for conflict: democratisation. If states can be democratised then they will be pacified. Arguments on behalf of this type of peacemaking strategy were much easier to articulate and justify than peacemaking strategies that entailed warfare or military intervention in the period up to 9/11. This was especially the case in a number of complex political emergencies that followed the end of the Cold War and involved the organisation and maintenance of multilateral peace-support coalitions. The promotion of democracy was not a value-free exercise, and the type of democracy promoted, and the nature of its promotion, was often responsible for the fragile and frustrated peace that reigned in a number of societies coming out of violent conflict. A fourth implication of the democratic peace proposition is its self-affirmation of leading states and their own system of government. In its basic sense, it recommends the straightforward transfer of western notions of democracy and fails to consider their ripeness for export.

The democratic peace thesis has become an incredibly powerful intellectual tool for the justification of a particular type of peace. It is a major plank in the elevation of the liberal democratic peace to its position of dominance whereby it becomes the only brand of peace to be promoted and affirmed by the international community. But the democratic peace proposition is deeply flawed for a number of reasons. First, correlation is not the same as causation. As John Owen points out in relation to inter-state wars, 'Wars are so rare that random chance could account for the democratic peace, much as it could account for an absence of war among, say, states whose names begin with the letter k.'[42] The precise reasons for the seeming association between democratic states and warlessness are unclear and are likely to reside in such a complex matrix of reasons (enduring alliances and patterns of trade etc.) that it is difficult to promote one war-restraining factor such as democracy above others.[43] Second, while advocates of the democratic peace theory attest to the power of democracy in restraining war between democracies, the proposition does not apply to war-making and intervention by democracies on non-democracies. The interventionist history of the United States in the twentieth and twenty-first centuries is testament to the extent that democracy can co-exist with high levels of intervention. Third, the advocacy of democracy and democratisation that has followed the internalisation of the democratic peace thesis among leading states and international organisations has not been complemented by an interrogation of the nature and varieties of democracy. Instead, there has been a tendency towards the blithe promotion of democracy and its attendant institutions without due care towards the political culture and behaviour within states and their suitability for the importation of democracy. The democratic peace thesis has encouraged the extension of technocratic 'solutions' to the problems of post-civil war societies, particularly in the emphasis on electoral democracy. The focus of many internationally sponsored democracy assistance interventions has been on the polling process rather than the wider issue of embedding a culture of democracy into political relationships.[44]

The most fundamental criticism of the democratic peace thesis is its irrelevance to the pressing reality of the prevalence of ethnonational tension and war. The thesis only applies to inter-state wars. War between states is a rare phenomenon, comprising less than 10 percent of the total number of armed conflicts.[45] Thus, the democratic peace paradigm, the object of a substantial academic industry and a means of justification for the policy of some leading states and major international organisations, is largely irrelevant to the cause and maintenance of intra-state war. Moreover, its focus on overt warfare also misses the need to focus on conflict and peacemaking as more than the termination of direct violence.

The components of the liberal democratic peace

In order to more fully understand the liberal democratic peace it seems sensible to unpack its core elements: liberalism and democracy. This section is not a critique of liberalism and democracy *per se*; both sets of values have provided the motive force for much human emancipation and social progress. The contention here is that peculiar, and at times harmful, versions of liberalism and democracy have been promoted by leading states, international organisations and IFIs. In particular, the idea of free markets has been central to the version of liberalism found in the liberal democratic peace, while a narrow focus on electoral politics and western-style political organisation has dominated much democracy promotion. This double concentration on free markets and electoral democracy has done much to give the liberal democratic peace its distinctive and at times contradictory character. It is worth repeating though that this section is not an assault on the ideas of liberalism and democracy, instead it is a critique of the manner in which they have been championed by the most powerful actors in the post-Cold War international political system as part of peace-support operations. It is also important to note an awareness that liberalism and democracy do not constitute discrete conceptual categories nor do they necessarily entail particular policy outcomes. Instead, they comprise broad categories capable of change and contradiction.

Central to the idea of the liberal democratic peace is the complementary relationship between each of its components. The components are mutually reinforcing and whether one takes 'liberalism', 'democracy' or 'peace' as an intellectual starting point, it is possible to make a procedural linkage with the other components. For example, if we begin with liberalism, then it is possible to argue that the emancipation of the individual demands democratic representation and results in pacific relations between citizens within and between states. The ideas of liberalism and democracy require a more detailed scrutiny, particularly to explain how their respective embrace of the primacy of free-market economics and western-style electoral politics has awarded the liberal democratic peace its peculiar character.

Liberalism

Clearly, the spread of liberal ideas has had a profound impact on the social and political organisation of human relations. If the objective of 'the liberal project' is taken to be 'enhancing human freedom and dignity', then it is clear that liberal advances have been made in many societies in terms of political, economic, religious, cultural and inter-personal rights.[46] Liberalism has provided the intellectual rationale for the elevation of the individual to the position of a citizen with prior rights over the sovereign or state (often expressed in a human rights discourse in the contemporary era).[47] According to this liberal view, many of these rights relate to freedoms of expression that are best guaranteed by political systems able to ensure peace and human enjoyment. Central to liberal claims is the negotiated restraint of the state in its interference in the realm of the individual. Liberal ideas present an optimistic challenge to the idea that warfare and anarchy are the natural state of humankind. MacMillan provides a useful summary of this vein of political thought: 'Liberalism's stress upon human freedom, the potential of agency over structure, the power of reason, and faith in the reconcilability of interests, equips it to be a distinctly pacifistic political philosophy.'[48] Liberalism has the capacity to impact on both the domestic and foreign policy spheres with a domestic liberal political order (invariably democratic) encouraging pacific inter-state relations.[49]

While the dominant post-Cold War strain of liberalism still emphasizes individual rights and emancipation, it also stresses the importance of the free market. The inclusion of the market in notions of liberalism is by no means new (it has been a central feature of some strains of liberal ideology throughout the twentieth century and before) but the reach of the market has never been so widespread.[50] This dominance has contributed to the distinctive character of the contemporary liberal democratic peace both as an idea and a practice. Free markets, and particularly the tendency of free markets to contradict social justice, have played a key role in the frustration of public expectations in the wake of many peace accords. Many post-civil war societies are hamstrung by market penetration and unfavourable global economic structures that render them consuming rather than producing societies. The principal problems in a number of societies emerging from violent conflict tend to be economic rather than political or security-related. Unemployment and under-employment, a lack of investment and savings, a contracted tax base and unfavourable trading regimes comprise the typical features of many post-war societies. A lack of restraint on capital is seen as an integral part of liberalism and one that contributes to the fulfilment of other social and political goals of the liberal canon. Mandelbaum neatly summarises the supposed virtuous circle by noting that 'free markets make free men'.[51] According to this view, the market provides a route for the further emancipation of the individual; the withdrawal of the state from the realm of the individual and the market go hand-in-hand. The view is liberal in its fundamental principles through a respect for 'individual desires and voluntary transactions' and a reliance on self-enforcing exchange relationships.[52] The recipe for the perfect market is:

> A liberal, market-enhancing state that protects property rights and encourages investment; freedom for firms to enter and compete in markets; openness to trade with and investment from the rest of the world; sound monetary and fiscal policies with modest deficits and low inflation; and measures to enhance the health and levels of education of the population.[53]

That 'there is no empirical basis for the argument that economic performance is necessarily tied to constitutional democracy and human rights' has done little to dampen the enthusiasm of the cheerleaders of market-led liberalism and democratisation.[54] A significant number of states (in the Arabian Gulf and East Asia) have pursued free-market economic development while limiting individual rights. For champions of free-market liberalism, a key obstacle to the fulfilment of the market was seen to be the 'overextended' state. The prescription advocated by IFIs was to 'pare down the size and responsibilities of the state, augment its capacity to fulfil its minimal economic role, and correct a variety of "domestic policy deficiencies" that waste resources and suffocate market resources'.[55] The manifestation of these policy prescriptions, although liberating for some, was often contrary to cohesive social values and human needs. Although institutions such as the World Bank have stepped back somewhat from the strict adherence to the 'market fundamentalism' that characterised their interventions of the 1980s and early 1990s, the market is still triumphant and its justification is often dressed in the language of liberalism.[56] A good example of the melding of liberalism with the free-market economy comes from women's empowerment programmes across the developing world. Explanations of these programmes and their constituent projects highlight the emancipatory and empowering potential of the market in awarding women with capacities for self-reliance and individual autonomy. Yet, what is remarkable is the high degree of marketisation at the core of such schemes, with participants encouraged to achieve further individual and gender emancipation through economic activity. Thus, computer skills are learned to make participants more employable and handicrafts produced for sale. Doubtless, such skills training can help liberate, but the extent to which market 'solutions' have a core and unquestioned role in the empowerment strategy is noteworthy.[57]

The contribution to peace made by free markets has been mixed. The correlation between free trade and the absence of inter-state war is undeniable. Nor can we easily dismiss the creativity of the market and its ability to emancipate some individuals and groups. But the market does not have a natural social conscience and bold claims on its behalf, such as 'Market forces can help fight AIDS', require caution.[58] Profits must come from somewhere, and private profit, in many circumstances, comes at the expense of public goods. Holistic and inclusive versions of peace that transcend attention on direct violence and tackle underlying restraints on human opportunity are expensive and require long-term intervention by states and other institutions, thus contradicting the inclinations of the market.

Profit and peace are very different things. Kenneth Good launches an excoriating attack on the tendency of the market to diminish rather than enhance human opportunity. Taking the United States, 'the home, and global progenitor, of an extensively deregulated market economy', as the prime example, he notes how the 'new flexible capitalism creates inequalities and injustice which the liberal polity, with its largely alienated, non-participatory electorate, is unable to address.'[59] In this view, the market has contributed to a 'totalitarian' penal policy, 'the militarization of policing', the deregulation of industry leading to 'disposable work and disposable workers', 'one of the lowest voter participation rates in the world' and the 'constant amoral manipulations ... [by] ... populist political elites'.[60] Rather than a panacea, this perspective regards the market as an obstacle to positive peace. Indeed, it can be no coincidence that many of the communities held up as embodiments of positive or holistic peace have been resistant to marketisation. Many are traditional societies that are not fully monetised and are physically removed from modern commercial centres.[61]

Direct linkages between free markets and ethnonational conflicts are commonplace. Market-dominant minorities in numerous states (for example, Chinese in Burma, Ibo in Nigeria and Lebanese in West Africa) have been victims of majorities who perceive themselves to be excluded from economic opportunities and exploited by the out-group.[62] In such circumstances, the imbalances of the market become suffused with wider grievance agendas to provide a powerful engine of division.

Similar dynamics can be found in post-peace accord societies in which any peace dividend seems more tangible for one group than another, sparking a sense of relative deprivation in the midst of a peacemaking process. Yet, for all of the potential complications that the market brings, it has gained an unassailable position as a core part of international peace-support operations and post-war reconstruction.

Democracy

The second component of the liberal democratic peace, democracy, has also become skewed to favour a particular variant of democracy that does not always contribute to positive peace. It is worth reiterating that this is not an attack on democracy as a means to represent the opinions of citizens, mediate disputes and share resources. Instead, the argument is made that a western version of democracy is promoted in such a way that it can be counter-productive to the pacific management of conflict. The extension of democratic forms of government since the end of the Cold War has been startling and has reinforced the notion that democracy is universally applicable. By 2003, 121 out of the world's 192 governments 'met the minimum standard of a fair vote count in conditions of secrecy and relatively open election campaigning'.[63] Yet, many democracies (a good number in societies emerging from civil war) can be described as 'thin', 'pseudo' or 'low-intensity' democracies.[64] They may have the outward appearance of democracy in that they mimic the procedural features of western representative democracies in their staging of electoral contests, but they may lack the political ethos and culture that embeds democracy in wider society. The past decade has seen many elections marked by spectacular incivility, whether in the form of the jailing and intimidation of opposition candidates (Zimbabwe and Azerbaijan) or the use of extreme language to characterise an opponent (Zimbabwe). Two aspects of post-Cold War peace interventions by leading states, international organisations and IFIs deserve attention: the concentration on electoral processes in place of attempts to foster a more deep-rooted democratic culture and the promotion of a western notion of civil society. Electoral assistance and support for civil society have been the mainstays of international intervention in war-torn societies from at least 1989 onwards and have been central to the emergence and peculiar character of the liberal democratic peace.[65]

Elections offer multiple advantages in post-civil war societies: the validation of a political transition; the legitimisation of processes of democratisation and peacemaking; the broadening of the base of popular participation in politics; the arbitration of disputes underlying an ethnonational conflict; the embedding of institutions and processes that aid non-violent dispute resolution and the affirmation of a peace accord or post-conflict constitution.[66] As Bratton observes, 'While you can have elections without democracy, you cannot have democracy without elections.'[67] In western societies, elections are regarded as a routine and insoluble part of democracy and their worth is often unquestioned. Elections by themselves do not make democracy; they form only part of wider processes of embedding democratic norms and values into society. Yet, much of the democracy assistance efforts spearheaded by leading states and international organisations in response to the civil wars of the 1990s and beyond concentrated on electoral support without due attention to the attendant norms and values of participation and transparency that characterise democracy in the four to five years between electoral cycles. Bastian and Luckham note the ability of democracy to be 'Janus-faced':

> As well as empowering citizens, overcoming exclusion and contributing to good governance, it can also become the tool of powerful economic interests, reinforce societal inequalities, penalise minorities, awaken dormant conflicts, and fail in practice to broaden popular participation in government.[68]

Election-specific pitfalls for the post-civil war society and the international community abound: the failure to provide adequate security for campaigning; the absence of an accurate electoral roll and organisational capacity to stage an election; the danger that the electoral process becomes an arena for the continuation of the ethnonational conflict and a premature election that precedes the establishment of mass participation political parties. However, there are three more fundamental problems with the expansion of the democracy project. The first is the limited ability of democracy assistance programmes to effect large-scale structural change in anything but exceptional cases of regime change or a transfer of sovereignty.[69] Electoral democracy may facilitate a change in government and leadership, and 'some institutional features and discursive trappings of democracy' may be incorporated into the manner of governance, but the overall structure of power relations in society may remain unchanged.[70] In many cases, rather than challenge authoritarianism, elections can consolidate it via the ballot box – a not unreasonable proposition in societies emerging from civil war in which groups are easily mobilised around ethnonational issues. In many cases, electoral democracy amounts to an essentially conservative device that replicates existing power relations. While leaderships change, much else remains the same. The virtues of stability are clear, particularly for societies emerging from civil war, but electoral devices by themselves may be unable to reform or restructure power relations in order to confront the underlying causation and maintenance factors behind a conflict. Yet, externally supported electoral assistance programmes are likely to be so fixated on the goal of holding an election that more profound issues of conflict causation may be overlooked. The nature of ethnonational disputes often calls for fundamental structural change so as to protect minorities, promote pluralism and redistribute resources.

A second problem with the expansion of the democracy project is the unsuitability for export of the western version of democracy. Mohammed Salih notes that there are 'no serious grounds' for the comparison of democratisation in Africa with democracy in western societies, and that 'democracy is a process that can be encouraged and enhanced, but not engineered'.[71] Yet, substantial energies from western states and international organisations have been invested into democratic transfer, or the attempt to supplant western notions of democracy, that emphasise electoral processes in societies emerging from violent conflict. The almost messianic promotion of electoral democracy as part of internationally supported peace interventions has meant that, in many cases, there has been little serious policy discussion of the suitability of electoral democracy to a particular post-war environment. For example, the extent to which a political and social culture can adapt to electoral democracy is crucial. Societies with deeply entrenched means of decision-making (patriarchal, consensus or warlordism) may struggle to accommodate electoralism.

The third fundamental problem with democracy promotion is that elections are frequently the scene of political violence. Although once established, democracies offer the prospect of orderly transitions between governments, electoral processes and transitions towards democracy in post-civil war scenarios can spark insecurity, tension and violence.[72] While the October 2003 Presidential election in post-Taliban Afghanistan was remarkable for its smooth running, the story was very different in the 2005 Iraqi parliamentary elections. Here, militant groups exploited the increased international focus on the election to illustrate their opposition to foreign occupation and their sense of exclusion from the puppet regime. In other cases, for example, Bosnia-Herzegovina, Kosovo and Northern Ireland), militant groups have hastily transformed themselves into political parties. Clearly, electoral rather than violent contests are to be encouraged, but hastily formed parties are often characterised by exclusive agendas that risk continuing the war by other means and their approach to campaigning and candidate selection may inflame rather than dampen inter-group tension.[73]

One feature of western democracy promotion strategies that has done much to define the nature of the liberal democratic peace in the post-Cold War world is the idea of civil society. Regarded as both an arena of political and social interaction, and as a sector of political and social actors, civil society has the capacity to act as a restraint on, and scrutiniser of, government and its institutions.[74] Comprised of non-governmental groups such as churches, trades unions and the media, civil society organisations can play crucial roles in deeply divided societies or those societies attempting to manage violent conflict. Civil society may provide a space for centreground political actors to interact, attempt to safeguard the rights of minorities or vulnerable groups, or resist government attempts to maximise its power. In semi-closed and repressive societies, for example Burma or Turkmenistan, civil society organisations play a role in bearing witness, or recording abuse and injustice. The principal problem with the western-inspired and funded promotion of civil society in the context of post-civil war societies is that a particular type of civil society is promoted. This civil society is usually urban, English-speaking, receptive to western ideas and ready to overlook traditional sources of power and counsel. Somewhat ironically, civil society organisations may form an elite just as exclusive to wider participation as a government in a deeply divided society. Adamson warns of this danger in relation to Uzbekistan and Kyrgyzstan:

> An international funded 'democracy sector' that has no deep roots in local society, is in danger of exacerbating tensions between the small elite that is able to benefit from international assistance and the majority of the population, which is struggling for economic survival.[75]

The chief point is that western interveners often have highly specific notions of what civil society 'should look like' and are intolerant of more locally inspired variants. This tendency has influenced the distinctive nature of the liberal democratic peace in the post-Cold War era and explains why much of the international peacemaking and supporting activity in societies emerging from civil war fails to connect with large sections of the population. Gagnon comments on one case: '... Some international NGOs have actually made it less possible and much harder to rebuild civil society because many Bosnians have the impression that civil society projects are really a sham by well-paid internationals.'[76] Indeed, societies emerging from ethnonational conflict often have very strong civil society organisations, usually a by-product of political mobilisation around an ethnic cause or grievance. Conflict is often a powerful energiser of bonding (rather than bridging) social capital. The problem is that this is often regarded as the 'wrong type' of civil society. While it may be unable to foster reconciliation and promote the politics of accommodation among hostile groups, it still retains a worth in that it can facilitate the distribution of public goods and services to those in need, albeit usually only those in the in-group. In many Muslim societies, the mosque acts as the focal point for social capital and as a centre for resource distribution. Yet in the western mindset, such civil society may be regarded as exclusive and antithetical to pluralism. As Barakat and Chard note, 'the definition of civil society adopted by the majority of the aid community is too prescriptive and culturally biased to serve as a useful tool in the development of strategies for democratic and social change in developing [or] ... war-torn societies'.[77]

In sum, many advocates of the liberal democratic peace have failed to take on board two lessons. The first is that many civil war societies already possess a civil society (though according to western eyes this may be an 'inappropriate' civil society). The second missed lesson is the need to recognise the heterogeneity of civil society in many post-civil war societies. Rather than civil society, many post-war environments are host to a number of overlapping civil societies.

The liberal democratic peace and 'the international community'

The key to the domination of the liberal democratic peace above other versions of peace has been the confluence of key agents (leading states and international organisations) and structural factors (the institutions and processes that support the economic and geo-political objectives of the agents). This is not a vast Machiavellian conspiracy through which the agents conspire to deliver a poor quality peace yet maintain the verbiage of a liberal democratic peace. Rather liberal democratic peace results from a combination of the pursuit of rational self-interest by core elements of the international community, the promotion of peace guided by liberal optimism and a genuine belief that democracy and open markets provide the best route to its achievement. The chief agents in the construction, adoption and promotion of the liberal democratic peace are often amalgamated into the seemingly innocuous term 'international community'. Despite the constancy of its use, especially in the news media, much of the structure and behaviour of the international community lacks a communal or communitarian element. Clearly, some states and international organisations have more power and are able to project more legitimacy than others. What passes as the international community can be more precisely summed up as a combination of leading states (the United States and key allies), some international organisations some of the time (the United Nations, European Union, North Atlantic Treaty Organization (NATO) etc.) and the major IFIs. Elements of this community share an ethos that prioritises free markets, the maintenance of state sovereignty and their own continued dominance.

The central player in the 'international community' is the United States. This fact is not an excuse for 'America-bashing' which may begin as a critique of the foreign policy of the United States but slides easily towards racism. Instead, it is a recognition of preponderance of US power in the post-Cold War world and the profound implications of this power for the conceptualisation and pursuit of peace. The economic, political and military hegemony of the United States is unrivalled and fuels an immense social and cultural reach. The United States has by far the largest economy in the world, easily the most technologically sophisticated and well-funded military, and it organises its defence on the basis that it will be able to unilaterally fight two wars simultaneously.[78] The extent of US power preponderance amounts to 'a situation unseen since the premodern heydays of Tang China, the Mongols, and the Roman Empire.'[79] Despite its anti-imperial origins, the United States is an empire, but it is a very different type of empire than previous empires, with different types of structures, values and modes of imperial power projection. Ignatieff refers to it as 'empire lite, hegemony without colonies, a global sphere of influence without the burden of direct administration and the risks of daily policing'.[80] His account of the US empire notes how its essential aim is to ensure the security of the centre and how it is empowered to use violence with impunity, while the 'moral grace notes' are 'liberal and democratic'.[81] Less critical accounts of US hegemony are available and make the point that the US empire has shown restraint and contains key liberal elements that help explain the nature of the liberal democratic peace that dominates the societies emerging from civil wars. Ikenberry is persuasive in making the case for the exceptionalism of American predominance:

> This world order – perhaps best called the American system – is organized around American-led regional security alliances in Europe

and Asia, open and multilateral economic relations, several layers of regional and global multilateral institutions, and shared commitments to democracy and open capitalist economies. It is an order built around American power and a convergence of interests between the United States and other advanced industrial democratic states.[82]

Nested within this liberal version of empire, which depends on the complicity of other western states and a complex matrix of multilateral institutions, is the liberal democratic peace. The United States, along with international organizations, such as the United Nations and European Union, and IFIs is one of the key (if not the primary) institutions of the liberal democratic peace.

The main structural features that underpin the liberal democratic peace have been in place since the end of the second world war or before: US dominance, Bretton Woods agreements, United Nations, Marshall Plan and NATO. The end of the Cold War reinforced rather than challenged key elements of the institutional architecture. The institutions rested on a basic bargain in which the United States was recognised as the legitimate guarantor of the post-war order but that it would limit the exercise of its power and maintain the liberal features of its hegemony.[83] Importantly, there was 'not a singular strategy or purpose'. Instead, the American-centred order depended on 'an assemblage of ideas about open markets, social stability, political integration, international institutional cooperation, and collective security'.[84] The economic elements of the institutional order were crucial to its overall character, especially in the creation and maintenance of predictable and relatively open trading regimes. The World Trade Organisation (WTO) and International Monetary Fund (IMF) are the most important parts of a raft of other organisations that support and lubricate open economies. Mandelbaum describes the latter organisation as 'the Vatican of free-market economics, but more powerful than the Bishop of Rome.'[85]

At least three observations can be made about the American-dominated institutional architecture underpinning the liberal democratic peace. First, the institutions were originally intended to govern relationships between western industrial states (including Japan) and their writ was extended gradually and selectively to other states. Trading regimes have not been deliberately designed to be unfavourable to developing world states; this is merely a by-product of their original design to service and benefit western industrial states. To a certain extent, the damage wreaked to other economies has been collateral. The selective extension of the US-led institutional network is important in another respect. Not only does it illustrate the restraint and voluntary characteristics of the system, it also explains why the system was tolerant of states and regimes that so obviously bucked the trend of free markets, liberalism and democracy. In many cases, and particularly during the Cold War, adherence to free markets was enough, with liberalism and democracy optional virtues. Thus, for example, several Asian and Pacific states were able to combine sustained high levels of economic growth with authoritarianism but still benefit from their membership of the system.[86]

The second observation on the institutional matrix that has provided the essential structure for the liberal democratic peace relates to its durability. Not only did the institutions survive the end of the Cold War, they were reinforced by the failure of alternatives. The endurance of the institutions owes much to their flexibility, the ability of the market to find its own course, and – when the flexibility and apparent rationality of the market fail – adjustments by leading states, particularly the United States. Indeed, herein lies one of the chief contradictions of the liberal democratic peace: its reliance on intervention and artificial corrective mechanisms. Third, the institutions and associated norms and values have been monopolistic in leaving minimal space for alternatives. States and societies that have attempted to organise economic, social and political systems contrary to the orthodoxy of the free market have been 'disciplined by the flow of capital.'[87]

Concluding discussion

The Liberal democratic peace promises an attractive environment for post-civil war reconciliation and reconstruction. Through liberalism and democracy, routes are offered for political representation, the protection of minorities and the pacific management of conflicts and resource claims. Theoretically, the emancipation of individuals will allow them to pursue rational (namely pacific) courses of action. Yet, in reality, the liberal democratic peace model that has characterised many of the internationally supported peace interventions in the post-Cold War period has delivered poor quality peace. Rather than plural democracies comprised of optimised individuals, many peace accord societies are the scene of a grudging cessation of violence and the re-entrenchment of inter-group hostility. Yet, the dominance of the liberal democratic peace is unassailable, largely because of structural factors. Alternatives to the liberal democratic peace often occur by default, at the local level (below the radar of national initiatives) or in areas deemed too marginal by leading states to benefit from their largess and attention.

It is important to temper criticism of the liberal democratic peace with a recognition that it has brought significant rewards to many societies emerging from civil war. Moreover, it is prudent to conceive of a variable geometry of the liberal democratic peace rather than a strictly uniform version of peace implemented without deviation across a variety of post-war environments. There have been variations in the extent to which the liberal democratic peace has been promulgated, with some societies (for example, Bosnia-Herzegovina) enduring extraordinarily intrusive levels of external intervention as part of the peacebuilding process. Other societies have been the recipients of liberal democratic peace-lite.

Recognising the existence and extent of the liberal democratic peace-making model is crucial to understanding the failings of many attempts to reach peace and reconciliation in societies emerging from civil war. The seeming orthodoxy of the liberal democratic peace, the near ubiquity of its deployment in internationally sponsored peace accords and the co-option of NGOs and other potential 'alternative' actors as agents of the liberal democratic peace mean that it is increasingly accepted as the norm. Moreover, it is rarely explicitly labelled as a liberal democratic model. The notion that there is no alternative helps dampen critical scrutiny of the liberal democratic peace as a means of peacemaking and as a peace aim. It is crucial therefore to conceptualise and interrogate the liberal democratic peace before reviewing its implementation. In a similar vein, the next chapter critically examines the concept of conflict, or the context in which the liberal democratic peace is deployed.

3
Conflict

War does not determine who is right – only who is left.

Bertrand Russell

Introduction

In order to deal with violent conflict we need to understand it. Although obvious, this first step has not always been internalised by analysts and practitioners interested in the pacific management of conflict. This chapter has four parts, all contributing to the idea that conflict is often more complex than first impressions suggest and that ameliorative interventions need to be tailored to suit the precise type of conflict. In its first section, the chapter examines the incidence of conflict, discounting simplistic but commonly held views that 'with the end of the Cold War, the world is experiencing an increase in intrastate bloodletting.'[1] In fact, and as illustrated with empirical evidence, a more varied pattern of both conflict escalation and de-escalation has developed during the course of the post-Cold War era. Second, the chapter examines one of the most understudied components of conflict: violence. A failure to appreciate the nature and varieties of violence has limited our understanding of conflict. Not only does violence take direct and indirect forms, but it also provides important evidential clues on the nature of the conflict, its actors and dynamics and how to deal with them.

Third, the chapter provides a brief recap of the hotly contested issue of conflict causation, suggesting that composite theories of the origins of conflict are likely to offer the most fruitful avenues for research. Rather than favouring greed, grievance or any other theory as the primary explanation of conflict, a combination of theories is likely to be most rewarding. Moreover, the emphasis on conflict causation risks missing one of the key characteristics of violent conflict: its maintenance. Many contemporary ethnonational conflicts and civil wars are long-lasting and deeply embedded in societal structures and processes; to concentrate on conflict causation alone risks conveying an incomplete account of conflict. Finally, the chapter will consider the phenomenon of chronic conflict or conflict deeply embedded within the social and political organisation of a society and its cultural practices. The chronic nature of many contemporary conflicts plays a key role in the fragile, stalled and contested nature of many peace initiatives and processes. Often, peace interventions will deal with the acute manifestations of a conflict and its most visible manifestations, leaving intact the chronic characteristics of the conflict.

The sections in this chapter are guided by the assumption that conflict forms a crucial and unavoidable part of human life. John Darby posed the provocative question 'What's wrong with conflict?' to make the point that conflict is 'intrinsic in every social relationship from marriage to international diplomacy'.[2] Problems arise when conflict is violent, ineptly managed and inimical to the fulfilment of human opportunity. Crucially, conflict refers to processes far beyond direct violence. This is in keeping with the holistic definition of peace reached in Chapter 1: the facilitation of non-exploitative, sustainable and inclusive social relationships free from direct and indirect violence and the threat of such violence. In this view, conflict is taken to mean systems and actions of exploitation, exclusion, and the limitation of opportunity, as well as direct violence.

In order to maintain a broad focus on both direct and indirect violence, explanations of conflict must cast their nets widely, canvassing the structural as well as the proximate. Social, economic and cultural factors need to complement the political and military analyses that often predominate in conflict-mapping exercises. Just as holistic explanations of peace have greater purchase, holistic explanations of conflict enable a more accurate portrayal of the factors that cause, sustain and temper violent conflict. Moreover, the popular focus on acute conflict, or the violent peak in the trajectory of a conflict, risks overlooking the chronic nature of many contemporary ethnonational and civil conflicts. These long-lasting conflicts are often deeply embedded within societal structures. They may experience occasional violent upsurges, but a more common backdrop is of inter-group hostility that does not escalate into direct violence. This may take the form of attempts to exclude the out-group from economic and political resources, a lack of civility in inter-group politics such as the regular deployment of derogatory language to characterise other groups or a pervading atmosphere of tension stemming from a military presence or build-up.

The example of northern Uganda's 'night commuter' children helps illustrate that conflict often has an impact far beyond direct violence and that it is chronic or deeply embedded in cultural and political practices. An estimated 50,000 children travel from villages and rural areas to towns each night in order to escape abduction by the Lord's Resistance Army (LRA). The LRA, the main guerrilla group in Uganda's long-running civil war, forces its captives to work as child soldiers, porters and sex slaves. Each morning, the children return to their homes with the cycle of night commuting repeating itself daily.[3] In most cases, the safety of numbers enables the children to travel unmolested and free from direct violence. Yet, the freedom from direct violence does not guarantee freedom from indirect violence. The fear of abduction not only dominates the daily pattern of life, through the separation of children from parents and disruption of traditional family activities such as gathering around the fire in the evening, it also has a psychological impact, doubtless dominating the state of mind of many children.[4]

Tension, apprehension and fear dominate the daily experience of many people in deeply divided societies. Although such sentiments are difficult to identify and quantify, and sit uneasily with many of the more concrete measures favoured by political science, they remain crucial to explanations of conflict. They operate at the group and individual levels, are often masked by camouflaging factors and are vulnerable to exploitation by political opportunists. Political tension, and its attendant emotions and reactions, operate during the pre- and post-violent conflict phases of many ethnonational and civil wars and thus rhyme with the primary focus of this book: the frustrated and contested peace that follows the formal conclusion of the violent phase of civil wars. For many inhabitants of 'post-conflict' areas, 'peace' is shaped by the threat of a resumption of violence or residual tension between communities who were formerly at war. As such, sentiments such as apprehension, tension and fear of violence deserve a central place in explanations of contemporary conflict. Moreover, the study of conflict and violence needs to be at the centre of examinations of peace as well as war.

The incidence of conflict

Rather than a simple increase in intra-state conflict, the post-Cold War period has witnessed a more varied picture in which the number of civil wars has increased and ebbed at different times. Armed conflicts are also unevenly distributed, with Africa and Asia experiencing more organised violence than other regions. A number of datasets have attempted to identify, classify and track post-Cold War armed conflicts and have been extremely useful in helping elucidate patterns of contemporary conflict.[5] The initial post-Cold War years witnessed a significant upsurge in the incidence of armed conflicts, but the upward trend stretches back to the early 1960s.[6] In other words, it is possible that many factors contributing to the outbreak of armed conflict after 1989 pre-date the end of the Cold War and caution against a blithe acceptance of the novelty of post-Cold War phenomenon.[7]

The proportion of civil wars to inter-state wars has grown markedly through the post-Second World War period. Inter-state wars remain something of a rarity, and although cases such as the 2003 US-led invasion of Iraq attract enormous attention, they are atypical and may be of limited comparative value. What many observers have missed is that the rise in post-Cold War intra-state wars peaked in 1992 at 55 armed conflicts in 41 locations.[8] Thereafter, the number of armed conflicts has fallen sharply, with 2002 experiencing 31 conflicts in 24 locations.[9] In global terms, 31 conflicts (down from a highpoint a decade before) does not point to a phenomenon of epidemic proportions. As Brubaker and Laitin observe:

> Measured against the universe of possible instances, actual instances of ethnic and nationalist violence remain rare. The crucial point is obscured in the literature, much of which ... metaphorically mischaracterizes vast regions (such as post-communist Eastern Europe and Eurasia in its entirety or all of sub-Saharan Africa) as a seething cauldron on the verge of boiling over or as a tinderbox, which a single careless spark could ignite into an inferno of ethnonational violence. Ethnic violence warrants our attention because it is appalling, not because it is ubiquitous.[10]

The relative rarity of ethnic violence is all the more startling when measured against estimates of the number of ethnic groups coexisting on the planet.[11] Not only is civil war rare, as the decade after the Cold War demonstrates, its incidence is prone to significant variation over a relatively short time period. While the outbreak of civil war may be uncommon, this is not to say that indirect violence does not characterise inter-group relations in many heterogeneous societies.

Significant instances of post-Cold War conflict de-escalation risk being overshadowed by narratives of conflict escalation.[12] Many of the conflicts that spilled over into violence in the late 1980s and early 1990s proved to be unsustainable in their use of high levels of violence. In other cases, one side was able to suppress the other, while in others still peacemaking efforts (internally or externally inspired) had a measure of success. The post-1992 fall-off in the incidence of civil war also coincides with the highpoint of UN peacekeeping deployments. Importantly, many of the conflict de-escalations of the early and mid-1990s were successful in stemming levels of direct violence but had less success in dealing with underlying causes of conflict. Ceasefires, DDR and SSR (Security Sector Reform) programmes were successful in dealing with many of the technical issues associated with violent conflict but were less successful in addressing the perceptual and psychological factors contributing to inter-group conflict and mistrust.

A number of factors complicate discussion of the incidence of intra-state conflict. First, violent conflict has become more visible in the post-Cold War era and thus may be perceived as more pervasive regardless of actual pervasiveness. The continuing electronic and digital revolutions have eased the dissemination of information and images from conflict zones. The collapse of the Soviet Union meant that journalists, NGOs and others could gain access to parts of the world literally closed to outside scrutiny for decades. The use of neat yet often misleading labels such as 'ethnic war' or 'new war' allowed commentators and policymakers to make connections between wars in different regions and thus point to an international phenomenon rather than a series of discrete, local wars.[13] The past two decades have witnessed the 'rediscovery of ethnicity' as a labelling device with which to explain civil war.[14] Another factor that made post-Cold War conflict more visible was the outbreak of war in the former Yugoslavia which brought intra-state war to Europe and transformed it from something that only occurred on the easy to ignore global periphery. Some governments and international organisations endeavoured to make intra-state wars and associated humanitarian problems more visible. The growing army of NGOs, and international organisations attempting to carve out a new role in the post-Cold War era, were important in this regard and were aided by the increased legitimacy attached to human rights discourse. Intra-state wars also became more visible by default; the demise of East–West rivalry cleared space on news and political agendas.

A second factor complicating discussion of the incidence of intra-state war relates to methodological and classificatory concerns on what constitutes a war and what should be included and excluded from any census of armed conflict. The widely respected Uppsala dataset uses a three-part distinction to classify armed conflict according to the level of fatalities. War is taken to mean conflicts involving 1000 battle-related deaths per year and Intermediate Armed Conflict as 'at least 25 battle-related deaths per year and an accumulated total of at least 1000 deaths, but fewer than 1000 in any given year'. Minor Armed Conflict is taken as 'at least 25 battle-related deaths per year and fewer than 1000 battle-related deaths during the course of the conflict'.[15] Arbitrary points of demarcation between categories will always spark debate, particularly with regard to anomalous cases, but the distinction is useful in alerting us to the variegated nature of armed conflict and the rarity of war (five wars were active in 2002) in the overall context of armed conflict.[16]

The concentration on fatalities as the principal measure of the intensity of a conflict is understandable, but there is a risk that it produces an overly narrow view of armed conflict and, as a consequence, a narrow view of peace. The measurement of battle deaths, injuries, refugee flows and other quantifiable data is understandable and can be put to good use. But it cannot capture the totality of violent conflict, particularly the often hidden and affective consequences of war. The blunt recording of battlefield fatalities encourages a concentration on militants (usually young males). Unless augmented by other data, such as population size or number of militants in the field (data not easily gathered during armed conflict), it lacks the relative quality needed to put battle-related deaths into perspective. Measures deployed during complex health emergencies, such as deaths per 10,000 persons per day, provide a less crude method of data collection.[17]

A third complication for measures of the incidence of armed conflict, and one related to the above point, is that such measures necessarily concentrate on the overtly violent phase of a conflict. Public health emergencies that happen alongside violent conflict regularly kill more than those slain on the battlefield. Political tension, structural discrimination, campaigns of harassment and inter-group verbal intimidation are all actions short of direct violence, yet they constitute core elements of many conflicts. They can occur before and after, or alongside, the direct violence phase of a conflict. As a result, datasets on armed conflict are best viewed in conjunction with supporting evidence such as measures of human rights abuses, development or democratisation. Clearly all such measures are dependent on the frame of reference and the definition of variables. The United Nations Development Programme's Human Development Index, for example, regards the individual as the principal unit of measurement in its calculations of human development. In many respects this aligns with the western view of the atomised individual and clashes with other perspectives that may attach greater weight to groups, such as the extended family. Datasets of the incidence of armed conflict are best viewed as complementary to other measures of conflict that have a purview beyond direct violence. The PIOOM (Interdisciplinary Research Programme on Root Causes of Human Rights Violations), Freedom House or Minorities at Risk studies, for example, provide contextual information that can be used in addition to blunt fatality figures.[18]

A fourth point is that battle-related deaths may be insensitive to the type of conflict, the nature of its participants and the conflict causes. The concentration on baseline figures such as battle deaths may mean that a range of other salient variables are conflated or overlooked. For example, violent conflicts involving the armed forces of the United States may result in high numbers of battle deaths because of the technological superiority of its forces and their ability to project huge amounts of ordinance to the battlefield. One news report on the 2001 US invasion of Afghanistan noted that 'one special forces soldier directing smart bombs from the ground called in strikes that killed 3,000 Taliban in a single day.'[19] By contrast, other violent conflicts may be characterised by more sporadic and less technologically advanced forms of direct violence. For example, conflict between the Indian government and separatist militants in Nagaland (with a population of less than 2 million) involves a relatively small number of active combatants, with limited access to sophisticated weaponry, and the window of opportunity for offensives is limited by climatic conditions. The reduction of conflicts to baseline data thus risks overlooking the variety and subtlety of many violent conflicts.

A final caution with regard to measures of the incidence of armed conflict, and one that applies to all quantitative approaches to conflict, is that active conflict zones rarely offer propitious environments for the accurate collection of statistics.[20] While some conflict areas are relatively accessible, and the participants in the conflict may be relied upon for a measure of transparency in their reporting, other conflict areas remain relatively inaccessible. It is impossible, for example, to obtain accurate casualty figures on the conflict between the Karen National Union and the Burmese/Myanmar government, let alone other information on displacement and the limitation of human opportunities that would convey a picture of the totality of the conflict.

The importance of violence

Compared with the broader concept of conflict, violence is understudied. To dismiss violence as a manifestation or function of the more 'important' social process of conflict risks overlooking the evidential clues that an analysis of violence offers the study of conflict. In particular, a careful scrutiny of the violence involved in a conflict may encourage an understanding of the varieties of violence and the implications of different types of violence on intervention and reconstruction strategies. This appeal to take violence more seriously should not contradict the earlier point that analysts should be mindful of both the direct and indirect nature of violence. The high visibility of direct violence means that it will ordinarily attract most attention, yet the simple reporting of violence does not necessarily lead to an understanding of violence and its role within conflict. Indeed, in long-running conflicts, violence can attain an almost routine quality that discourages analysts from inferring any political or communicative meaning behind it.

Many analyses of conflict have conflated various types of violence under broad and under-conceptualised categories. Commonly used descriptions of violence, such as 'communal rioting', 'looting' or 'guerrilla warfare' offer a poor guide to the complexity involved in violence. Such terms are often labels rather than accurate descriptors that help delineate one type of violence from another. A conceptualisation of types of violence, or the development of typologies to help distinguish varieties of violence, can provide a more nuanced picture of the conflict, its actors, dynamics and duration. For example, the deployment of sporadic, low-technology, opportunist violence may point to low-capacity antagonists, bereft of a large support base or powerful sponsors. Or it may suggest a weak militant organisation that lacks the capacity to take and hold territory.

Whether the violence is horizontal (intra-group) or vertical (group versus state) may allude to the causes of the conflict, the extent to which the conflict has infected all levels of society and the extent to which groups or institutions are mobilised. Antagonists' level of target discrimination may allow observers to draw inferences about the sensitivity of the antagonists to political condemnation and the moral framework that guides their approach to the conflict. Similarly, the extent to which violence is accompanied by a fully formulated and widely disseminated political programme may be important in suggesting the seriousness of antagonists in their pursuit of a campaign of violence or investigation of peace initiatives.

Clearly, there are limits to the utility of analyses of violence. Militant organisations are often secretive and inaccessible to scrutiny. Moreover, a single incidence of violence may be open to wildly varied interpretation, with victims and perpetrators associating different motivations to the same act. Nevertheless, violence is often the shop window of conflict. At the very least, it is a form of communication, often brutal and blunt, but capable of conveying messages of intention, strength of various factions within a militant organisation and receptivity towards peace initiatives. Consider, for example, the case of the breakdown of the Irish Republican Army (IRA) ceasefire in Northern Ireland in 1996–1997. Frustrated at what they regarded as a lack of political movement in the nascent peace process, the IRA engaged in a series of attacks in England, Northern Ireland and the European mainland. But this violence was of a qualitatively different order to the violence that characterised the IRA campaign over the previous quarter of a century. There was a greater discrimination of the selection of targets, restraint with regard to civilian casualties and some care was taken so as to minimise the risk of antagonising pro-British loyalist militant groups into breaking their ceasefire. Crucially, this violence was moderated so as not to blow the peace process asunder and its primary objective was to gain re-admittance to a peace process that offered the IRA better terms. The example is by no means atypical: violence, and variations in the types of violence deployed during a conflict, can act as a barometer of antagonists' political intentions and receptivity to conflict management measures.

An analysis of the violence involved in a conflict is likely to lead to an awareness of the need for more sophisticated intervention strategies, thus guarding against 'one size fits all' template interventions. It seems obvious that different types of violence leave a different footprint and require tailored development and reconstruction assistance. Each conflict contains its 'violent peculiarities', whether landmines, child soldiers, rape and amputation, 'suicide' bombers or state-sponsored militias, and thus demands specialist ameliorative efforts. Often the violent component of the conflict, rather than the meta-conflict itself, will determine the population that requires most assistance and the longevity and nature of that assistance. In sum, violence cannot be regarded as a largely undifferentiated category that is merely a manifestation of conflict. Scrutiny of the types of violence deployed during a conflict can provide evidence on the nature of the conflict. Similarly, reactions to violence are important, whether it prompts political overtures or greater or more diffuse social capital. The proportionality of violent responses from one side to the other may signal (im)possibilities of conflict management or mitigation.

The causes of conflict

Appropriately, the academic literature on the causes of conflict lacks consensus; mono-causal explanations jostle with composite theories, and various levels of analysis (the individual, group, institution, state or region) are promoted as providing the best vantage point for understanding conflict. In recent years governments, international organisations and NGOs involved in peace and conflict interventions have invested great energy into conflict assessments or conflict analyses designed to equip staff with an initial sketch of the conflict origins, actors, dynamics and manifestations. The rationale is that appropriate conflict intervention must be based on an understanding of the conflict. The next chapter develops the theme of conflict analyses, arguing that in many cases peace analyses are also required to ensure the implementation of peace accords. It also stresses the need for a critical perspective in such peace assessment activities so that they go beyond attempting to 'fix' dysfunctional peace accords and ascertain the fundamental conflict causation and maintenance factors.

Attempts to discern the causes of conflict are beset with a number of challenges, the most fundamental of which is that in the absence of a precise science of conflict-causation it is left to the researcher to attach weight to various conflict-contributing factors. It is here that biases and preconceived ideas can take hold and provide explanations of conflict that exceed supporting evidence. Consider, for example, the case of a conflict in which the antagonists are explicit about the conflict causes. They may deploy a language of nationalism, moral righteousness or historical grievance to explain their involvement in the conflict, yet these explanations may be a wholly unreliable guide to the true causes of the conflict. The researcher is left with considerable agency and may discount the publicly given conflict cause to develop an alternative thesis of conflict causation. Moreover, many antagonists operate in closed decision-making networks that prevent a full disclosure of the 'real' conflict causes. Since few observers were privy to Slobodan Milosevic's discussions with his inner circle in the early 1990s, can we be absolutely confident in our analysis of the causes of the civil war in the former Yugoslavia?

The case of the Maoist insurgency in Nepal illustrates the complexity involved in identifying conflict causation.[21] Neither the Communist Party of Nepal (Maoist) (NCP(M)) nor the Nepalese government are opaque in their decision-making processes. While the Nepalese government has been beset by infighting and instability, culminating in a spectacular case of regicide in 2001 and a coup in 2005, the NCP(M) leadership is often restricted to rural hideouts and has an amateurish political profile.[22] Each side has employed a number of discourses to justify their involvement in the conflict and the ultimate aims of the antagonists are not always clear.[23] At one stage Prachanda, the NCP(M) Chairman, cast the conflict in terms of sovereignty and democratisation: 'The main issue of the ongoing civil war has remained whether or not the right to determine their own fate and future should be in the hands of Nepalese people.'[24] In other statements though, leftist ideology is given precedence: 'It is obvious to all that our party is a revolutionary Communist Party fighting for a people's republic',[25] or:

> the ultimate aim of our movement is to contribute towards the attainment of glorious communism by ending all forms of exploitation of man by man from the face of the earth only by marching forward under the guidance of Marxism-Leninism-Maoism, the invincible universal ideology of the proletariat, the last and the most revolutionary class in history, can this golden future of humankind be attained.[26]

The observer, confronted with a medley of ideological justifications, socio-economic grievances and pressure for constitutional reform, must attempt to prioritise conflict causes mindful that a political leader's concern with the 'invincible universal ideology of the proletariat' may not actually be shared by that proletariat. For the latter, the primary reasons for pursuing the conflict may lie in more prosaic goals such as land reform or better access to public services.

It is also difficult to ascribe precise motives to the Nepalese government in that it has employed a number of discourses (security, democracy, the maintenance of the constitutional order) in defence of the war. These discourses have been subsequently updated during the post-9/11 'War on Terror'. As a recipient of over $20 million as part of the US Anti-Terrorism Assistance Program, Nepal has attempted to characterise its conflict with the Maoist rebels as part of the global 'War on Terror'.[27]

The Nepalese example is useful in illustrating how publicly articulated conflict causes may be perplexing and misleading and how the reasons for enjoining a conflict may change over time. The example also suggests how a series of conflicts may overlay one another, resulting in a complex conflict strata that requires delicate excavation so that individual layers can be distinguished and relationships between them identified. It also suggests that actors on the same side may hold different reasons for pursuing the conflict. Many Nepalese may share the Maoist's demand for radical reform of the government but may be bemused by the Maoist ideology espoused by the NCP(M) leadership. Accounts of the insurgency in Nepal are typical of many analyses of other conflicts in that they concentrate on the escalation of conflict into direct violence rather than the evolution and continuation of the conflict past the initial upsurge in violence. The outbreak of the Maoist insurgency is often dated to February 1995. Yet, structural explanations of conflict that concentrate on factors embedded within the social, political and economic organisation of a society militate against the identification of precise conflict start dates. This raises an additional question: how far back do we need to go to find a convincing explanation of the causes of a conflict?

The factors causing the eruption into direct violence may be unusual or unforeseen events that are of limited worth in explaining the underlying dynamics of a conflict. The downing of a plane carrying the Presidents of Rwanda and Burundi in 1994 is often given as the key proximate factor in the unleashing of the genocide in Rwanda. This event though was only one of many conflict-contributing factors, some proximate and some structural, that combined in April 1994 and overcame other factors restraining violent conflict. Importantly, conflict-catalysing factors may be very different to conflict-sustaining factors; different tools may be required to explain the sudden escalation of a conflict and its later chronic nature.

While conflict is clearly a pervasive and universal phenomenon, it is not clear that we can reach universal explanations of conflict and related violence. The sheer variety of conflict types, actors, dynamics and manifestations invite circumspection with regard to universal claims on conflict. Can we compare the suppression of the Uighars by the Chinese government with Kurdish separatism or conflict between militants from Guadalcanal and Malaita in the Solomon Islands? Similarities in conflict causation between diverse cases may be so general as to limit comparative, conceptual or analytical claims. At the same time we may be discouraged from comparison by local factors and conflict peculiarities that actually mask common traits. Antagonists in, and witnesses to, a conflict are often convinced of the conflict's exceptionalism and intensity. It is in this context that the researcher has the unenviable task of identifying conflict causes.

Academic debate on conflict causation has crystallised around two main themes: greed and grievance. The greed thesis stresses economic predation as the chief cause and maintenance factor in civil war, while grievance explanations concentrate on a wide category of other factors ranging from identity, religion and group claims to unmet status needs. The greed and grievance categories are by no means exclusive, and the dividing line between them is blurred. Arguments rage on whether greed or grievance deserves precedence, but rather than greed *or* grievance, many violent intra-state conflicts are caused and maintained by a combination of greed *and* grievance. Paul Collier has been the most prominent proponent of the greed thesis of conflict causation, neatly summing up the greed argument thus: 'civil wars occur where rebel organizations are financially viable.'[28] In this view, groups and individuals seek to maximise economic gain via civil war. The maintenance of conflict is explained through a self-sustaining political economy of civil war in which membership of a militant organisation becomes the rational means of economic survival. The greed thesis casts elites as rent-seeking cliques primarily interested in using political organisations and institutions as vehicles for predation. In the extreme case of failing states, the leadership makes no pretence at the provision of public goods and services, and instead makes alliances with key private sector interests to harvest resources.[29]

According to the greed thesis, the principal reason civil war breaks out in some locations and not in others is varying rates of revenue generation. Collier juxtaposes the examples of a marginal survivalist group in the United States, the Michigan Militia, and the main leftist guerrilla group in Colombia, the Revolutionary Armed Forces of Colombia (FARC), to illustrate the logic of the greed thesis:

> The factors which account for this difference between failure and success are to be found not in the 'causes' which these two rebel organizations claim to espouse, but in their radically different opportunities to raise revenue. The FARC earns around $700 million per year from drugs and kidnapping, whereas the Michigan Militia is probably broke.[30]

The thesis encourages a cautious approach to explanations of conflict based on ethnic superiority, identity claims and historical grievances. These explanations may be cynically promoted by political entrepreneurs who use them to mobilise support, but they provide an unreliable guide to 'true' economic motivations. To support their case, the proponents of the greed thesis have amassed a formidable battery of quantitative data that makes associations between civil war and economic indicators such as income levels, dependence on primary commodity exports and low growth. The greed thesis has many attractions, not least its apparent rationalism in viewing antagonists as rational actors who pursue objective and measurable goals. As such it is far removed from the subjective relativism of morality and good versus evil contests. Moreover, the greed thesis has a predictive capacity, with quantitative models able to make associations between economic indicators and the likelihood of the (re)occurrence of civil war.

Greed explanations of conflict causation have attracted scepticism because of their dependence on unreliable data, the inaccessibility of much of its academic output and its tendency to make generalised claims on behalf of under-conceptualised labels.[31] Yet the greed thesis remains popular and has found powerful backing in the form of the World Bank.[32]

'Grievance' is perhaps too neat a categorisation for the broad array of non-economic conflict explanations, and there is a danger that it becomes a default category comprised of a hotchpotch of factors excluded from the economic category. Nor is the grievance label able to encompass explanations that rely on psychology and human proclivities towards violence. The view that humans' biological code in some way predisposes individuals to violence, or to react violently to external stimuli, is popular (though not in academia) and fits ready-made narratives of good versus evil. Within the mainstream grievance thesis though, four factors are commonly identified as contributing to conflict and so are worthy of further examination: ideology, ethnicity, and human needs inter-group competition. Ideology and ethnicity are unconvincing explanations of conflict causation, although they are powerful mobilisation tools that can parasitically latch onto true conflict causes. Inter-group competition and unmet human needs, on the other hand, are capable engines for the production of violent conflict.

Ideology

At first glance, ideology provides an attractive basis for explanations of violent conflict causation. Whether Prachanda's beloved 'Marxism-Leninism-Maoism' or socialism and fascism, it is possible to point to historical or contemporary examples in which political leaders have invoked ideological claims to justify or oppose violent conflict. Ideology can be an adept tool for the mobilisation of groups and is often malleable enough to make connections with contemporary concerns. Yet, scratch the surface of a conflict rationalised in ideological terms and more prosaic causes are often visible. While ideology can provide the intellectual validation, means of articulation and mobilising zeal for the escalation of conflict towards violence, it cannot be taken as a sufficient *cause* of conflict. To contribute to conflict, ideology requires prior mobilising factors such as advocates or grievances, and thus cannot be regarded as an independent conflict causation factor.

Ethnicity

Similarly, explanations of violent conflict causation that point to ethnicity, tribalism or the purity of the group can be misleading.

Conflicts can be 'ethnicised' in the sense that claims of the superiority or historical mission of the ethnic group can be used to boost prior-existing grievances, but ethnicity in, of and by itself is an unlikely initiator of inter-group conflict. The context and manipulation of ethnicity, rather than any intrinsic power associated with the ethnic group and its worldview can explain the escalation (rather than origins) of conflict. Social science has a particular antipathy towards ethnicity as an explanation for human behaviour because ethnic claims rely on nostalgia, myth and mysticism and thus run counter to the fundamental social scientific assumption: that we inhabit a rational world of explainable phenomenon. Yet, there are three compelling reasons why it is prudent to resist an over-hasty dismissal of ethnicity in explanations of conflict causation.

First, in a classic baby and bathwater dilemma, there is a danger that in the overwhelming desire to reject the essentialist or primordial claims made on behalf of ethnicity we overlook its instrumentalist potential. An important distinction needs to be made between ethnicity as a mobilising factor on the one hand and as a conflict-priming factor on the other. Ethnicity lacks true catalytic power but is able to exploit prior-existing conflicts. A second reason why ethnicity demands respect rather than instant dismissal in explanations of violent conflict causation lies in its incredible instrumentalist potential. Few other claims possess a similar ability for the 'historicization of the collective self', group mobilisation and counter-mobilisation.[33] As Smith points out:

> Without a widely accepted myth of ethnic descent, without shared ethno-historical memories, including those of one or more 'golden ages', without a sense of ethnic election and mission, only a revolutionary civic nationalism with exemplars drawn from widely accepted canons of virtue and grandeur ... could provide that criterion of political solidarity and social cohesion that can sustain political community and stabilise the sense of national identity. In this respect, ethnic nationalism possesses advantages denied to other modes of national identification: a definite standard of authenticity, a clear criterion of communal belonging and a powerful basis for a sense of collective identity.[34]

The third reason why ethnic claims of conflict causation demand serious attention is that despite the social science community's belief that we live in a rational world of measurable certainties, there is something at the heart of ethnicity that we simply don't understand. Walker

Connor referred to this as 'the nonrational core of the nation' that operates at the level of emotion and sentiment.[35] Social science has been unable to help us explain the success of 'appeals not to the mind but to the blood'[36] through which ethnic entrepreneurs evoke symbols, poetry and myth to connect with the emotional subconscious:

> Rational would-be explanations have abounded: relative economic deprivation; elite ambitions; rational choice theory; intense transaction flows; the desire of the intelligentsia to convert a 'low', subordinate culture into a 'high', dominant one; cost-benefit calculations; internal colonialism; a ploy of the bourgeoisie to undermine the class consciousness of the proletariat by obscuring the conflict class interests within each nation ... All such theories can be criticized on empirical grounds. But they can be faulted principally for their failure to reflect the emotional depth of national identity: the passions at either extreme of the hate-love continuum which the nation often inspires, and the countless fanatical sacrifices which have been made in its name.[37]

In the absence of understanding, a complete dismissal of ethnic claims would be imprudent.

Human needs

The next major theory of conflict causation, human needs, is attractive in making a clear connection between conflict and the socio-economic condition of groups and individuals. It is also somewhat liberating in its optimism of humanity, moving away from notions of mankind as aggressive or power-seeking towards a notion of 'necessitous man'.[38] The theory is also able to operate in conjunction with other theories of conflict causation and by taking the human being as the basic unit, promises universalism and an ability to transcend local and cultural peculiarities. Developed by Maslow, the theory identified a hierarchy of human needs, ranging from basic physiological requirements to more complex psychological needs of esteem and self-actualisation.[39] Much human behaviour, it was argued, was a function of attempts to fulfil these needs.

Although originally designed to explain psychological development, human needs theory has attracted the interest of conflict theorists because of its potential to explain 'seemingly different and separate social problems, from street violence to industrial frictions'.[40] The hierarchy of human needs expands far beyond the tangible necessities needed to maintain human life, such as food and shelter, to include the relationships and identity affiliations thought to be necessary for psychological fulfilment. This enables ethnic or religious claims to be recast as human needs – commodities desirable for the attainment of human satisfaction. Human needs are not necessarily innate, instead they can be socially constructed in the form of bonds of identity.[41] Unmet human needs, according to the theory, can lead to competition and conflict.[42] Moreover, human needs theory is compatible with structural explanations of conflict and peace. It encourages an examination of the nature of societal organisation and related institutions that regulate and possibly frustrate the fulfilment of basic needs.

The logical conclusion of human needs theory is a holistic notion of peace based on the fulfilment of the whole array of social, cultural and economic needs crucial to human contentment. In this view, conflict management calls not for the address of essentially symptomatic violence but the identification and satisfaction of unmet human needs. While traditional conflict management techniques may lead to a concentration on those actors responsible for violence, human needs theory lends itself towards a revision of the underlying causes of conflict, namely those institutions and norms of social organisation thought to be frustrating human needs. Consequently, it leads to a focus on the condition of the bulk of the population, rather than what Tilly terms 'the violence specialists' who often hog most intervention limelight.[43] Human needs theory also lends itself towards a focus on the prosaic but crucial matters of social and economic development and the distribution of resources. Azar notes the compatibility of human needs theory with identity politics in that the 'deprivation of physical needs and denial of access are rooted in the refusal to recognize or accept the communal identity of other groups. Formation and acceptance of identity may thus also be understood as a basic development need.'[44]

Inter-group competition

Human needs theory is wholly compatible with the next major category of conflict causation: inter-group competition. At one level, inter-group competition may be regarded as a conflict manifestation, a result of conflict arising from other issues rather than a conflict cause by itself. However, at another level, by including the variables of esteem and status, inter-group competitions are able to develop a conflict-causing and conflict-sustaining dynamic of their own. Theories of social categorisation and social identity are useful in explaining the formation, maintenance and evolution of identity groups, and competition between these groups. The basic premise is that individuals are engaged in constant cognitive processes of categorisation to understand and systematise their social environment.[45] Crucial to the formation of social identity is the recognition of, and affiliation to, social groups that are viewed positively.[46] This is a relational and discriminating process in that other groups (out-groups) are viewed negatively. The group is capable of the simultaneous occupation of a number of mutually reinforcing roles that illustrate the melding of human needs theory and inter-group competition as conflict explanations. Thus, the group may act as a source of identity, mobilisation, discourse and fellowship in grievance.

The sentiment of esteem adds particular potency to social categorisation and identification, and resulting inter-group calculations. All humans attach a high salience to esteem, or positive self and group evaluation. The pursuit of positive self-esteem 'is dependent upon the discrepancy between how a person perceives herself and how she thinks she should be' and is a major motivating factor in human behaviour.[47] This search for social approval and the identification of positive distinctiveness operates at both the individual and group level.

Social comparison and the resultant cognitive calculations of esteem often take the form of innocuous discrimination between groups, but this can become more serious in contexts with deep societal fissures, such as a location with competing groups who define themselves by race or ethnic affiliation. Negative perceptions of the self or group will result in attempts to attain positive self-evaluation. One strategy may be for individuals to join another social group, but such inter-group mobility is rarely possible in deeply divided contexts: an individual who formerly supported Palestinian independence with little regard for Israel's security (or even existence) cannot easily become a hard-line Zionist. In the absence of opportunities to move between groups, individuals and groups locked in status competitions may seek to review the inter-group comparative framework. A number of peace processes have attempted to offer formulae through which groups attempt to put their competition on hold and forge cooperative relationships through power-sharing or the management of relations on functional issues (for example, the Ta'if Accord in Lebanon and the Belfast Agreement in Northern Ireland). In the long-term, it is hoped, the strength of the functional bonds between the groups, perhaps cooperation for mutual economic benefit, would overshadow the salience of the inter-group competition. But opportunities for a fundamental revision of the inter-group comparative framework come along rarely, are easily derailed by spoilers, and only operate in the long term. This leaves two related options for groups who feel that their status position is inadequate: to compete more strenuously with the out-group and to engage in violence against the out-group. Thus, it is legitimate to regard inter-group esteem competition as a cause rather than manifestation of conflict.

Having reviewed a range of factors that contribute to the escalation of conflict towards violence, the crucial point to make is that no single explanation is able to account for civil and ethnonational war. Instead, a composite of complementary explanations is to be recommended. Violent conflict is a complex social phenomenon that can only be explained via a complex matrix of causal factors. Structural and proximate factors must be reviewed alongside evaluations of the relevance of economic factors, human needs and inter-group competition. Causation factors must be distinguished from manifestations, and analysis must be mindful of the dynamic nature of violent conflict and its ability to evolve with time. The Israeli–Palestinian conflict provides a good example in this regard. While many of the structural factors underlying the conflict have remained basically intact for several decades, many proximate and ancillary factors have changed markedly. The al-Aqsa Intifada, the terminal collapse of the Oslo process, the Hamas suicide bombing campaign, the construction of Israel's security wall and other incidents presented the current generation of Israelis and Palestinians with a different set of politicising (and possibly radicalising) events, images and terminology than previous generations. While some of the bases of the conflict have remained more or less stable (e.g., the central contention between two peoples and one territory), other bases such as the international political environment have changed considerably. Indeed, given the longevity of the conflict, it is legitimate to ask whether it is the same conflict, or a series of conflicts, inherited but moulded by each successive generation.

A final factor to bear in mind when reviewing the causes of violent political conflict is that we may neglect those factors restraining conflict. Like the dog that didn't bark in the Sherlock Holmes story, the conflicts that have not erupted into violence are significant in themselves and may provide lessons for the management of conflict. In a similar way to analyses of conflict causation, there is no exact science of conflict restraint, especially since it can draw on the realm of the counterfactual.

Chronic conflict and conflict maintenance

A key reason why so many contemporary peace processes are stalled and peace accords thwarted is because of a fundamental mismatch between the nature of the conflict and the conflict management strategies deployed. Although many contemporary intra-state and ethnonational conflicts are chronic in nature, many peace intervention strategies attempt to deal with the acute features of the conflict. This final section of the chapter attempts to sketch the core features and implications of chronic conflict. Five features of chronic conflict are worthy of mention. First, these conflicts are long-term, often having a trans-generational character stretched over decades if not centuries. Chronic conflicts are capable of displaying extreme variations in intensity over the longer-term, with violent peaks giving way to extended periods typically characterised by tension and fear of violence rather than direct violence. Such conflicts are capable of being re-energised by incidents and sudden shocks that connect with and aggravate the underlying conflict. The protracted nature of chronic conflict means that they may have a cumulative effect, with an extended series of crises denuding an area or group of its resources, capacities and optimism. Moreover, the nature of the conflict 'lull' may limit the opportunity to repair damage to resources, capacities and optimism. At first glance, the term 'chronic emergency', favoured by NGOs, may appear as an inappropriate oxymoron to describe the situation in areas suffering from chronic conflict.[48] Yet the term is appropriate in that it captures the serial nature of the problems in chronic conflict areas in which resources are denuded and resolve sapped over an extended period as the result of multiple factors.

Second, and following on from the last point, chronic conflict contains both direct and indirect violence. Indeed, indirect violence in the form of apprehension at the resurgence of direct violence or the structural exclusion of certain groups from access to public resources may constitute a typical experience of chronic conflict, with direct violence being the exception. Such violence may be so firmly embedded in social processes that it is regarded as unexceptional. It may also take subtle or not easily visible forms such as sexual violence.

A third feature of chronic conflict is the manner in which it becomes embedded in the social, political and economic *systems* of the conflict area. A chronic conflict is capable of operating at multiple levels of society and infecting multiple issue areas. The world wars were described as 'total wars' because they represented a quantum leap in the scale and extent of warfare. Chronic conflicts are also worthy of the 'total war' description because of their all-embracing character that inhabits the totality of life in the conflict area. Thus, the conflict will infect local and national politics, political discourse, access to resources, livelihoods, daily life patterns and cultural activities such as sporting competitions.

This all pervading nature of conflict means that neutral space becomes squeezed, if not irrelevant or even irrational. Since access to resources or positive social identity may depend on aligning with one side or the other in a chronic conflict, there may be few advantages for those who want to champion a third way. Fourth, chronic conflicts often operate in clusters with a number of conflicts occupying and destabilising a geographical region. For example, the Horn of Africa, or Sudan and its neighbours Chad and Uganda are host to a number of conflicts that feed off each other. Fifth, chronic conflicts often coincide with other chronic vulnerabilities in society and contribute to a vicious cycle of increasing social needs and declining capacities. Thus, inter-group conflict might be accompanied and reinforced by natural and man-made disasters, the deterioration and destruction of livelihood systems, the collapse of state provision and environmental degradation.[49] The key point is that the 'chronic' nature of the conflict extends far beyond issues of inter-group violent conflict to embrace a wide range of social and economic factors.

Chronic conflict has profound implications for states, international organisations and NGOs interested in the management of protracted conflict and the amelioration of its impact. It is immune to superficial peace interventions that deal with conflict manifestations. Instead, it demands more sophisticated approaches that are long-term, development focused and concentrate on systems of governance, resource distribution and modes of inter-group interaction. But these prescriptions are easier said than done. They are expensive, reversible and can take decades to show results. While governments and aid agencies can mobilise resources in response to a specific emergency, chronic conflicts have no such appeal. In a sense these conflict areas become victims of the 'normality' of their conflicts. The constant association of Sierra Leone or Somalia with violence, disease and social dystopia means that western publics and international organisations suffer from a 'compassion fatigue', and it is difficult to summon the fire brigade to a fire that seems to be perpetually smouldering.[50]

Peace intervention in cases of chronic conflict often requires the prior intervention of an orthodox or 'superficial' peace process to create a secure environment in which deeper-level development activity can then take place. For example, mine clearing or disarmament programmes must first attempt to remove the obvious weapons of war before the less obvious 'weapons' of food insecurity and inter-group suspicion can be dealt with. The sheer immediacy of relief needs means that they are understandably prioritised by aid agencies and other intervening organisations. Yet, rather than a strictly linear relief-to-development continuum, with relief activities necessarily preceding development activities, it is possible to envisage a combination of relief with development.[51] In such circumstances, relief planning would internalise the need to address long-term development needs and confront those factors making the conflict sustainable and chronic.

The prevalence of chronic and long-term conflict calls for an understanding of conflict maintenance. The tools of traditional conflict analyses, more often accustomed to explaining the blip of violent conflict escalation, may not always be appropriate for this task. A key conflict-maintaining factor is the particular dynamic that a violent conflict is able to generate. Some conflicts develop sophisticated war economies that provide combatants or elites with a powerful rationale for the continuation of the conflict. The agents and systems of war may become so institutionalised over the long-term that they promote war and conflict by virtue of being. Thus, for example, the Israeli Defence Force or Hezbollah may rarely pause to consider fundamental questions on their role and purpose. Instead, their roles are largely prescribed by a combination of their environment, history and the inertia of institutionalism. Another conflict-maintaining factor linked to the dynamic that conflicts can generate is the ability of elites, states, groups and individuals to create conflict coping mechanisms that can help insulate themselves from the worst effects of the civil war. A conflict may be largely contained in a certain geographical area (for example, the north and east of Sri Lanka) or be largely confined to certain social categories (working class males in Northern Ireland). Actors can develop insulation mechanisms to bypass the direct costs of the conflict. For example, Israel used Christian militias to protect its border with Lebanon thereby lessening the Israeli body count.[52] Technology and the use of 'disposable' young males from the margins of society comprise other ways in which actors protect themselves from the costs of conflict and thus find the continuation of conflict more sustainable. A final conflict maintenance factor arising from the dynamic of the conflict stems from the nature and pattern of the violence deployed. Some types of violence necessarily lend themselves to short campaigns (e.g., the deployment of overwhelming force, or the decision by an insurgent group to 'make a stand' in the open and thus present themselves as an easy target). Other types of violence, for example, low-level hit-and-run attacks may contribute to more sustained campaigns of violence.

Conflict maintenance is very much related to perceptual and psychological factors or the extent to which elites, groups or individuals are motivated to engage in retaliatory or incendiary activities. In some conflicts, a dynamic of revenge (often disproportionate or symbolic) can develop, with cultural or political expectations that the in-group must exact revenge if attacked. Esteem and honour may make violent reaction a necessity and preclude peace initiatives. A sense of hopelessness, that the continuation of the conflict is in someway inevitable, may also contribute to conflict maintenance and permanently depress expectations that the conflict can be interrupted. While conflict-related belief systems inhabit the realm of the intangible, they can be modified over time with, for example, political elites preparing constituencies to accept sacrifices over the longer-term and to regard such sacrifices as honourable.

Concluding discussion

Understanding the nature of violent conflict is crucial for any critical examination of post-peace accord societies. The 'no war, no peace' situations prevailing in many post-peace accord societies are characterised by a continuation of the conflict (often through indirect rather than direct violence) regardless of the provisions of the peace accord. The dangers of conflict recidivism also necessitate that peace research is mindful of the factors behind the causation and maintenance of violent conflict. Many contemporary peace accords, despite the transformative promises of the liberal democratic peace, freeze conflict rather than challenge it. This is especially the case in its concentration on the technical aspects of peacemaking and peace accord implementation rather than on the belief systems that perpetuate conflict. Rational actors respond to incentives, and an understanding of the motivations behind conflict behaviour may allow third parties to develop (dis) incentives to encourage pacific behaviour.

The next chapter proposes an innovative and experimental approach to assessing the 'success' or 'failure' of peace in post-peace accord societies. Crucial to this is a critical lens that moves beyond the mere evaluation of the implementation of a peace accord against the limited standards set by the liberal democratic peace. Instead, a critical peace assessment aims to examine the extent to which a post-peace accord society has attained a holistic and sustainable peace. In order to undertake this assessment task, a sophisticated understanding of conflict is required.

4
Critical Peace Assessment

> People who live in the post-totalitarian system
> know only too well that the question of whether
> one or several political parties are in power, and
> how these parties define and label themselves,
> is of far less importance than the question of
> whether or not it is possible to live like a
> human being.
>
> Vaclav Havel

Introduction

The problems and opportunities presented by stalled and unfulfilled peace require specialist diagnosis so that peace-supporting interventions and initiatives may be better targeted. To that end, this chapter proposes that conflict assessments, the diagnostic tool used by intervening NGOs, international organisations and development-minded third party governments to analyse conflicts, are modified and extended to post-peace accord scenarios. To a certain extent this is already happening, with some organisations involved in peace interventions conducting Peace and Conflict Impact Assessments (PCIA) to gauge the extent to which their activities excite or temper conflict.[1] This chapter advocates a more specialist and fundamentally critical approach. 'Critical peace assessments' have the potential to play a major role in the analysis of post-peace accord societies, allowing internal and external actors in a peace process to identify those factors restraining and facilitating the fulfilment of peace. Information gleaned via a critical peace assessment exercise should allow intervening agencies and local actors to prioritise issues and sectors deserving of attention and encourage the strategic coordination of peace-support activities. Crucially, a critical peace assessment is an opportunity for a *critical* analysis of a peace process or accord and should help identify the inadequacies of a peace accord as well as deliberate attempts to thwart peace. A critical peace assessment should not be seen as a compliance tool to be used by supporters of a peace accord to ensure that their opponents fulfil peace accord promises regardless of the flaws in that accord. As such, the critical peace assessments proposed here mark a major departure from many of the currently available peace and conflict assessment tools.

The critical peace assessment model proposed in this chapter aims to identify the shortfall between the implementation of a peace accord and positive peace as imagined by the inhabitants of the post-peace accord society. The active inclusion of the recipients of the peace, or those people for whom peace is declared and maintained, differentiates this model of peace assessment from many others. Critical peace assessments should offer guidance on how the shortfall between real and imagined peace or 'peace gap' can be addressed. As such, it is more than an information gathering exercise, and is capable of aiding the coordination of development and peace-support policy. The critical peace assessment framework relies on public participation to first imagine a better peace, and then assess how the peace accord, peace-support activities, and external factors thwart or facilitate the attainment of the better peace. Other, more traditional, informants and sources of information are used, but the participatory aspect of peace assessment is designed to help address a common failing in many post-peace accord societies – a disillusioned public.

In recent decades, donor governments, international organisations and NGOs have pioneered increasingly sophisticated conflict analysis or conflict assessment models designed to collate information in support of their interventions. These conflict assessment tools were designed to capture the essential catalysts, dynamics and actors in conflict and have been further developed to take account of the impact of peace and development initiatives. This chapter makes two arguments. First, it suggests that stalled or thwarted peace requires specialist diagnoses that are not available from standard conflict analysis tools. Bolting a 'peace' or 'post-peace accord' element onto an orthodox conflict analysis model is not enough. Instead, the intricacies of a part-peace and part-conflict situation demands a more finely calibrated analysis tool. The second argument is the need for those involved in peace assessments to maintain a critical stance. The peace that follows peace accords may not necessarily be just or sustainable. It may reinforce division, award legitimacy to militant actors and minister to conflict manifestations rather than causation or maintenance factors. Peace accords are capable of generating a moral firewall that insulates the accord and its proponents from scrutiny. To ask awkward questions risks being tainted as 'anti-peace' or unwilling to recognise the benefits accruing from a peace accord. A critical peace assessment is only subversive to the extent that it challenges dysfunctional aspects of a peace accord and the actors, practices and institutions that support it. Third party governments, international organisations and NGOs engaged in peace-support activities may have invested their energies and resources so heavily into a particular peace process or accord that they find it difficult to maintain a critical stance. Critical peace assessment exercises offer the opportunity to pierce the moral firewall surrounding peace accords and pose basic questions on the benefits and failings of peace.

The chapter begins with an overview of five core principles or assumptions that underpin existing conflict assessment exercises and examines how these may also apply to critical peace assessments in post-peace accord scenarios. Second, it proposes three additional assumptions required to enable critical peace assessment exercises to be applied effectively after civil wars. Third, the chapter discusses the practices of conflict and peace assessment, noting how modifications may be required in methodology if it is to have a critical element. Fourth, the chapter will outline the stages of a critical peace assessment exercise. Here, it is argued that a key role of a critical peace assessment is to identify restraints on conflict recidivism or those factors that may retard slippage back towards civil war. These redoubts against the recurrence of civil war call for particular attention in the strategies of actors and institutions interested in promoting peace.

The aim of merely understanding the extent and dynamics of a stalled peace, rather than heroically rushing in to save the day, may seem modest. Yet, in order to rejuvenate a peace accord, it is important to fully comprehend its extent and limitations. Stalled and dysfunctional peace is easily relegated among the priorities of governments, international organisations, NGOs and the media. Once the bulk of direct violence ends, it is understandable if the attentions of news editors, foreign and development policy analysts in national governments and the directors of aid agencies are drawn elsewhere. As one politician noted from the context of a moribund peace process:

> The world's media no longer descend on Northern Ireland the way they did at the time of the Good Friday Agreement six years ago.

For many, the absence of violence on TV screens every night is an indication that the conflict in the province has ended.[2]

The slow leaching of popular faith away from a peace accord is unlikely to compete with a violent crisis in terms of public attention. The winding down of peace-support operations in the former Yugoslavia by international organisations and aid agencies in the late 1990s illustrates the phenomenon of 'attention flight'. Quite patently, the peace heralded by the 1995 Dayton Peace Accord and supported by the international community was deeply dysfunctional and had left many problems unresolved.[3] Yet, the attentions and budgets of the international organisations and aid agencies moved on from the unfinished business of Bosnia-Herzegovina. First attention was diverted to nearby Kosovo, and then to East Timor, Afghanistan, Iraq, Darfur, the Asian Tsunami and Niger. Even 'good news' stories, such as the repatriation of the one millionth refugee in Bosnia and Herzegovina, received scant international attention.[4]

Ungenerous caricatures of stalled peace can prevail and help promote the view that some post-peace accord societies are undeserving of further attention. The following characterisations of post-peace accord societies are not uncommon in the news media: that antagonists have somehow squandered peace; that they lacked the wherewithal to turn pacific statements into actions; that they ungratefully wasted the largess and attentions of the international community or that they were never genuinely interested in peace. Continuing violence (political or criminal), electoral support for nationalist or extreme candidates, or a refusal to cooperate with international criminal court proceedings are all taken as evidence of a local cynicism towards peace.

While some of these 'squandered peace' observations can be applied to certain cases, and particularly to political, economic and militant elites, their blanket application may be inappropriate in many post-peace accord societies. The sins of the elite are not necessarily those of the bulk of the population, particularly if citizens lack the agency to shape the post-peace accord environment. Moreover, the 'squandered peace' viewpoint may fail to take account of the chronic nature of a conflict and the inability of many orthodox peace processes and peace accords to address the structural causes of conflict. The root causes of a stalled peace may not lie principally in the failed implementation of the peace accord and the unwillingness or inability of political actors to fulfil the aims of that accord. Instead, the key problem may lie in the nature of the peace accord itself or its progenitor peace process; they may lack the capacity to deal with the underlying and chronic nature of a conflict. A peace accord may minister to conflict manifestations and ignore conflict causes or discount particular groups and their grievances. It may even exacerbate the conflict or spark new sites of contest. It is in this context that a critical peace assessment provides a useful analytical tool that can help peace process participants and observers reinvigorate and re-orientate a stalled peace. Problems with an accord may only become visible or pressing in the years after an accord has been reached so the critical peace assessment process is able to provide an opportunity for an ongoing evaluation of an accord's relevance to evolving problems and effectiveness in addressing grievances.

Many of the problems facing post-peace accord societies are generically similar despite local variations. Common problems include a disjuncture between the elite and popular experience of peace, the replacement of optimism with cynicism among what was originally a pro-peace constituency, continuing violence (often in the form of crime), the uneven distribution of any economic peace dividend, incomplete disarmament of combatants and stalled security sector reform, and a lack of state capacity to translate peace accord goals into reality. This generality in examples of stalled peace allows for the utilisation of a common critical peace assessment method across cases. The emphasis on comparison though does not preclude the adoption of flexible methodologies to suit local exigencies.

Principles and assumptions of conflict assessment

The five principles and core assumptions of conflict assessments outlined in this section are gleaned from the conflict assessment models employed by leading international organisations or the development agencies of selected governments. Summarised in Table 4.1, they have application to critical peace assessments to be conducted in the aftermath of civil wars.

The first principle of conflict assessment that can extend to critical peace assessment is an understanding that complex political conflicts do not have a single cause. Conflict, as a multi-causal phenomenon, demands a comprehensive analytical framework that reviews a wide range of conflict-contributing factors. The analysis must also examine the various levels that may host or contribute to conflict: local, regional, national and international. The acceptance of the complexity of conflict causation has clear application to critical peace assessments. Mono-causal explanations for the failure of a peace accord to fulfil its promise

Table 4.1   Principles and assumptions of conflict and critical peace assessments

Principles and assumptions of conflict assessment that apply to critical peace assessment

- Conflict has multiple causes
- The importance of interaction effects
- Prioritise conflict causation factors
- Flexible methodologies are required to take account of local circumstances
- Analyses need to be aware of both direct and indirect violence

or deal with continuing conflict are frequently put forward by antagonists and often amount to self-absolution and a blaming of opponents. Thus, for example, the problems of a post-peace accord society may be conveniently blamed on one group's failure to implement certain aspects of the peace accord or 'turn their back on terrorism', while, with equal convenience, the action or inaction of other parties may be overlooked. A critical peace assessment demands a systematic review of factors inhibiting peace. Some of these factors may pre-date and remain unaffected by a peace accord, while other factors may have been sparked by the peace process and accord. The result should be a layered picture of the multiple factors that restrain positive peace.

A second assumption underpinning conflict assessment that also has application to critical peace assessments is that conflict causation often relies on 'interaction effects'. In other words, the mere existence of multiple conflict causation factors is insufficient to trigger (violent) conflict. As USAID note, 'the simple existence of poverty is not enough, nor is ethnic difference, nor is competition over natural resources.'[5] Not only do such factors require deliberate activation by elites and others, they also depend on the 'potential to interact and multiply up'.[6] Just as conflict causation is very much due to the interplay between a volatile cocktail of factors, the stalling of a peace accord and the dissipation of the optimism required for peace, relies on the relationship between factors. Thus, critical peace assessments require not just an awareness of the manifold nature of peace impediments, but also the often cumulative and interactive nature of these factors. So, for example, the high crime rates that are often cited as the major element in the popular disaffection with peace in Guatemala are best viewed alongside complementary factors such as the lack of capacity of law enforcement institutions and the uneven distribution of wealth.[7] In sum, critical peace assessments must identify the complex interplay between factors responsible for the leaching of faith away from a peace accord. This rhymes with a holistic view of peace that emphasises inter-group relationships and the integration of needs with resource distribution. The logic of a recognition of the inter-connectedness of conflict causation and maintenance is a recognition that peace also requires an integrated approach.

The third principle underpinning existing conflict assessment exercises that may have relevance towards post-peace accord peace assessments is the need to prioritise those factors contributing to both conflict causation and the hindrance of peace. While the identification of conflict-causing factors constitutes an important first step, it must lead to a prioritisation or ranking of factors through which the analyst distinguishes between principal and other conflict-causing factors. Similarly, with critical peace assessments, the object is to identify and prioritise the key peace-hindering factors. This will help with strategic programming by internal and external actors interested in addressing the problems of a frustrated peace. In the optimum scenario, it will encourage the targeting of tailor-made initiatives and interventions, with core problems receiving more attention than subsidiary ones. In some post-peace accord situations, interventions in support of peace processes and accords have reflected the capacities and skills sets of the intervening actors rather than the needs of the society. In other cases, peace-support activities have concentrated on the most easily addressed problems rather than those that are most urgent, while in others still, the most visible problems attract precedence. The identification and prioritisation of peace-retarding factors can have profound implications for a post-peace accord society. It may be that structural factors are identified as the primary impediments to the enjoyment of peace thus challenging powerful actors and calling for reforms far in excess of tinkering within existing peace-support programmes.

Not only will a critical peace assessment methodology encourage greater discrimination in policy interventions by identifying the most significant peace-retarding factors, it may also lead to policy agility. Regular reviews of the implementation of a peace accord may reveal that different issues or sectors require different levels and types of attention at different stages of the emergence from violent conflict. For example, a peace assessment may reveal a long list of security factors denying the fulfilment of peace, ranging from the partial success of a disarmament programme and spiralling crime rates to the inability of many former combatants to find employment. A common element in all of these issues may be the youth sector, and particularly its alienation from society, exclusion from politics and lack of absorption into an underdeveloped

civilian economy.[8] A peace assessment should enable analysts to identify the need for strategies to address youth exclusion. Moreover, it may
also illustrate that lack of capacity (in disarmament programmes, crime
reduction and economic initiatives) lies at the heart of many problems,
thus suggesting the need for a strategic and coordinated focus on capacity building across sectors. It may also become apparent that certain
issues require greater attention at different times during the post-peace
accord period, thus calling for the choreography of peace-supporting
initiatives. This 'joined-up' policy approach, through which strategic
linkages are made across sectors, is a key advantage of a comprehensive
approach to peace assessment.

The fourth principle of conflict assessments that has relevance for
post-peace accord critical peace assessments is the need for flexibility in
methodology so that local circumstances can be factored into initiatives
and intervention. Differences in the scale, intensity and complexity of
conflicts and emerging peace situations demand that conflict and peace
assessments are aware of local circumstances. For example, in some situations the state may be a principal actor in the conflict and its management. It will act as the key source of patronage and resources, the centre
of capability in terms of the provision of security and the main 'prize' in
the conflict between warring groups. It may also possess that indefinable
political elixir: legitimacy. Yet, in other conflicts and emerging peace situations the state may have less significance. Lemke notes that 'there are
many examples of developing world political elites actually dismantling
the edifices of state power.'[9] The state may be remote from people's lives,
having extremely limited capacity in social provision and little ability to
project its will beyond the capital city. The presence of alternative
sources of power and legitimacy, such as kinship or religious groups,
associations of former combatants or international organisations, may
mean that the state is relegated to a lowly position among the networks
and institutions most relevant to people's lives.

This will have significant implications for conflict and peace
assessments, and steer analysts towards sub- or supra-state actors. Yet the
notion of the state as the principal unit of political organisation is
deeply ingrained into western political consciousness. This near fetishi-
sation of the state in western analyses (and thus the analyses of leading
states, international organisations and international financial institutions) is evidenced in the strong interest in institutional design and
reform. Attention to political behaviour or culture and how local political customs interact with political institutions, is less evident, yet this is
precisely the lens required in some circumstances. The key point,

however, is that critical peace assessments must retain a flexibility that allows a recognition of the circumstances prevailing in the post-peace accord society. This flexibility must be mindful that western models of political organisation do not always explain political phenomenon in the rest of the world.

The final principle underpinning conflict assessments that can have continued value in critical peace assessments is the need to see beyond direct violence. Just as a conflict situation is comprised of both direct and indirect violence, a post-peace accord situation may contain both types of violence. Indeed, a peace accord and orthodox peace-support activities such as peacekeeping may be successful in staunching most direct violence among organised groups. Yet, the indirect violence of harassment, militarism and the retention of weapons may persist. Thus, critical peace assessments must be equipped to take account of structural impediments to peace that continue regardless of the cessation of direct violence.

Additional principles and assumptions for critical peace assessment

While existing models of conflict assessment offer peace assessments useful principles and guiding assumptions for the diagnosis of post-peace accord societies, three additional principles are required in order to tailor the analysis to the specificities of a post-peace accord situation and award it a critical dimension (Table 4.2). The first of these is that the analysis of stalled peace must have no sacred cows or individuals, issues or institutions that are beyond examination. In other words, a critical peace assessment must be capable of recommending fundamental revision in a post-peace accord society. It must resist the temptation to reify a peace accord as a document written in stone and the final word on how peace is to be achieved. The assessment must not regard external 'friends of the peace process' as necessarily helpful and altruistic in all circumstances. Neither must it view commissions and institutions originally created in support of the peace accord as off-limits. It may be difficult to achieve this critical distance from a peace accord, especially if it has assumed a privileged place in the psyche of some groups within the post-peace accord society. While peace assessments must examine the impact of existing development and peace support programmes on progress towards peace, they must not be beholden to existing programmes. The mere inclusion of the word 'peace' in an initiative sponsored by an international organisation, government organisation or an

Table 4.2 Additional principles and assumptions of conflict and critical peace assessments

---

Additional principles and assumptions of conflict assessment that apply to critical peace assessment

---

- No sacred cows
- Critically examine the impact of development and peace-support activities
- Identify positive factors preventing conflict recidivism

NGO is an insufficient guarantee that the sponsored activity will actually enhance peace. A critical peace assessment must be prepared to recommend radical change if it identifies ineffective or counter-productive development and peace-support activities. Circumstances do change, and what may have been appropriate in the infant years of a peace accord may lose its relevance or even become counter-productive as time progresses. Since the framers of peace accords cannot be expected to have complete prescience in anticipating implementation problems, it seems prudent to integrate a review mechanism into a peace accord.

Crucially, a critical peace assessment should be regarded as a much more fundamental exercise than a routine peace accord 'health check' that attempts to judge the success or failure of peace against the promises made in a peace accord. Instead, the assessment needs to look beyond the accord. It may be that the peace accord was limited in its ambitions, ministered to conflict manifestations while overlooking conflict causes and excluded key conflict actors or sections of the population. In some conflicts, for example Colombia, governments have attempted to conclude separate peace deals with individual militant groups rather than work towards a comprehensive peace settlement.[10] A peace assessment that uses a peace accord as the essential yardstick for the attainment of positive peace misses the point. Instead, it should be open to critiquing a peace accord and exploring the shortfall between actual and ideal peace.

The second additional principle of critical peace assessment is the need to examine the impact of development and peacebuilding activities established by the peace accord. Most conflict assessment models already examine the impact of aid and development activities on the conflict. A post-peace accord situation requires an extension of this practice to examine the effects of development and peace-support actions on the implementation of the peace accord *and* the fulfilment of positive peace. Development and peacebuilding interventions do not always fulfil their intended consequences and can even exacerbate conflict. For example, one group in a deeply divided society may feel that other groups are benefiting disproportionately in terms of development assistance. Alternatively, they may feel that truth recovery exercises, ostensibly designed to help a society come to terms with a fraught past, heap blame on themselves but absolve others. The key question for a critical peace assessment is to establish the extent to which, if any, that peace-support activities contribute to the embedding of peace and the peace accord. Other questions include the extent to which these activities are coordinated, are correctly targeted at key areas and sectors of society and have the potential to become sustainable.

The tendency towards a standardised template approach in internationally supported peacebuilding activities compounds the need for a critical examination of the efficacy of peace-support activities and their actual contribution to a peace that is widely enjoyed. A number of peace processes and post-peace accord situations have come to resemble one another in terms of formulaic contributions from external actors. This donor-driven 'conveyor belt' of DDR, SSR, truth recovery and institutional reform may continue apace but may not always match the precise needs of a society emerging from conflict. A critical peace assessment can provide a valuable service in challenging superfluous interventions and re-orientating others to address actual needs.

An advantage of including a review of development and peacebuilding activities in peace assessments is that it demands the inclusion of local-level analyses. Thus, the quality of peace is not only viewed through an exclusively national lens (which is often inappropriate given the propensity of many conflicts to be restricted to one geographic region of the state). If a peace dividend is more visible in one area than another then it suggests the direction of additional resources to the less favoured area, and an examination of the positive lessons to be learned from the more successful case. Moreover, by examining a post-peace accord society at both the national and local levels, a peace assessment should be able to identify the transmission routes and mechanisms whereby ideas and resources are transferred from the elite to the local levels and vice versa. A recurrent problem in post-peace accord societies is that the benefits of a peace accord agreed at the elite level fail to materialise at the local level. Development and peace-support activities can play a role in helping such dividends materialise and in helping local communities make the connection between macro-level political change and local conditions. In such circumstances, a critical peace assessment requires an honest appraisal of the experience of peace at the local level and the role of peace-support activities in embedding or blocking peace.

The final guiding assumption to underpin critical peace assessments is the need to identify the positive factors that restrain slippage back towards violent armed conflict or the erosion of attempts to tackle structural conflict. Societies emerging from civil war experience a high risk of conflict recidivism.[11] A critical peace assessment can perform a valuable role in identifying key 'redoubts' that promote inter-group tolerance and provide restraint in the face of temptation to resume violent hostilities. For example, an independent media, a parliament with real powers of oversight or a church hierarchy may act as bulwarks of restraint against those motivated to go back to war. These redoubts may remain largely intact when other elements of a peace accord become weakened. A critical peace assessment can also help identify those actors that pose a threat to peace. Superficial analyses of militant organisations often inflate the homogeneity of armed groups and overlook internal fissures. Darby notes that individuals in militant groups during peace processes can be categorised as moderates, opportunists, dealers and zealots according to their reactions to the peace process or accord.[12] A critical peace assessment exercise may help identify those elements in a militant organisation that are minded towards moderation and help assess factors that may encourage or reinforce this moderation. Thus, a peace assessment should not be restricted to the identification of risk factors that contribute towards conflict. Instead, it should also help identify the opportunity or safety factors that support the implementation of a peace accord or attainment of positive peace.

Practices of critical peace assessment

The primary reasons for conducting critical peace assessments are to contribute towards better targeted development and reconstruction policy, and to re-orient stalled peace accords towards broad-based sustainable peace. In the optimum case, peace assessments become a regular (though not routine) activity conducted by development-orientated international organisations, NGOs, third party governments and other actors within a post-peace accord society. Nested within development programmes, they become a tool for policy coordination and the strategic direction of programmes rather than reactive fire brigade evaluations that respond to the latest crisis. By regarding peace assessments as an integral part of development strategy, policymakers are able to make permanent the linkages between peace, conflict and reconstruction.

The use of critical peace assessments as part of policy formation should help guard against one of the most common failings of development and peacebuilding policy: its basis in faith and hope rather than observed evidence. Sentiment is a poor guide for policy regardless of how well-meaning its proponents may be. Liberal optimism, the philosophical basis of many development and peace-support activities, is inherently prescriptive and fuels the 'something must be done' mentality. Such motivations are often noble, but the urge to intervene, or 'do something', may precede a calculation of what is necessary, feasible, sustainable and locally acceptable. The sentiment that formerly warring groups should reconcile and peacefully integrate is understandable but often unrealistic given the extent of division. Indeed, in the immediate aftermath of a violent conflict it may be irrational for groups of antagonists to trust each other. Critical peace assessments operate according to observed evidence rather than hoped for reconciliation, and grounded by an evidential base, their policy implications are likely to operate in the realm of the possible. The recommendation that policy is realistic should not be taken as a lowering of expectations. Nor should it be taken as an extension of the 'new barbarism' literature that proposes a judicious selectivity in conflict management intervention (restricting interventions to the most amenable cases).[13] Instead, a critical peace assessment based on what is realistic and feasible calls for tough and often radical policy prescriptions. For example, a recurrent failing of orthodox peace-support activities is that they often invest in those already committed to peace.[14] Frequently the urban dwelling liberal middle class, this sector is often the most accessible to third parties rather than in most urgent need of attention. Given that this sector may already support peace initiatives, efforts by international actors to co-opt them may prove superfluous.[15] It is important that the pro-peace sector is shored up and maintains a position as stakeholders in peace, but the sector should not be the main focus of peace-support activities. The findings from critical peace assessments should encourage the targeting of peace support activities beyond the 'already converted' constituency and an engagement with groups sceptical or indifferent towards the peace process and accord. In sum, a critical peace assessment should guide needs-driven interventions rather than activities based on hope and ease of access.

While comprehensive peace assessments are resource expensive, thoroughness is essential. A peace assessment needs to be conducted at all levels of society so that the connections and disjunctions between the local and state levels can be tracked. Peace assessments restricted to a single layer of society will give an incomplete picture and fail to reveal the crucial transmission or blockage points at which violence, intolerance and disobedience of the provisions of a peace accord are transferred between levels of society. Unfortunately, this means that the resources required to conduct a comprehensive peace assessment are usually only available to international organisations, third party governments and larger NGOs. There are strong arguments however for the sharing and wide dissemination of the results of peace assessments. First, the critical peace assessment process may arouse suspicions of partiality and raise sensitive issues – not uncommon responses to research in societies emerging from violent conflict.[16] By publicising the results of the critical peace assessment exercise, and making it clear that the primary focus is on development and reconstruction, some suspicions may be allayed. A second reason for the sharing of the findings of peace assessments is that smaller NGOs, bereft of the capabilities required to conduct their own peace assessments, would be able to benefit. This would allow them to orientate their policies so that they complement those of other peace and development-minded actors. Third, since multiple critical peace assessments will have different methodologies and rely on different sources and informants, the sharing and dissemination of information would aid comparison and the refinement of methodology. If duplication of resources became evident, it may also encourage aid agencies or donor governments to cooperate in conducting peace assessments.

There is a fourth argument in favour of the public dissemination of the results of a critical peace assessment in a post-peace accord society: the (public) identification of actors, dynamics and structures that are impediments to peace may mobilise efforts to address the problems identified. This task requires delicacy and there is a fine line between the identification of problem issues, policies and actors on the one hand and the politics of blame on the other. If a peace assessment is seen to reinforce the position of one political party or group of parties then it may risk losing its advantage as a diagnostic tool. Absolute objectivity is an impossible goal in a socially constructed world, let alone a society emerging from a violent internal conflict and retaining deep fissures. Concepts such as reconciliation, socio-economic development or post-war reconstruction regularly become the site of bitter inter-group conflict in post-peace accord societies so there is likely to be little neutral ground for a critical peace assessment to occupy. In such an environment openness and transparency with regard to motive, mode of operation and findings is perhaps the best strategy. In this regard, it is important that a critical peace assessment does not become the possession of one sector or institution and that it strives to maintain a sense of independence.[17]

The establishment of peace monitoring mechanisms and units has become standard practice in many peace processes and accords. Indeed, the history of such monitoring stretches back to the early UN deployments which were concerned with ceasefire monitoring and the identification of those responsible for breaches.[18] As White observed, the United Nations 'realised the necessity of having accurate, neutral information' in conflict situations.[19] Lightly armed, these missions relied on the moral authority of the United Nations to act as a deterrent and traditional peacekeeping and monitoring missions have often been criticised for freezing conflicts or 'making provisional measures permanent' thereby hindering conflict transformation.[20] The monitoring provisions of contemporary peace processes and accords have varied from the oversight of ceasefires to the more expansive task of monitoring the implementation of a peace accord. While some, such as the Peace Zone Monitoring Committees in Mindanao, have been in the main inspired and staffed from local resources, others, such as the Implementation Monitoring Group in Liberia, have drawn on the resources of the Economic Community of West African States, the United Nations, African Union, European Union and the International Contact Group on Liberia.[21] The ill-fated October 2000 Townsville Peace Accord for the Solomon Islands combined a locally constituted Peace Monitoring Council with an International Peace Monitoring Team. An Independent Monitoring Commission was established in 2004 as an afterthought to Northern Ireland's 1998 Belfast Agreement when it became clear that the peace accord had not staunched all political violence. The Peace Monitoring Group established as part of the 1997–1998 Bougainville peace process was empowered not only to monitor the ceasefire, but also to 'promote and instil confidence in the peace process through its presence, good offices and interaction with the people of Bougainville'. Importantly, it was also empowered to 'provide people in Bougainville with information about the ceasefire and other aspects of the peace process'.[22]

Monitoring can have the advantage of making clear that peace accords are dynamic and open to evaluation and re-evaluation. But many of the monitoring mechanisms established as part of contemporary peace accords are narrow in their remit, limited to policing the implementation of a peace accord and unable to raise wider questions of the quality of the peace and the fitness for purpose of the original peace accord. Issues germane to positive peace (socio-economic exclusion and

potential, public health, structural violence etc.) are often not mentioned in peace accords and thus fall outside of the remit of a monitoring committee. The neutrality or independence of such committees has
raised concern in many peace processes, with antagonists anxious to
secure a place on the committee or unwilling to afford the committee
legitimacy lest it demands uncomfortable concessions. Peace accord
monitoring bodies risk becoming yet another arena of competition in a
peace process. As was the case in Northern Ireland, the continuation of
inter-group conflict despite a peace accord meant that the adjudications
of the monitoring body became a weapon of blame rather than a 'neutral' means for the rectification of the failings of a peace process.[23]

Monitoring institutions and mechanisms of this type are not the
same thing as critical peace assessments. While the interest of the former is restricted to judging respect for a ceasefire or the implementation of a peace accord, the latter should adopt a much more holistic
stance and concern itself with the wider issues of the development and
maintenance of positive peace. By necessity the former may be reactive,
responding to violence or allegations of bad faith, while the latter
should adopt a comprehensive outlook, reviewing all levels of society
and processes within it. The composition of peace accord monitoring
bodies and those charged with critical peace assessments may also differ. In some cases, the former contain nominees from the main antago-
nist groups, while a critical peace assessment should be removed, as far
as is possible, from party political interests. This is not to suggest that
critical peace assessments should not be informed by political parties
and militant organisations. They should not, however, be beholden
to actors with a vested interest in an unchanging version of a peace
accord. It could be that a critical peace assessment identifies aspects of
a peace-support programme sponsored by a major NGO as posing a significant obstacle to the fulfilment of a holistic version of peace. Since a
critical peace assessment must be enabled to identify obstacles to peace
from whatever quarter, the composition and resourcing of the critical
peace assessment teams has a peculiar delicacy. Evaluations are an
accepted element of internationally supported development and peace-
support activities and have helped ensure effectiveness, value for
money and transparency at the programme and project levels.[24] While
arguments can be made that the marketisation and contracting out of
evaluation activities helps lower costs and encourages independence,
the evaluation 'market' may also have a disciplining effect on evaluation agents and restrain their willingness to criticise the hand that
feeds them.

Notionally the practicalities of a critical peace assessment should present fewer problems than a conflict assessment. It might be expected that the post-peace accord stage of a conflict would offer a safer and more open environment for the research needed for a peace assessment. Yet, many of the obstacles and dangers facing the researcher in a conflict environment may persist in the post-peace accord era. Information gathering in a conflict area cannot be regarded as a neutral activity, and antagonists are likely to harbour suspicions on the purposes and implications of the research.[25] This is particularly the case if the critical peace assessment is conducted on behalf of donor organisations or third party states that have the capacity to invest significant financial or symbolic resources in the post-peace accord society. By its very nature, a critical peace assessment is a political act, though not necessarily a party political act. In the optimum scenario, it is conducted in favour of an expansive notion of peace and is antithetical to groups supporting direct and indirect violence.

Continuing dislocation as a result of armed conflict may mean a dearth of baseline data that could complement a peace assessment and help contextualise its findings. Lebanon, for example, has not conducted a census since 1932, fearing that an ethnic headcount would fuel inter-group claims and shatter the consociational balance constructed by the 1989 Ta'if Accord.[26] Other post-peace accord states simply lack the capacity to collect basic statistics, thus hampering the provision of public goods and policy planning.

Imagining Peace

A participatory methodology that encourages local communities to think critically about the quality of the peace they have experienced after a peace accord is the fundamental basis of a peace assessment. A peace assessment attempts to identify the shortfall between experienced and imagined peace. To do so, it must take as its starting point a canvassing of public aspirations of peace. Imagining peace may sound naive in the extreme, particularly given the immediacy of some post-peace accord problems. Yet, inviting participants in a peace assessment exercise to imagine peace, or discuss the concept in an idealised form, has a number of advantages. First, a broad-based exercise to assess local opinions on idealised versions of peace, may mean that varieties of peace (including indigenous notions of peace) become apparent. In other words, the exercise may help guard against homogenised versions of peace that may be envisaged by powerful internal and external actors. As such, it has the capacity to act as an antidote to the standardised liberal democratic peace and the mechanistic deployment of its constituent parts regardless of need and local circumstances. Second, imagining peace has the potential to tap into creative thinking that could offer ways to reinvigorate the stalled or dysfunctional peace process. By widening the range of actors and informants beyond political parties or militant groups, the peace imagining exercise provides a forum for a range of less well heard voices in post-peace accord societies (for example, women, small businesses and rural communities). As imagined from these perspectives, peace may have a very different character from that negotiated at a conference table or legislated through a new constitution.

The third and most fundamental advantage from the imagining peace exercise, is that it can free participants' thinking from the immediacy of temporal political disputes. The language and conceptual breadth used to describe imagined peace may be very different from the language and conceptual breadth used to describe a peace linked with a particular peace process, peace accord or political controversy. An imagined peace that is at all times grounded in political realities, and the positions that go with them, will be constrained by political boundaries. Imagined peace that attempts to transcend these boundaries and think conceptually in terms of human needs and aspirations may be of a different order. In the Palestinian case, for example, peace envisaged through a political or constitutional lens may include a fully formed Palestinian state and shopping list of Israeli concessions such as the release of prisoners or restitution for land seizures. It is likely to imagine peace as a relational concept, at all times mindful of the Israeli 'other', rather than imagine peace as a concept in its own right. Imagined peace that attempts to think beyond the shopping list of gains and concessions, and expresses peace in terms of human needs and aspirations may be empowered to connect with peace-sustaining concepts such as inter-group dignity, tolerance and respect.

The much used, and critiqued, participatory rural appraisal and participatory development techniques can be utilised to maximise public participation in critical peace assessment exercise.[27] Cooke and Kothari have noted pitfalls of the 'tyranny of participation' and its tendency to have less radical policy effects than advertised.[28] Attempts to acquire direct citizen input into policymaking processes and cut through the stodge of mediated and consensus decision-making have had well-documented undemocratic side-effects.[29] Yet, we should not be over-hasty in our dismissal of the empowering and transformative potential of participatory methodologies, particularly in their ability to open up new political spaces and hear previously unheard voices.[30]

A critical peace assessment framework

Having outlined the core assumptions and practices underpinning conflict assessment, and how these can be modified to suit the purposes of post-peace accord critical peace assessment, this section will illustrate peace and conflict impact assessment tools already utilised by the UK Department for International Development (DFID) and the United States Agency for International Development (USAID). It will then propose a critical peace assessment framework. The DFID strategic conflict analysis model has clear application to post-peace accord environments and is used to assess the 'risks of negative effects of conflict on programmes; risks of programmes or policies exacerbating conflict; [and] opportunities to improve the effectiveness of development interventions in contributing to conflict prevention and reduction'.[31] The model has three stages (briefly summarised in Figure 4.1): analysis of the conflict, analysis of the international responses to the conflict and the development of strategies and options.[32] Rather than portraiture of the main actors and structures in a conflict, the DFID methodology is concerned with 'dynamic profiling' or capturing the interaction between actors and the incentives and triggers behind actions.[33]

While acknowledging the difficulty of predicting the onset of escalation of conflict, the DFID guidelines point to the interaction between three factors as critical to conflict: a society's structural vulnerability, the opportunity to benefit from instability and violence and a society's capacity to manage or contain violence.[34] The final stage of the conflict assessment is to identify strategies and options for conflict management

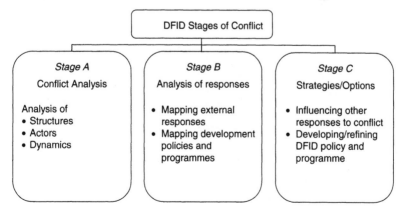

Figure 4.1 DFID–three key stages of conflict assessment.

and to ensure that development approaches are conflict sensitive.[35] Crucial here is a need to ensure coherence and cooperation in the strategies of all external donors, international actors and their local agents. The conflict assessment is designed to help adjust current development activities and to suggest new initiatives.

The USAID conflict assessment model (summarised in Figure 4.2) attempts to illustrate the motives, means and opportunities behind conflict. Comprehensive, and concerned that it does not overlook 'less obvious' conflict-contributing factors, the conflict assessment model provides a checklist of questions organised around the categories of motives, means and opportunities.[36] Thus, for example, in order to clarify the means or mobilising factors behind a conflict, the model asks the following under the heading 'Regime type and legitimacy': Is the regime democratic, authoritarian or mixed; how long has it existed in its current forms; is it in a period of transition or erosion; are there generally accepted rules for political competition and what is the overall level of respect for national authorities?[37] Impacting on all three main categories in the conflict assessment (motive, means and opportunity) are external factors in the form of 'bad neighbours'[38] and the adverse effects of globalisation. The USAID model also points to the importance of 'windows of opportunity' or catalytic events such as elections or natural disasters that trigger latent conflict factors towards violence.

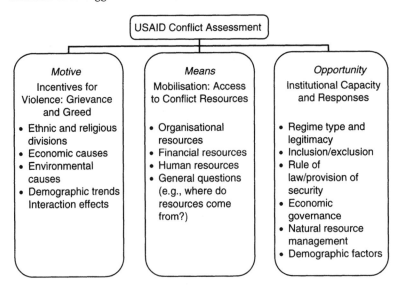

Figure 4.2 USAID conflict assessment framework.

As with the DFID template, emphasis is placed on the impact that development and peace-support activity has on peace and conflict. The conflict assessment model is particularly interested in identifying chains of interaction between conflict-contributing factors and sectors in society, and ways in which these interaction chains can be broken. It is hoped that this multi-level approach will encourage policy interventions to take a strategic viewpoint, mindful of how peace-support activities can be mutually reinforcing. The USAID conflict assessment framework has been developed alongside programme 'toolkits' that are designed to examine why some issues (e.g., youth unemployment or competition over land) become particularly salient in some conflicts, and develop programme options, and monitoring and evaluation tools, to deal with them.[39]

Having outlined existing peace and conflict assessment frameworks, this section can now move on to introduce a six-part critical peace assessment framework for use in post-peace accord scenarios. It develops existing peace and conflict models in three ways. First, it is consciously designed for the post-peace accord phase of civil wars. In this phase, the leading protagonists in the conflict will be party to the accord (with varying degrees of enthusiasm and reluctance) and the accord may have the blessing or practical support of major international organisations and third party states. The post-peace accord phase also assumes that large-scale inter-group violence has ceased, but does not assume that all violence has ended. Second, the primary target of a critical peace assessment model is the population in the war-affected zone. This marks a departure from many peace and conflict impact assessment tools that are primarily targeted at donor agencies. In the case of a critical peace assessment, the supposed recipients of the peace act as both the key informants and 'consumers' of the assessment exercise. The main dialogue in many orthodox conflict assessment exercises is often within organisations, for example, between the field stations and headquarters of donor agencies or involves external donor governments and the central government of the state in question. The third way in which critical peace assessments can be differentiated from the peace and conflict assessments currently used by many organisations is their attempt to transcend the mere evaluation of existing programmes and projects. Many such evaluations and audits lack the critical perspective required to address the failings of a peace accord. Instead, for a range of often prosaic reasons (such as continued access to funding or the tightly written remit of evaluation activities), they are often complicit with the aims and objectives of existing projects and programmes and bereft of any motivation to criticise or challenge them. The critical peace assessment methodology has the advantage of adopting a holistic approach to the post-peace accord society.

The overall aim of critical peace assessments is to identify and address the shortfall between idealised and experienced versions of peace. A critical peace assessment aims to transcend what can be described as 'the project trap' or the tendency of many observers to view a post-peace accord environment in terms of existing projects and programmes, and the institutions, terminology and goals that support them. Existing projects and programmes can rapidly become imbued with inertia (the most obvious sign of which is the need to secure additional funding once the initial project-cycle reaches an end regardless of whether the project or programme has a peace-supporting added value). Peace-support activities that are counter-productive or superfluous need to be identified as such – a difficult task given the moral energy associated with the word 'peace'. Many peace-support programmes and projects concentrate on issues and sectors that are most amenable to peace-support intervention, leaving aside trickier issues and sectors. They may, for example, cater for 'natural engagers' or moderate groups and individuals who already occupy the political centre-ground and are thus in little need of peace-support activities. The lens of existing programmes and projects may only afford a partial view of the post-accord society. A critical peace assessment must take a more holistic approach and include issues and sectors that may be unpalatable or obdurate. It is precisely these areas that are most likely to contain the main obstacles to the fulfilment of peace.

The critical peace assessment framework outlined here has six stages, with the first stage of imagining peace acting as the initial stage and principal referent against which the other elements are measured (see Figure 4.3). The next four stages of the framework (assessment of peace accord implementation, assessment of peace-support activities, identification of factors restraining conflict recidivism, identification of peace influencing external factors) examine peace-enhancing and peace-hindering elements of the post-peace accord society. These factors lead to the final stage of recommendations for policy interventions. Key informants for the conduct of the peace assessment are government and political figures, local government officials, NGO and civil society personnel, media commentators and business stakeholders. But since a central part of the critical peace assessment exercise is the organic or local reception of the peace process and accord, the network of informants must spread further and encompass the local level. An engagement with

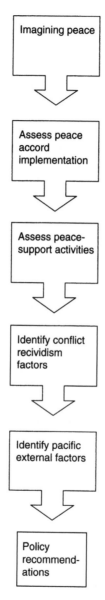

Figure 4.3 Critical peace assessment model.

the community level may be resource expensive and methodologically problematic, but it will provide the crucial baseline evidence (imagined peace and observations of 'peace' in action) against which the peace process and the peace accord will be measured.

Like much research in deeply divided societies, the critical peace assessment is likely to produce highly divergent visions and experiences of peace. Moreover, it may also produce contradictory policy recommendations. For example, constituencies who imagine peace in a minimalist way, such as the provision of greater physical security and an end to a post-peace accord crime surge, will differ from those who harbour notions of peace as a more inclusive form of socio-economic development and political organisation. As with the case of orthodox conflict assessments, those conducting the critical peace assessment will have considerable agency as to how to interpret and react to the critical peace assessment findings. Yet, since the critical peace assessment framework goes beyond a mere checklist of the implementation of a peace accord, there is at least an opportunity for notions of positive peace to be considered.

The second stage of the critical peace assessment framework is an assessment of the implementation of a peace accord. This includes questions on the extent to which provisions of the peace accord have been implemented, contested or ignored. It may be that implementation on some issue areas, for example the establishment of new political institutions, is more advanced than other areas, for example security sector reform. Respect for the provisions of a peace accord may also vary according to geographic area or community, with one group in a deeply divided society perceiving the peace accord to be to their advantage and thus abiding more faithfully to its provisions. An assessment of the peace accord should also review the extent to which an accord has been endorsed or rejected by popular vote or demonstration, contested or renegotiated. Importantly, a critical peace assessment is not an aid for the full implementation of a peace accord. Its principal purpose is to map the shortfall between optimal positive peace, as imagined by inhabitants in the relevant territory, and actual peace, as experienced by those inhabitants. The exercise is predicated on an understanding that peace accords are not carved in stone. Instead, accords are highly political documents that rely on interpretation and the spirit in which they are received. Stage two of the peace assessment exercise is measured against stage one.

Stage three involves an assessment of peace-support activities in the wake of the peace-accord. This stage measures the impact of the peace support activities against *both* the aims of the peace-accord and the ambitions of imagined peace. While the ultimate aim is to assess the extent to which peace-support activities contribute towards the attainment of positive peace, measuring the extent to which peace support activities contribute to the aims of the peace accord is a valuable exercise. It may be the case that the peace accord contains many ambitions in tune with the idea of positive peace, or that it contains important restraints that guard against conflict recidivism.

Peace-support activities are defined as those initiatives and programmes conducted by third parties and local agents (including the state) that are deliberately designed to enhance peace. Thus, for example, a World Bank or government micro-credit scheme that allows internally displaced women to establish small businesses, but which is publicly linked with the wider goal of peacebuilding, can be considered as a peace-support activity. For the sake of manageability it is necessary to include only those initiatives and programmes that explicitly mention a peace-support or peacebuilding aim. Other activities that produce peace-enhancing benefits as a by-product can be covered in the fourth stage of the peace assessment exercise that examines restraints against slippage back towards violent conflict.

The fourth stage of the critical peace assessment framework aims to identify factors successful in restraining a return to conflict and assess if they reveal positive lessons that can be applied to other sectors or issues. Restraints on conflict recidivism may include external actors able to offer security guarantees and a civil society enabled to act as a check on government. Perhaps the most powerful restraint on a return to overt political violence may come in the form of demonstrable signs that the peace accord environment offers greater advantages than war. Such signs may include political institutions (local and national) that are able to service basic needs in a manner perceived to be efficient and equitable (a tall order in a deeply divided society in which calculations of relative group status have an ethnonational dimension and are all pervasive). The reconstruction of infrastructure and public policy provision are grossly understudied in post-war contexts yet they have the potential of offering a powerful bulwark against a return to conflict. It may well be that significant political engineering is required to safeguard minority rights in such situations, which risks alienating groups who wish for majoritarianism to prevail. Yet would-be political engineers should note that political actors and their support constituencies cannot be 'made' to be moderate. The mere advocacy of pluralism, 'common sense', inclusion and reconciliation is rarely convincing. Instead, there must be demonstrable advantages associated with the holding of moderate political positions, and these advantages must outweigh those promised by advocates of political extremism. Lebanon, Northern Ireland, Israel and Sri Lanka have all shown how hard-line or nationalist parties have profited electorally after peace accords or initiatives through the exploitation of public disappointments and fears.

Stage five of the critical peace assessment framework identifies those external factors that influence a post-peace accord society. Stedman and others point to the fundamental role external actors can play in the success or failure of peace accords.[40] Such external factors serve as a reminder that many of the factors contributing to peace and instability lie beyond the control of political elites and their followers in a society emerging from protracted internal conflict. A presidential election in the United States, the ending of a civil war in a neighbouring state that prompts the circulation of weapons and combatants, or fluctuations in international commodity prices, can all have conflict catalysing or calming effects regardless of the agency of local antagonists. States and societies emerging from protracted armed conflict often lack the capability to resist external interventions and influences. This incapacity may range from an inability to police a border to an economy so enfeebled that it has virtually no autonomy with regard to how it connects with the global economy or controls its currency. Stage five calls for an audit of the extent and strength of external influences on the society, how they facilitate or hinder the implementation of the peace accord and how they facilitate or hinder the goal of positive peace. Many external factors will be structural, deeply embedded into the organisation of international political and economic life. As such they may not be immediately obvious and may even seem innocuous. Yet, the principal referent of imagined peace calls for a fundamental and critical assessment of all levels of society and relationships impacting upon it.

The final stage of the critical peace assessment framework calls for policy recommendations that attempt to redress the shortfall between imagined and stalled peace. A peace accord that fails to deliver positive social change, perpetuates division or is accompanied by a crime surge is in need of revision. The extent to which a critical peace assessment translates into a feasible plan to rejuvenate a stalled or dysfunctional peace accord depends on at least three factors: the first relates to the identity of those organising and conducting the critical peace assessment and the extent to which they possess the leverage power to encourage significant revisions in the peace accord. Realistically, only major international organisations or third party states are likely to have such powers of compliance. The second factor relates to the willingness and ability of the main stakeholders in the peace accord to conduct or resist revisions to the peace accord. Following exhaustive peace negotiations, and the possible endorsement of an accord through an electoral process, political actors may be understandably unwilling to countenance major revisions of a peace accord.

Similarly, a large electoral majority or the support of a powerful client may insulate actors against pressure to revise an accord. A third factor governing the extent to which the recommendations arising from a critical peace assessment can materialise in the form of policy changes stems from the degree to which the critical peace assessment can harness the post-peace accord public mood.

Concluding discussion

As an experimental diagnostic tool, the critical peace assessment model is prone to criticism for its lack of realism when faced with the highly political constraints of a society emerging from civil war. Yet, the value of this analytical framework lies in its ability to maintain a critical perspective. The danger with many assessment and evaluation exercises is that they act as compliance tools for the peace accord or elements of the peace accord (such as a national solidarity programme). The critical peace assessment methodology must be free to identify elements of the peace accord as presenting obstacles to the fulfilment of a widely enjoyed peace. The concentration on the identification of those factors that limit the quality of peace in a post-peace accord society risks that observers may overlook the existence of positive peace promoting factors, particularly restraints on conflict recidivism. Many such pacific bulwarks have a subtle quality, deeply embedded within social and cultural norms to the extent that they may not be immediately obvious. The policy recommendations stemming from a critical peace assessment may be advised to build on these redoubts against backward slippage into civil war, to examine how they can be bolstered and replicated in other areas or sectors of the post-peace accord society.

The next three chapters concentrate on three factors that have thwarted the enjoyment of peace in many societies emerging from civil war despite the existence of a peace process or peace accord: violence, poverty and external interference. Malign impacts from all three sources can co-exist, or even be facilitated by, the liberal democratic peace (the variant of peace most commonly promoted through internationally supported peace initiatives).

5
Peace Accords Thwarted by Violence

Only the dead have seen the end of war.

Plato

Introduction

By 2004, Kosovo was in its fourth year of UN administration. Secured by 18,000 NATO peacekeepers and 3,500 UN police officers, it had experienced the whole panoply of peacebuilding measures that often follow peace accords. Under international supervision, elections had been organised, war crimes proceedings had resulted in the indictment of senior Serbian military and political figures, and complex programmes of security sector reform and combatant demobilisation and disarmament were underway. It was by no means a perfect peace, but it represented the combined efforts of the most capable organs of the international community: NATO, the World Bank, the European Union and United Nations.[1] Moreover, Kosovo was able to benefit from the 'lessons learned' by international organisations and NGOs in the 'proving grounds' of complex political emergencies earlier in the 1990s. In March 2004, reactions to a single incident illustrated the fragility of peace in Kosovo. Three Albanian children drowned in the River Ibar near the divided town of Mitrovica. The story quickly spread that the children had drowned after being chased by Serbs. The rumours prompted attacks by ethnic Albanians on the minority Serbian population. Over the course of two days, 33 major riot incidents were reported, involving an estimated 51,000 participants. Over 4,100 people were displaced from their homes, 550 homes were destroyed and 27 Serbian Orthodox churches were burned (which in turn prompted attacks on mosques within Serbia). Nineteen people were killed and over 1,000 were wounded.[2]

A UN investigation later found no evidence of malicious involvement in the drowning – it seemed to be a straightforward accident, but one which aggravated latent tensions that had been left unaddressed by elite-level attempts to reach a *modus vivendi*.[3] Tensions between Serbs and ethnic Albanians were stubbornly immune to the admonishments of the international community and were not helped by a 60 per cent unemployment rate, the persistence of residential segregation and reports that some among the majority Albanian population were exacting revenge for the excesses of decades of Serb domination. This pattern in which violence persists despite a macro-level political accord is observable in Northern Ireland, El Salvador, Solomon Islands, Chechnya, Israel–Palestine and many other divided societies undergoing transition. The violence adopts different forms and intensities depending on the location (e.g., spoiler violence by Hamas in Israel–Palestine or criminality in the Solomon Islands) but in all cases it has the capacity to damage the quality of 'peace' once agreed or secured. In some cases, it has the capacity to derail the peace and spark a full-blown resurgence of the conflict.

This chapter reviews violence after peace accords or in stalled peace processes. Its main aim is to illustrate the *totality* of violence in post-peace accord environments thus keeping in tune with the wider definitions of peace and violence maintained throughout this book. It argues that analysts must look beyond the relatively narrow confines of the category of 'spoiler violence' or deliberate attempts to undermine a peace process or accord through direct violence. Unsurprisingly such spoiler violence attracts significant popular, media and scholarly commentary. The 1998 Omagh bombing in Northern Ireland and the Hamas bus bombing campaign in Israel in the mid-to-late-1990s illustrate the grim human harvest of such violence and its potential to have a deleterious effect on a peace accord or peace process. But other types of violence hold a similar capacity to derail or thwart peace accords and often attract less attention. Intra-group feuding, crime, militarism in society, private or 'domestic' violence and inter-communal tension contribute to the broader tapestry of violence in post-peace accord societies. These types of violence can be described as 'accidental spoiling' in that their primary purpose is rarely political in the sense of attempting to impede the elite-level peace process. They may, however, thwart or harm peace as a by-product of their primary purpose. Thus, for example, pervasive crime and lawlessness may fatally puncture the optimism of the pro-peace constituency.

The chapter begins by surveying the inheritance of conflict that often accompanies societies emerging from the violent phase of ethnonational conflict. It makes the point that many of the violence-related factors that define a civil war society persist into the post-peace accord period and are resistant to quick fixes or the ameliorative programmes (e.g., security sector reform) that often form part of internationally supported peacebuilding exercises. In its second part, the chapter considers deliberate spoiling activity, especially spoiler violence that continues after a peace accord has been reached. Here, it is argued that the term 'spoiler' brings with it normative baggage and demands careful application. It is also suggested that the category of spoiling is restrictive and fails to capture the totality of violence in post-accord societies. The third part of the chapter adopts a broad view of spoiling behaviour to consider 'accidental spoiling' or activities such as criminality or indirect violence that have the capacity to undermine the peace.

The inheritance of violent conflict

Once a peace settlement is reached, there is little guarantee that violence can be controlled or terminated. The complexity and intertwined nature of many of the violent processes attendant to ethnonational conflict means that they remain resistant, and at times oblivious, to efforts to reach a peace settlement.[4] Consider Nicole Ball's list of seven security characteristics in war-torn societies (Table 5.1). Such factors are impervious to quick fixes and often necessitate messy, expensive, long-term and *ad hoc* approaches to their management. Many of the issues are archly political and connect with perceptions of post-accord relative group status (i.e., inter-group gains and losses). Although they may appeal for

Table 5.1   Security characteristics in war-torn societies[5]

Security characteristics in war-torn societies
• Bloated security forces
• Armed opposition, paramilitary forces
• Overabundance of small arms
• Need to reassess security environment and restructure security forces accordingly
• Lack of transparency in security affairs and accountability to civil authorities and to population
• Political role of security forces
• History of human rights abuses perpetrated by security forces

technical responses, for example the rapid downsizing of the security forces, political considerations may render such responses dangerous. Many of the characteristics are embedded within the political culture of the society and require behavioural changes from key sectors capable of blocking the implementation of a peace accord.

There can be no doubt of the potential of violence to interrupt peace processes, harden attitudes, puncture public optimism, caution against security sector reform and negate the good intentions of the framers of a peace accord. A ceasefire is normally the minimum prerequisite for entry to formal peace negotiations, allowing the talks to transcend furious reactions to the last atrocity and inter-party confidence to take root.[6] In a number of cases, peace process participants have positively exploited ceasefires as something more than a negotiation-enabling stopgap in violent conflict. In Aceh (where the ceasefire was called a 'humanitarian pause') and in Sri Lanka some progress was made on development issues in the interregnum provided by the ceasefire. The advantage in such cases was the possibility of identifying – in the public consciousness – the peace process with improvements in quality of life. In Mindanao, joint ceasefire monitoring between the Government of the Philippines, the Moro Islamic Liberation Front (MILF) and third parties including Malaysia has provided an important platform for the development of inter-group trust. But there is a danger that a ceasefire becomes a substitute for more fully developed peace processes and peace accords. In 'frozen peace' situations, antagonists and civilians benefit from the respite provided by the ceasefire, but antagonists may lose incentives for further pacific engagements with each other. In other words, there is a danger that the ceasefire ossifies into a protracted 'no war, no peace' situation in which essential conflict causation and maintenance factors remain unaddressed.

The 'security dilemma' is rarely far from the calculations of participants in peace negotiations. Simply put, each side will be anxious not to let its guard drop until sure that the threat from the other side is reduced. Political leaders, armed groups and inhabitants of war-affected states must *feel* secure enough to enjoy and invest in peace. As a result, much depends on the perception of security and the information and discourse that informs perception. Crucially, the security dilemma will persist into the post-peace accord phase of a conflict. Many key implementation stages of a peace accord, such as the disarmament of armed groups or new political oversight measures for military forces, will be designed to address the security dilemma. Post Good Friday Agreement Northern Ireland provides two signal lessons on security issues for other societies emerging from conflict. The first is that Northern Ireland had relative success in creating technical mechanisms (e.g., principles of non-violence, a ceasefire monitoring body, commissions on security sector reform etc.) to deal with a series of security-related issues. Yet there was a failure to deal with issues of chronic mistrust that underpinned security problems. The second lesson was that inter-group perceptions of insecurity can be independent of objective changes in the security environment. While the IRA and other militant groups were largely faithful to their ceasefires, political discourse by other parties on the threat posed by these organisations reached new levels of shrillness despite the declining body count.

Many security issues may be more precisely described as 'insecurity' issues and are peculiarly prone to exploitation by political entrepreneurs in delicate post-accord environments. Licklider cautions that

> The importance of the security dilemma can be exaggerated. Many civil war settlements collapse, not because of real fear of attack, but because one or more of the antagonists were unhappy with the outcomes and felt violence was a preferred alternative.[7]

Moreover, actors discontented with the outcome of a peace accord may be willing to exaggerate the perceived threat from opponents and exploit the fears of constituents. A state, for example, may choose to defer the security sector reforms demanded by a peace accord and use continuing insecurity as a pretext for its tardiness in downsizing its security establishment. As the case of Northern Ireland shows, violent incidents that would have been regarded as relatively minor in the midst of the violent phase of a conflict may be regarded in a more serious light in the post-peace accord period.[8]

The key point to make in this section is that violence is not switched off like a tap by the mere agreement of a peace accord. Much violence is structural in nature and often immune to the provisions of a peace accord that may only relate to the manifestations of violence or its most visible agents in the form of organised armed groups. The *ad hoc* and semi-formal nature of many armed groups, and the horizontal or opportunistic inter-group nature of the violence they use, may mean that they are not amenable to formal chains of command and instructions to ceasefire. For some groups and individuals, peace accords may be cathartic and signify a decisive break between a past in which society was characterised by large-scale political violence and the 'fresh start' of a future characterized by a new political dispensation in which violence is illegitimate. Others may not be so easily convinced and may observe a different reality in which a peace accord agreed at the elite level does little to change their security and perception of security. The actors and systems that pose the greatest obstacle to their security needs may be left untouched, or may even be reinforced, by the peace accord. Others still may regard a peace process or peace accord as a threat to their position or aspirations and refocus their violence in order to undermine attempts to reach or implement peace.

Spoiling

The seminal conceptualisation of spoilers was developed by Stephen Stedman who identified spoilers as 'leaders and parties who believe that peace emerging from negotiations threatens their power, worldview, and interests, and use violence to undermine attempts to achieve it'.[9] Importantly, this violent opposition to peace can extend into the post-peace accord period. Stedman formulated a typology of spoilers according to their goals and their commitment to these goals. Thus, he identified 'limited', 'greedy' and 'total' spoilers, with limited spoilers having limited goals such as the redress of a specific grievance though not necessarily a limited commitment to achieving these goals.[10] The goals of greedy spoilers vary according to calculations of cost and risk and thus are context dependent. Stedman's use of the term 'greedy' does not imply that actors are entirely profit-seeking in the way that the greed thesis explains conflict causation.[11] Instead, he emphasises that greedy spoilers expand and contract their ambitions according to opportunity. Total spoilers lack this flexibility and see the world in 'all-or-nothing terms and often suffer from pathological tendencies that prevent the pragmatism necessary for compromise settlements.'[12]

Stedman also highlights the importance of the position of the spoiler (inside or outside the peace process), the number of spoilers and the locus of spoiler behaviour (or whether the spoiler group can change from one type of spoiler to another).[13] In terms of the management of spoilers, Stedman attaches most weight to the role of external guardians of the peace process and peace accord:

> The crucial difference between the success and failure of spoilers is the role played by international actors as custodians of peace. Where international custodians have created and implemented coherent, effective strategies for protecting peace and managing spoilers, damage has been limited and peace has triumphed. Where international

custodians have failed to develop and implement such strategies, spoilers have succeeded at the cost of hundreds of thousands of lives.[14]

Crucial too in the management of spoilers are the dynamics within the spoilers' constituency and whether hawks or moderates make the most convincing case for the continuation/escalation of conflict or accommodation. The primary bulwark against spoiling comes not from the state security apparatus but from within the spoilers' own community and the extent to which their potential core support can be persuaded to engage with the new political dispensation and abjure the methods, if not the cause, of the spoilers.[15] Critics have suggested that Stedman's typology lacks the flexibility displayed by many actors in peacemaking processes.[16] Political and militant actors are able to simultaneously hold seemingly pacific and threatening positions. Indeed, the strategy of many actors during a peace process and the post-peace accord implementation phase is a finely calibrated balance between the aspiration to engage with an opponent in a new or restructured political dispensation and the capacity to engage in violence. Some members of an armed group (or their political representatives) may be delegated to 'test the waters' by publicly airing pacific ideas or initiatives that contravene the organisation's doctrine. Others may maintain hard-line positions in order to reassure supporters that there will be no sell-out. Such Janus-faced positions (perhaps kindly termed 'deliberate ambiguity') are commonplace in peace processes and post-peace accord situations and mean that political opponents and observers must sift through conflicting signals to interpret the real intentions of a movement or to identify if the hawks or doves are in ascendance. Moreover, there is a danger that observers can ascribe too much coherence to their opponent's thinking and actions. Policy may be made in an *ad hoc* manner and retrospective wisdom can grant it a prescience and coherence unworthy of hastily made decisions. Thus, for example, spoiler groups may act primarily in anger and frustration than according to a sophisticated plan.

Two fundamental criticisms can be made of the conceptualisation of spoilers. The first relates to the normative implications of the label 'spoiler' and the second posits that the spoiler category is much too narrow and exclusive to convey the totality of violence in many post-peace accord societies. The term 'spoiler', when applied to actors in a peace-making process, is pejorative and inherently condemnatory. The use of the sobriquet goes much further than merely labelling an actor or group of actors as anti-peace. It involves the labeller adopting a normative position in relation to the peace process or accord that is broadly supportive of the peace on offer and critical of those opposed to it. It risks identifying the user of the term with the peace process and may make a judgement on the righteousness of the proposed peace and the wickedness of those against it. In other words, the term spoiler is not – at first glance – a precise and technical description of violent actors in the context of a peace process or post-peace accord environment.

A key argument of this book is that the blithe acceptance of a peace process or peace accord as 'a good thing' is not enough, particularly when the quality of peace experienced by inhabitants in the war-affected area is poor. A critical examination of the nature of the peace process and accord will help guard against an oversimplified commentary that considers peace as 'good' and opposition to that peace as 'bad' regardless of the quality of peace on offer. It may be that an iniquitous peace is on offer and the label spoiler is a wholly inappropriate description for those who continue to pursue a grievance agenda. As a blunt label it also risks conflating varied opposition positions and methods into a single category.

The use of the term 'spoiler' denotes a 'naming power' or the possession of a social and political power that can deem certain groups or activities as deviant and others as orthodox. In simple terms, those groups with most power will be advantageously placed to promote their worldview and associated terminology. During a conflict or a peacemaking process, actors with access to the media, international support and the organs of the state (should they exist) will be better placed to project their preferred terminology. They may be able to paint their opponents as political deviants who are opposed to the peace process by the use of labels such as rebels, irregulars, peace wreckers or spoilers.[17] A vivid example of naming power comes from the post-Saddam Hussein insurgency in Iraq, with the US military branding their opponents as 'anti-Iraqi forces' even though the majority of the militias who resisted US occupation were Iraqi![18] This bizarre interpretation then found its way into some media outlets.[19]

The label 'spoiler', rather like the discourse associated with terrorism, is capable of conjuring up two-dimensional images crazed desperadoes who are beyond the moral compass of any 'right-thinking' observer. Such an analysis may disregard the rationality underlying the actions of groups who calculate that the peace process and peace accord represent a bad deal for their cause or community. Indeed, it may be that the group labelled as a spoiler is simply holding out for an improved deal. The example of Hamas and their opposition to the Oslo peace process between Israel and the PLO in the 1990s is useful in helping us transcend an oversimplification of violent actors in post-accord situations. Understandably, much attention has focused on the organisation's murderous opposition to the peace process and particularly its attacks on the softest of Israeli civilian targets. But the portrayal of Hamas as mindless wreckers of peace interested only in the ruination of a peace process or accord and immune to reasoned deliberation risks missing the rational core behind much spoiler violence. As Richards notes,

> The confused accounts of terrorised victims of violence do not constitute evidence of the irrationality of violence. Rather they show the opposite – that the tactics have been fully effective in disorientating, traumatizing and demoralizing victims of violence. In short, they are devilishly well-calculated.[20]

The Hamas opposition to the peace process was based primarily on coolheaded analysis rather than angry impulses or fundamentalist interpretations of scripture. They derided the 1993 Declaration of Principles on Interim Self-Government Arrangements as 'self-rule under Israeli control on two percent of the Palestinian territory', a 'new security belt' for Israel, a 'conspiracy' to halt the Intifada and an attempt to co-opt the PLO into policing Hamas.[21] Their calculation was that the Oslo process offered a poor deal for Palestinians, fell well short of their traditional political objectives and offered kudos for the PLO but little to Palestinians aligned with other groups. Indeed, the Hamas analysis of the peace process was broadly similar to those of Edward Said and others who regarded the peace process as a con-trick that bought peace for Israel, co-opted a corrupt Palestinian leadership, offered few material benefits for most Palestinians and ultimately failed to deliver Palestinian objectives.[22] According to Said,

> [PLO Chairman] Arafat has mortgaged the future of his people to their oppressors. It is as if in his haste to get things for himself and a few symbols for his Authority, Arafat has thrown away his people's future, leaving it for later generations to try to extricate themselves from the mess he has now created.[23]

Clearly, Edward Said and many other opponents of the peace process abhorred Hamas tactics, but their critiques of the Oslo process were largely similar to those of an organisation labelled as a 'spoiler'. This raises important questions on the utility of the 'spoiler' label, not least on whether the term can be applied to peaceful actors. To guard against the indiscriminate use of the term 'spoiler', it seems prudent to distinguish between the noun 'spoiler' and the verb 'spoiling'.[24] While it is possible to identify violent spoiling behaviour, the term 'spoiler' is too much of a broad brush and risks labelling an actor or group of actors as 'anti-peace' regardless of whether the opposition is to a particular peace at a particular time or anti-peace *per se*. Moreover, many groups that strenuously oppose peace processes and accords lack the capability to fulfil their threats, particularly in the ultimate aim of derailing a peace process or destroying a peace accord. To label them as 'spoiler groups' may give an inflated impression of their competence and capacity (something that many such groups crave).

The rush to label opponents of peace processes as spoilers is often aided by the tremendous moral energy that peace processes and initiatives garner. Many third party governments, particularly those guided by western liberal optimism, are anxious to believe that peace initiatives are the 'real deal' and offer genuinely once-in-a-generation opportunities for the pacific management of seemingly intractable ethnonational conflicts. This was certainly the case in much of the international reaction to the emergence of the Oslo process. The Clinton White House, for example, was eager to host the signing ceremony for the mutual recognition between the PLO and Israel and was well aware of the potential 'political boon' of reflected glory that the ceremony offered to the US President.[25] Against the backdrop of a vicarious international clamour for peace in someone else's conflict, a simplistic black and white pro- and anti-peace discourse could develop without a critical interrogation of the nature of the peace on offer and its ability to address the structural causation and maintenance factors behind the conflict. Thus, for those international actors championing peace from the sidelines, the term 'spoiler' has the attraction of providing a neat conceptual compartmentalisation.

The timing and targeting of spoiler violence often displays a great deal of concern with maximising its political impact, again cautioning against its mischaracterisation as unthinking rage. For example, in the months leading up to and following the 1998 Belfast Agreement in Northern Ireland, militant pro-united Ireland groups who regarded the peace process as a 'sell-out' set off a series of car bombs in town centres across Northern Ireland. Most of these groups had split from the IRA which was on ceasefire. At a superficial level, these car bombs can be interpreted as murderous and reckless and an expression of anger at a changing political situation. Yet, on closer examination, and despite the very real human tragedies caused by the bombings, the bombing campaign was a sophisticated attempt to influence the political process. They were mainly targeted against towns with pro-United Kingdom Protestant majorities and were designed to goad this constituency into pressing its political leaders into withdrawing from the peace process or disavowing the peace accord when it was reached. This would have resulted in the 'win, win' situation of the collapse of the peace process and the blame for the collapse falling on their political enemies. The bombing campaign was also designed to embarrass their erstwhile colleagues from Sinn Féin and the IRA who had called a ceasefire in order to engage more fully with the peace process. Ultimately, this bombing campaign ended in failure when a bomb in the centre of Omagh killed 28 civilians and united public opinion against groups prepared to use violence after the Belfast Agreement had been reached.

Islamic Jihad provides another example of an armed group that is labelled a 'spoiler' but whose attention to target discrimination and timing suggests a level of sophistication that the term 'spoiler' fails to capture. In November 1998, just as the Israeli cabinet was meeting to consider the Wye River Memorandum, a key US-brokered modification in the ailing Oslo peace process, Islamic Jihad set off a bomb in a Jerusalem market.[26] The aim was to bounce the Israeli government into rejecting the memorandum and overreacting in its security response thus further endangering the peace process. The essential point to make is that violence labelled as the work of 'spoilers' is often sophisticated in its political purpose despite the often brutal nature of the violent acts it entails.

Accidental spoiling

Although caution is required in the use of the term 'spoiler', this should not be taken as a denial of the very real phenomenon of direct and indirect political violence during peace processes and once peace accords have been reached. Ultimately, however, the label 'spoiler' is narrow and exclusive and risks overlooking the entirety of post-peace accord violence. John Darby's four-part categorisation of violent actors during peace processes (Dealers, Zealots, Opportunists and Mavericks) is useful in classifying actors according to their actions and motivations.[27] Darby is careful to acknowledge that the boundaries of these categories are never entirely clear and that movement between categories is possible. In his typology, Dealers are groups who are prepared to renounce violence and cut a deal. Their willingness to strive to reach a political accommodation makes the peace process possible, but it is also likely to antagonise other actors, many of them former allies. Zealots are the fundamentalist radicals who believe that the Dealers have sold out. Often comprised of break-away or splinter groups, 'Their aim is not to influence the content of a peace agreement. It is to ensure that an agreement is not reached or, if reached, is derailed.'[28] Opportunists can be persuaded to cut a deal under certain circumstances. They may simply be holding out for a better deal, and so may be regarded as temporary spoilers. While Darby's first three categories are defined according to their reaction to the peace process or peace accord, no such stricture applies to his fourth category: Mavericks. These are groups who may have been once committed to the political cause but 'who now carry out unauthorized crimes for personal gain or from habit.'[29] Importantly, Mavericks may not have a conscious political programme even though their violence may have a real political effect in undermining public faith in a peace accord. So Darby points us towards a crucial distinction, and one that is almost entirely absent from the academic literature on groups involved in spoiling: the distinction between direct spoiling deliberately aimed at undermining a peace process or accord and indirect accidental spoiling that may derail a peace accord as a by-product of its primary purpose.

The first category (deliberate spoiling) can have catastrophic effects on a peace accord and its host society.[30] It can puncture the space required for parties to reach a political accommodation and undermine public optimism that the pacific management of the conflict is possible. It seeks to exploit the security dilemma or the delicate psychology that attends peacemaking. Spoiling of this type often seeks to spark a security overreaction and retard the security sector reform provisions of a peace accord. It deliberately seeks political outcomes that are damaging to the peace process or accord. But the second category of spoiling, indirect accidental spoiling, can be no less damaging to a peace accord. Although not expressly calculated to have meta-political effects in terms of the overall peace process, this type of violence can 'spoil' a peace accord just as effectively as deliberate spoiling. Peace accords have been 'spoiled' by intra-group feuding, crime surges, the persistence of militarism or inter-communal violence and other types of violence. In Chechnya and the Solomon Islands, for example, public faith in peace accords was eroded by the pervasive nature of crime. In both locations, the crime sprees were conducted by loosely coordinated militia groups and were not part of a conscious political project. Yet, the effect on the peace accord was much the same as a concerted campaign of spoiling purposively designed to bring down a peace accord. The quality of the peace on offer to the bulk of citizens was compromised to the extent that previously agreed peace accords were fatally damaged.

The distinction between purposeful and accidental spoiling is more than semantic: different types of post-peace accord violence (and threats of violence) necessitate different management strategies. Three types of accidental spoiling (inter-communal violence, intra-group feuding and crime) will be discussed to illustrate the potential of violent processes to derail peace accords as a by-product of their primary purpose. This violence often has an insidious quality, is deeply embedded in societal structures and may be overlooked by the security provisions of formal peace accords which often concentrate on armed groups.

Inter-communal violence

That a peace accord does not instantaneously transform inter-communal perceptions should not be a surprise. Ethnonational conflicts are deeply embedded in societal structures and modes of operation and so remain resistant to quick fixes. Physical separation during conflict may mean that opposing groups have relatively little exposure to each other, resulting in the development of unflattering myths about 'the other'. Each group may be served by its own media and develop its own discourse with which to rationalise the conflict and describe opponents. Added to this, the atrocities that pepper violent conflict, together with the grinding indignities imposed by a mutual inability for pacific co-existence, may make it irrational to trust erstwhile opponents. Thus, a peace accord agreed at the elite level is unlikely to prove a sufficient balm to negate deeply ingrained enmity. Inter-communal tension presupposes a post-peace accord political dispensation more advanced than the simple separation of communities through physical barriers or population transfers. In such situations, minorities may live among majorities or federal provisions may legislate for local-level autonomy within a unitary state.

A significant number of post-peace accord environments have witnessed a continuation of serious inter-group tension and violence despite the ending of most large-scale violence between armed groups. Ceasefires and programmes of disarmament, disbandment, cantonment, ex-combatant reintegration and security sector reform can help manage the reduction of direct violence between organised groups of antagonists and may be monitored by third parties such as the United Nations. But more informal inter-group violence between individuals and groups of individuals may persist, or take over from more formally organised violence. This violence may be an expression of dissatisfaction with the peace accord and the perception that it has failed to address key grievances. It also tends to be horizontal in nature, often involving inter-communal clashes rather than vertical group versus state violence. While former members of militant groups (state or non-state) may be involved in this violence they may act in an individual capacity or ignore central commands to respect ceasefires.

Post-Belfast Agreement Northern Ireland provides a good example of an escalation of informal group-on-group violence despite the existence of a major peace accord and the general observance of ceasefires by the main militant organisations.[31] Although there was a marked decline in the formal violence between organised groups, inter-communal violence increased in terms of sectarian street assaults and localised rioting. In 2003, the public housing authorities recorded that over 1,200 households were forced to move as a result of intimidation.[32] While this violence was largely sectarian and conformed to the traditional Catholic-nationalist versus Protestant-unionist rubric, it was not accompanied by a formally expressed political project. Instead, local grievances predominated and were able to slot into the overall framework of inter-group enmity. The violence tended to be informal, localised and opportunistic and lacked much of the organisation and division of labour that had characterised earlier phases of conflict.

In many ways, Northern Ireland's post-accord violence was similar to the rioting in Kosovo described at the beginning of this chapter. It was illustrative of the inability of a macro-level political accord to address grassroots concerns and antipathies. Moreover, the participants in the intimidation and rioting were unlikely to have been unduly concerned with the wider political ramifications of their actions: local concerns trumped national and international considerations. Yet, despite the spontaneous and relatively contained nature of this violence it still had the capacity to contribute to the 'spoiling' of the peace. Doubtless the violence marked a further undermining of public confidence in the peace on offer and raised questions on the quality of peace.

Three factors will influence the extent to which inter-communal mistrust persists into the post-peace accord period and threatens to spill over into violence to undermine that accord. The first factor is the presence of political actors prepared to dissent from the peace accord and make capital from any public disappointment with peace. Whether originally opposed to the accord, or disillusioned with it once in operation, such actors may be tempted to fuel inter-communal mistrust and thereby undermine the accord. A key element in the exploitation of inter-group tension will be the perception of relative group benefits and losses from the peace accord. Of course, such interpretations operate in a subjective realm and political entrepreneurs can find a ready discourse to paint in-group concessions as extraordinary and damaging, and out-group concessions as grudging, minor and overdue. The presence of political actors prepared to dissent from the peace accord and stoke inter-communal tensions will depend on the extent to which a community is dissected into factions and the determination and capability of the dominant faction to thwart internal dissent.

The JVP (Janata Vimukthi Peramuna/People's Liberation Front) in Sri Lanka provide a good example of a group who have exploited Sinhalese fears that the peace process is a 'sell out'. They have stood on the side-lines while the main Sinhalese political parties (People's Alliance and United National Party) pursued peace initiatives, at all times warning that the peace process amounted to a betrayal. A memorandum of understanding between the Sri Lankan Government and the Tamil Tigers was thus described as 'surrender with an icing of peace ... which makes the Sri Lankan state kneel down before Tiger Terrorism.'[33] A sim-ilar pattern (with almost identical hyperbolic tendencies) was observ-able in intra-unionist politics in Northern Ireland. While the Ulster Unionist Party (UUP) formally supported the 1998 Belfast Agreement, substantial elements dissented and the rival Democratic Unionist Party (DUP) was able to undercut the UUP's conciliatory discourse with a more shrill discourse of suspicion towards traditional enemies.[34] Much of this opposition to the peace accord did not deliberately seek to inflame communal tensions, but the continued use of a sectarian lens and the constant interpretation of the agreement in inter-group win/lose terms had this effect.[35] The 'auction politics' whereby groups from within one community seek to portray themselves as the 'true defenders' of the community clearly provide fertile ground for the undermining of peace accords through the inflammation of inter-communal tension.

A second factor that may encourage the continuation of inter-communal resentment after a peace accord has been reached is the extent to which political and militant leaders communicate with their own constituencies before and after a peace accord has been reached. If a grassroots constituency has an early awareness of the implications of a peace accord, and that it is likely to involve concessions as well as gains, then the chances of a popular backlash against a peace agreement can be minimised. The provisions of peace accords formulated behind closed doors may come as something of a shock if constituencies are not prepared for the realities of post-peace accord life and may be grist to the mill for ethnic entrepreneurs.

A third and related factor is the balance between the public expectations attached to a peace accord and the observed evidence or perceptions of that agreement. An onus rests with the framers of peace accords to manage expectations and temper optimism. This may be a difficult feat to achieve since elite-level peacemakers must also be convinced that a peace accord contains enough positive elements to enable them to recommend it to their constituency. Moreover, if a peace accord or resultant constitution relies on public endorsement through an election or referendum, then proponents of the accord must accentuate the positive in any campaign. Yet, if public expectations of the peace accord are left unfulfilled, then citizens will have little reason to support the accord. Consider the opinion of one young Albanian in Kosovo after the 'peace' brokered between Albanians and Serbs: 'We have no jobs, no money, guys just hang around here waiting for trouble. Nothing has changed for us since the war ended and we've got nothing to lose.'[36] From this perspective it is understandable why any attachment to a peace accord may be tenuous and conditional on material advantages accruing from the accord.

Disenchantment with a peace accord can be accentuated if one group believes that the benefits of peace are unfairly shared. Clearly such perceptions are malleable and open to political manipulation, but if a community believes that its rivals are the chief beneficiaries of peace then the peace process and accord may be regarded as a continuation of the conflict. In such a context, grassroots inter-group tension will find ample fuel. In Northern Ireland, for example, survey evidence shows a marked sectarian differential in public support for the 1998 Belfast Agreement. Many Protestant-unionists were suspicious of the Agreement from the outset, regarding it as pro-Catholic-nationalist in origin and design. As implementation of the Agreement progressed, however, negative Protestant-unionist perceptions of the Agreement deepened to the extent that 70 per cent of Protestants thought that their opponents were the chief beneficiaries from the accord by 2003.[37] The extent to which a peace accord is implemented and the perception of how this implementation is conducted becomes a key determining factor in the persistence of inter-group disharmony after a peace accord is reached.

Post-peace accord inter-group violence can be low-volume, localised and relatively contained. The types of violence utilised may lack sophistication and the deployment of heavy weaponry, and the violence may have no obvious political ambition. Yet, such violence can have a profound political impact through re-energising the conflict, reinforcing negative perceptions of the out-groups and acting as a brake on the implementation of the peace accord and inter-group encounters. Rather than a single catastrophic event shattering the confidence and optimism of those who have placed their faith in a peace accord, the drip-drip nature of this violence can have a long-term corrosive effect. It also provides 'ammunition' for political leaders opposed to the accord.

Intra-group feuding

Peace processes and accords confront all political actors in a conflict with tough choices, many of which have ethical as well as practical implications. Decisions to call and maintain a ceasefire, to engage with an adversary in a negotiating process or to accept a peace agreement that falls short of traditional goals can all place strain on the cohesiveness of political and militant groups.[38] Armed groups that seem homogenous to outsiders are often more accurately characterised as coalitions borne of necessity in the midst of conflict. When the urgency of the violent conflict recedes in the context of a peace process and accord, the group's cohesiveness may dissipate.[39] In some cases, the peace accord and associated issues may prompt internal dissent within the militant organisation and cause some members to break away and actively attempt to spoil the accord. Splintering of this kind can be bloody, with factions using violence to claim resources, legitimacy and support. An organisation's command structures may loosen, as priority is afforded to political rather than military activities, and group members may become less disciplined in their use of weapons and influence. Intra-group feuding may organise itself around personalities, territory, resources (such as weapons, finances or the mantle of an organisation's name) and crucially the legitimacy to act on behalf of a community.

While the direct violence emanating from the feud may be largely restricted to members of militant and political groups, the fall-out from such violence may have much wider ramifications, particularly on public perceptions of peace. Community members may feel pressurised to display loyalty to one faction or another. The feud may prompt a security crackdown or provide a government with an excuse to delay or dilute the security sector reform provisions of an accord. The end result may be an increase in public insecurity despite the institution of a peace accord.[40] By virtue of its in-group nature, many of the manifestations of a feud may remain obscured from the view of outside observers. This lack of visibility makes the effects of feuding no less pernicious and devastating to peace accords.

Feuding between Chechen nationalist leaders had a profound effect on the public enjoyment of 'peace' in the interregnum 1996–1999 period when Russian forces had withdrawn from Chechnya.[41] The Chechen President Aslan Maskhadov was able to exert little control over other guerrilla leaders, in particular the increasingly extreme Shamil Basaev.[42] Indeed, Basaev even suggested that Maskhadov be tried in a *sharia* court for treason because of his pragmatism in relations with Moscow.[43] One commentator noted that Maskhadov's '... influence does not go further than his bodyguards.'[44] Indeed, when Maskhadov was killed by Russian troops in March 2005, rumours abounded that he had been betrayed by associates.[45] For many Chechens, the experience of 'peace' was less than positive and was characterised by the lawlessness of armed groups.

Crime

Post-peace accord crime surges have become common, though by no means guaranteed, features in societies emerging from protracted armed conflicts.[46] Peace deals in Bosnia-Herzegovina, Chechnya, Guatemala, the Solomon Islands and many other locations have been seriously compromised by the persistence, and escalation, of crime. Lawlessness and criminality have mocked peace accords secured at the elite level and undermined the confidence of the pro-peace constituency. In the cases of the Solomon Islands and Chechnya crime has been a major factor in the outright collapse of peace accords, while in other cases it has acted as a cancer that inhibits the institutionalisation of the peace accord.

Exactly what constitutes crime is by no means clear in many post-war societies.[47] The state (or authority) may lack the legitimacy to designate certain activities as criminal and the capability to enforce the law. A peace accord may entail a revision of the legal code and there may be genuine confusion as to new laws (and possibly a cynical exploitation of this confusion by some). A society can become so brutalised by warfare that its tolerance threshold is raised to the extent that activities deemed 'criminal' in largely peaceful societies may be regarded as 'normal' or at least unremarkable. The fact that lynching and vigilantism has become a relatively common community response to crime in Guatemala reflects the internalisation of violence in society and is doubtless related to the state's 25-year civil war.[48] Moreover, a societal moral code fashioned in the midst of a protracted ethnonational war is unlikely to change overnight as the result of a peace accord. The persistence of informal 'policing' by militant groups in Northern Ireland *after* the Belfast Agreement had been reached indicates that some citizens regard militant organisations rather than the police force as the most legitimate crime management body.[49] A final point to bear in mind when considering what constitutes a crime in a society emerging from war is that the nature of the violence employed in many ethnonational conflicts blurs the distinction between politico-military and criminal activities. Theft, rape and kidnap – activities commonly regarded as purely criminal in 'peaceful' societies – can become core tools in an ethnonational war. The peculiar culture of violence sustained, and justified, as part of the intergroup conflict may persist in the post-accord period, although the violence may adopt a more informal character. Indeed, the key to understanding crime in a post-peace accord context lies in the 'persistence factors' through which the elements and dynamics of wartime persist into the post-peace accord period.

Five persistence factors capable of contributing to post-peace accord crime are worthy of further exploration: state incapacitation, cultural permissiveness towards crime and violence, the presence of former combatants, the recycling of military weapons for criminal purposes and uneven economic development.[50] State weakness constitutes a common ailment in post-war societies with many such states lacking legitimacy and capacity, and facing rivals in the form of armed groups, ethnonational groups or private businesses. In the case of state incapacitation, groups and individuals may calculate that their chances of apprehension for crime are low. Indeed the provisions of a peace accord may actually weaken the state and embolden those tempted to engage in crime: for example, a peace accord may provide for the downsizing of a police force or its withdrawal from a certain area. The second persistence factor, a cultural permissiveness towards criminal activity, may be deeply embedded into the psyche of a group or society. During a protracted violent conflict, areas and communities may become acculturated to the notion that certain activities are socially acceptable (rather than criminal) or that the police will be uninterested in certain types of law-breaking or law-breakers or will lack the capacity to intervene. Some groups may expect leniency from law enforcement agencies, perhaps because the groups and agencies share similar ethnic profiles. Such patterns of social habituation are unlikely to diminish quickly and a culture of violence (with its associated behavioural norms and perceptions of deviance and acceptability) may help foster crime.[51] Indeed, under such circumstances, cooperation with the law enforcement authorities may be regarded as deviant or disloyal to the in-group.

The third and fourth persistence factors (the presence of former combatants and weapons) are inter-related. The mobilisation associated with
ethnonational conflict produces large numbers of 'violence specialists'
whose skills are more suited to wartime than the needs of the civilian
economy.[52] Post-war economies are rarely able to absorb the large
numbers of young males 'freed' through the downsizing of the security
sector and the disbandment of non-state militant groups. Although
demobilisation campaigns regularly include re-training and business
enterprise schemes to help former combatants better integrate into the
civilian economy, they cannot counter the harsh realities of unemployment, underemployment and a chronic lack of economic opportunities.[53]
In such a context, the informal and illegal economy may offer the most
attractive route for advancement, especially if former combatants have
become acculturated to 'the Kalashnikov lifestyle'.[54] During wartime,
combatants may have survived through banditry and theft, and given
the dearth of alternatives in the post-peace accord environment, these
survival strategies may retain an attraction. Moreover, the group bonds
forged during wartime may persist after the conclusion of a peace accord
and provide former combatants with ready-made social and economic
networks. Former combatants may also have, or expect, an exalted or
privileged status in the post-accord society that entails a prior claim over
resources or a certain latitude where the rigidity of law is concerned.
Former combatants' associations in Kosovo and Zimbabwe conform to
this pattern, with veterans in the latter a key factor in agitation for land
reform.[55]

Compounding the problem of large numbers of former combatants
skilled in activities that can easily lend themselves towards crime is the
issue of the prevalence of military style weapons.[56] Post-conflict disarmament programmes have become increasingly sophisticated and have
attempted to adopt a holistic approach, linking the removal of weapons
to political transitions and the provision of economic alternatives. Yet,
the motivations to retain weapons may be strong for many actors in a
society emerging from violent conflict. Some may be suspicious of the
peace accord and regard disarmament as premature. In other cases, guns
may have a symbolic or socio-cultural value that disarmament programmes are unable to counter. For instance, gun ownership may confer
incredibly valuable affective qualities such as esteem, machismo or
group membership. Of particular relevance for post-peace accord crime
surges is the economic worth of small arms and their use as a means to
economic survival or advantage. Since weapons have a market value in
many conflict societies (or neighbouring societies), it is irrational for

their owners to merely submit them at a weapons collection point. If a disarmament scheme lacks a 'buy back' facility then it becomes rational for the weapon owner to attempt to sell the weapon on the market.[57] Alternatively, the weapon can be retained and employed as part of criminal ventures. While disarmament programmes supervised by the United Nations and other international organisations usually concentrate on the arsenal and personnel of formal and semi-formal armed groups, they may overlook the weapons held by individuals, loose associations and groups not privy to the peace accord.

The combination of military style weapons with former combatants who are used to operating in groups, have some military training and are habituated to the use of violence can award post-peace accord crime a particularly violent character. Thus, in some post-peace accord societies violent crime has an almost casual nature and clearly diminishes the quality of peace. It may prompt punitive populism in the form of vigilantism, the privatisation of security and calls for robust policing, thus countering any provisions of a peace accord that involved the 'softening' of security. Uncontrolled crime may also discourage potential investors and so inhibit any post-war economic recovery.[58]

The final 'persistence factor' to consider in relation to crime is uneven economic development. Underdevelopment and uneven development often feature heavily in the matrix of factors that contribute to civil war, and the war itself may bring further disparity to wealth and income levels. This will especially be the case if certain geographical areas, ethnic communities or social sectors escape the war unscathed while the burden falls more heavily on others. While development and reconstruction aid may follow a peace accord, most post-war societies possess few advantages in the face of an open global economy and unevenness within society may become further compounded. In blunt terms, peace will bring clear economic winners and losers, and for those for whom a peace dividend proved illusory, the informal or illegal economy may offer more easily earned opportunities. Uneven economic development by no means guarantees crime, but unmet economic needs combined with a perception that other groups (perhaps ethnic rivals) have gained advantages in the post-war period may make the informal and illegal economies more attractive options.

The case of the Solomon Islands provides a good example of crime and lawlessness undermining attempts to implement a peace accord. Tensions between Isatabus people on the main island of Guadalcanal and Malatian settlers from a neighbouring island spilled into serious violence in 1998. The settlers were perceived to have prospered at the expense of their hosts.[59] Approximately 20,000 people were forced to flee their homes as rival armed groups took to the streets. A number of ceasefires and peace accords were brokered between 1999–2001 but they failed to staunch growing lawlessness. Armed groups ignored calls to disarm (or only abandoned their homemade weapons while retaining their high-powered weapons) and continued to show little regard for human rights. A government strategy of 'buying off' the militants by offering compensation merely encouraged greater demands for 'compensation' and attempts to co-opt militants by appointing them as 'special constables' merely compounded the problems of lawlessness. The growing factionalisation of the militant groups also contributed to their uncontrolled nature. The chief point is that, despite an official peace process and the rhetorical declaration of 'peace', crime rates soared and undermined public and international faith in the peace.

It is worth noting that increasing levels of reported crime may not automatically indicate rising levels of actual crime. New crime recording systems introduced as part of a peace accord transition and a greater public confidence in the police may result in increased reporting of crime. Some sectors may even be tempted to inflate the threat from crime. The downsizing of the security sector that is common in many peace accords may prompt security employees to emphasise their own utility in the face of a crime wave. Those opposed to a peace accord may also point to increased crime (real or imagined) as a peace deficit and a further argument as to why a peace accord should be revised or ignored. Crime may also be more visible (as opposed to prevalent) in the post-accord period and occupy a vacuum formerly filled with the war. For example, media organisations and political parties that had been preoccupied by the ethnonational war may be free to devote attention to crime in the post-war period.

Concluding discussion

Attempts to make peace in the context of civil wars are obviously prone to deliberate violent attacks. Political and militant actors may calculate that a peace process and ensuing peace accord may be unable to fulfil traditional constitutional or political goals. They may calculate that the time is not right to sue for accommodation (perhaps assessing that greater gains can be made on the battlefield) or that the projected costs of peace may outweigh the known income of war. As Zahar notes, 'warring factions that benefit from the war have no interest in a peace that may unravel the war economy, especially if they have not negotiated side agreements that allow them to partake in the financial benefits of peacetime.'[60] Deliberate spoiling is often designed to make it impossible for certain political actors to remain in peace negotiations or to remain party to a peace accord. It is often calculated to provoke an overreaction or a clamour for revenge. Given the political ambitions, and at times effects, of such deliberate spoiling it is understandable that it has garnered significant academic and policy attention. Yet other types of violence can be just as effective in spoiling peace or devaluing it to the extent that popular perceptions of the post-peace accord environment are characterised by disaffection, political apathy and a lack of faith in the material benefits of peace.

Charles Call has pointed to the 'counterintuitive phenomenon' in which the peace is more violent than the war it succeeds.[61] Much of the violence that contributes to the 'violent peace' of many post-peace accord environments can be described as secondary or accidental spoiling. Such violence is often disjointed, localised and structural in nature, lacking the political purpose and publicity-seeking spectacular attacks of deliberate spoiling. It can often be chronic, in the sense of being deeply embedded within societal norms and unlikely to flare into acute violence that would demand international attention. A sense of militarism, for example, may be ingrained into societal consciousness to the extent that few notice it.[62] It may take the form of a military presence on the streets (often fulfilling civil roles), conscription and an inflated military budget, and the insulation of military figures (past and present) from critical scrutiny or effective political oversight. The effects of the seeming normalcy of embedded militarism may be difficult to identify but may include the stunting of civil society, the reinforcement of patriarchy and a sense that 'peace' comes with soldiers. A peace that coexists with militarism may require the constant negotiation of a delicate civil–military balance and the conditioning of new generations to the routine nature of military interference in politics.

Although not deliberately targeted at undermining a macro-political peace accord, secondary or accidental spoiling can have an insidious impact, connecting with prejudices and polluting the quality of peace. Crime, feuding and low-level inter-communal violence comprises of the bulk of political violence in many societies emerging from civil war. Much of this violence is indirect, taking the form of fraud, intimidation or the promotion of inter-group tension. It is rarely accompanied by publicly articulated political programmes, and its apparently disjointed nature, and failure – in many cases – to mount a serious challenge to the legitimacy of the state, may mean that it attracts little attention. Yet, such violence holds enormous capacity to pollute peace, particularly if we hold a holistic view of peace that concerns social development and wide participation in the polity. Peace accords can leave substantial human insecurities and vulnerabilities untouched through their concentration on direct violence and organised militant groups.

DDR and SSR programmes in many internationally supported peace processes and accords have had a technocratic quality. A number of such schemes have had considerable success in withdrawing weapons from circulation, providing alternative means of livelihood for combatants and reforming institutions and practices associated with compromised regimes. Many DDR and SSR schemes have benefited from best practice observed from other conflict locations and have been coordinated with other peacebuilding activities such as economic regeneration and human rights promotion. Yet, there remains a danger that an overly technocratic approach deals with the legacy of civil war violence in terms of quantities of weapons to be collected, former combatants to be processed and institutions to be reformed. The perceptual factors that are fundamental to post-war recovery may remain unaddressed. Individuals and groups that retain perceptions of grievance, victimhood and insecurity into the post-peace accord period are likely to hold conditional (or negative) attitudes towards peace.

6
The Elusive Peace Dividend

The shepherd leaves his mellow pipe,
And sounds his trumpet shrill;
The workman throws his hammer down
To heave the bloody bill

William Blake

Introduction

In the four years following the 1993 Israeli–Palestinian Declaration of Principles, Palestinian income declined by almost one-quarter.[1] In the eight years following the 1990 *de facto* split between Moldova and Trans-dniester, Gross Domestic Product (GDP) in Moldova fell by three-quarters.[2] Income disparities in post-1989 Taif Accord Lebanon were worse than those of the 1960s.[3] Unemployment in Bosnia-Herzegovina in mid-1997, 18 months after the Dayton Accord had been reached, affected 65–75 per cent of the workforce.[4] In such circumstances, it is understandable if many citizens in societies emerging from civil war associate peace with poverty and economic degradation. As Addison and colleagues note starkly, 'Ending the mortality and morbidity associated with war may be the only significant benefit of peace for large numbers of people unless poor communities and poor people are helped to recover their livelihoods and build their human capital.'[5]

Travel around any post-war society and one is often struck not by the obvious signs of war damage, but by the signs of a depressed economy that has failed to recover from the depredations of war. Physical war damage is often quickly repaired, especially in urban centres or major thoroughfares, or it gradually blends into developing world contexts of chaotic urban planning. Signs of poverty, underdevelopment and uneven development are conspicuous through poor infrastructure, empty and unproductive rural landscapes, urban unemployment, an economy geared for consumption rather than production, the absence of young people because of out-migration and a lack of external investment.[6] Very few societies emerging from civil war in the past 20 years have succeeded in economic reconstruction. Woodward notes the 'mounting evidence that countries that have experienced a civil war never fully recover to the economic level they had before the war began'.[7] The persistent failure of post-war economic recoveries is despite the concentration of immense national, international and NGO effort on economic rehabilitation. It is also despite the vast quality-of-life sacrifices made by citizens in the name of austerity programmes, rightsizing, marketisation and other schemes apparently designed to rehabilitate post-war economies and harmonise them with the global economy. Most fundamentally of all, the actual experience of contemporary post-war reconstruction contradicts the view promoted by advocates of the liberal democratic peace that prosperity is a core element of peace.

The rhetorical linkage between peace and economic development is a cardinal point of the dominant version of the liberal democratic peace. Proponents of the liberal democratic peace (among them states, international organisations and IFIs) regularly highlight economic development as the prize to be won by the acceptance of peace-support interventions.[8] Yet, the translation of a promised peace dividend into the tangible benefits of increased earnings, improved social expenditure and the public perception that any dividend has been distributed in a transparent and equitable manner is more difficult to achieve. Literature on post-Cold War defence conversion provides a useful service in adopting a critical stance on the notion of a peace dividend. Keith Hartley dissects four 'myths' of the peace dividend (it is large and instantly available, it solves a country's social and economic problems, disarmament threatens a country's economy and adjustment problems will be limited and localised) and illustrates the high costs of transition.[9] As Braddon notes, 'In the imperfect world that surrounds us, labour and capital resources do not switch easily between alternative uses.'[10] The expectations and disappointments that attended the economic fall out of reduction of conventional forces in post-Cold War Europe are also relevant in post-civil war environments. Peace accords with a poorly distributed or delayed economic peace dividend have become commonplace and present a real threat to the sustainability and enjoyment of peace.

This chapter assesses the extent to which peacemaking processes and peace accords can be thwarted by a failure of economic development. The chapter begins by outlining the economic impacts of war, observing how economic factors often contribute to the causation and maintenance of conflict. The illustration of the economic impacts of war is important for our purposes because of the proclivity of these impacts (and the factors that promote them) to persist into the post-war period. The chapter then examines the reconstruction challenge, noting how many of the economic problems facing societies emerging from violent conflict are structural and exogenous, and largely beyond the control of political and economic actors at the national level. Yet, there is only so much mileage in wailing at the inequities of IFIs and the in-built biases of trading regimes. Short of radical global economic reform, societies emerging from civil war must face up to attempting to survive and develop in the context of an unforgiving global economy. This requires real policies and strategies to deal with real problems. Protest politics, though worthy, is unable to provide a substitute for economic strategies designed to maximise productive capacity, retain at least some national control over the economy and reinforce peace. The chapter then considers the trend towards the privatisation of post-war reconstruction whereby reconstruction is conceptualised as a profitable activity for foreign corporate interests or national elites. Such privatisation has profound implications for the nature, quality and ownership of the peace that follows contemporary civil wars. The chapter's final section reflects that there is no yet-to-be-discovered formula for economic and social recovery in the context of a sustainable peace. Instead, key ingredients of post-war reconstruction are well-known; indeed many of them played a key role in the post-Second World War Marshall Plan and still retain contemporary relevance: sustainability, local ownership and participation, an emphasis on production rather than consumption and the judicious timing of reconstruction activities.

Methodological constraints limit our ability to make sweeping comparative generalisations on economic performance in societies emerging from civil war. For example, some conflicts are restricted to specific geographical areas within a large state (Manipur or Nagaland in India), while others dominate the entire state (Democratic Republic of Congo) or region (Israel–Palestine). Would-be comparativists are also faced with the problems of vastly differing pre-war economic baselines or the differing extents to which combatants exploited or targeted different sectors of the economy. Moreover, societies in the midst of civil war offer a poor platform for the collection of reliable economic data.

While sources such as the United Nations Development Programme (UNDP) Human Development Reports provide an invaluable time series resource, health warnings must apply to data collected in adverse environments.[11] For example, reliable data was unavailable for Bougainville during the 1990s as it emerged from conflict. Instead, for the purpose of statistical measurement it was subsumed within Papua New Guinea.

The key point in any discussion of economic development in peace-making processes or in the aftermath of civil war is the extent to which it can reinforce or retard the pacific management of conflict. Economic development has the potential to lift communities and societies out of conflict and can provide common ground that allows other shared activities to take root. It can also fund reconstruction, reconciliation and pluralism, all of which are resource greedy activities. But the pitfalls of deficient, delayed or unevenly shared reconstruction and recovery can be cavernous. The fears and jealousies of civil war environments mean that it becomes rational to monitor resources (aid, loans, government expenditure and initiatives) disbursed to the out-group. In some cases, economic recovery can become war by other means as groups seek to maximise their advantages and deny rehabilitation opportunities to the other side. Yet, it is possible to conceive of pro-peace economic development that can help promote social and political cohesion, can be disbursed sensitively and transparently and can help mitigate the adverse effects of sectarianism and division.

The economic impact of war

The 'typical' civil war costs $50 bn, with most of the economic costs falling on neighbouring states, and lasting well after any cessation of violence.[12] The variegated nature of civil wars, not least the differing methods through which they are pursued and therefore impact on the economies, means that we should be wary of over-generalising the economic impacts of civil wars. Nevertheless, some economic costs of civil war are observed with depressing regularity. An initial point to make is that many societies descend into civil war in the context of an already declining economy. Indeed, proponents of the 'greed' thesis cite economic downturns as a contributory factor in the outbreak of civil war. Paul Collier highlights the importance of three economic criteria in predicting civil war: low per capita income, low economic growth and a dependence on primary product exports.[13] He notes how the doubling of per capita income halves the risk of civil war, and how each percentage point of economic growth diminishes the risk of civil war by a percentage point. Other authors reflect on the confluence of ethnonational or sectarian politics with resource competition, especially in the context of a declining pot of resources.[14] In many conflict locations, the principal reference point in calculations of relative deprivation is how well the other group is doing. Thus, for example, Sinhalese and Tamil fishermen may express their grievances in terms of the advantages (real and imagined) on offer to the other group but denied to them. It is also clear that economic resources comprise an explicit object in many conflicts: for example, oil in Aceh, Nigeria and Sudan; coltan in the Democratic Republic of Congo and water in Ethiopia.[15] Ethnic entrepreneurs find it effortless to suffuse nationalist narratives with claims to resources or grievances that resources have been appropriated by the out-group or a rapacious state. Thus, for example, much of the discourse from the Moro Islamic Liberation Front in Mindanao (Philippines) stresses the exclusion of indigenous groups from resource extraction by corporate interests and the Filipino government.[16]

When war starts there is little doubting its debilitating effects on the economy. Four interlinked features of a wartime economy are highlighted here because of their ability to persist after a peace accord has been reached and to retard the embedding of any peace: the distortion of government spending patterns; the decline in government capacity to manage the economy; the expansion and entrenchment of the informal economy and war damage (both tangible and intangible). The most obvious war-induced distortion of government spending priorities is an increase in defence and security expenditure (often at the expense of social expenditure). In 2002, for example, 23.5 per cent of Eritrean GDP was devoted to military expenditure, amounting to six times the outlay on healthcare. In the same year, military expenditure in Burundi was over three and a half times the health budget.[17] Brück describes increased defence spending as a 'double burden'. In the present it leads to a reduction in output, productive investment and welfare allocations, but in the future it results in increased debt and taxation, and deters investment.[18] In other words, much of the economic burden of the war does not fall on those who pursued and witnessed it, but on later generations. While the readjustment of government spending allocations in the aftermath of war may seem like a straightforward technical matter (reprioritising social investment at the expense of defence spending), it often faces immense political obstacles. Those ripe for 'downsizing' (the military, police or ex-combatants) may embody politically powerful constituencies and expect to be rewarded for their wartime service and sacrifices by their relatives. As Brynen observes, peacebuilding brings with it 'a very political economy' and one that may be resistant to rapid change.[19]

Crucial in the distortion of government spending patterns in the midst of violent conflict is the extent of dependency on external parties. Third party governments may directly finance the war through the provision of loans or military assistance. Pursuit of war can also be supported indirectly – even unwittingly – whereby third party donors (governments and NGOs) subsidise government social spending and thus free up a portion of the government budget for military purposes. Certainly, the Sri Lankan government, a long-term recipient of overseas development aid, was able to increase its defence budget because foreign governments and NGOs were, in effect, taking care of much social expenditure.

The second impact of war on the national economies is the decline in governments' ability to manage their economies. This feature is by no means ubiquitous in that some economies become more centrally controlled under wartime conditions. Yet, the meta-trends of globalisation, complex interdependence and the expansion of marketisation mean that all governments' abilities to control economies are compromised. The special circumstances of civil war, however, can further degrade governmental capacity to direct the economy. Emergency conditions may mean that the routine procedures of governance are bypassed or ignored. Thus, the government's ability to collect revenues (through formal mechanisms) may be eroded and its duty to collect economic data neglected. Losses of territory and control of boundaries, along with an erosion of the government's legitimacy as the state's chief economic agent, can all hamper the ability to administer and direct an economy. Relevant here is the importance that remittance flows can attain, in some cases overshadowing government expenditure.[20]

The third lasting economic impact of war, the expansion of the informal economy, is very much related to the loss of state control over the economy. Government attempts to mobilise capital in pursuit of the war, usually through increased taxation, may lead not only to capital flight but also the conversion of capital into less visible forms. Formal government economic agents may face competition from other actors such as soldiers and other militants imposing their own levies or private actors expanding into areas where formal government-regulated exchange networks no longer operate or have become inefficient. The potential scale and depth of informal economies is worth noting. It is estimated that 90 per cent of Angola's economy operates via extra-state exchange networks, a socially embedded phenomena that may be resistant to formalisation.[21] Shadow networks and street currencies become the only way of life and part of rational survival strategies that mock the inefficiencies and inabilities of formal markets.[22]

Some commentary is tempted to label shadow exchange economies as 'corruption'.[23] Yet, given that the legitimacy of governments is contested during civil wars, and that criminal justice and regulatory codes may be fluid, caution may be required when using normative labelling.[24] Moreover, as Nordstrom notes, the informal economy is rarely discrete and instead often becomes deeply interlinked with the formal (national and international) economy. Rather than 'small-scale, rural and low-tech' she suggests that informal economies be recognised as part of 'power-defining global systems' that are 'not marginal to the world's economies and politics, but central to them'.[25] The peculiarities of the merging of the legal and non-legal economic spheres is illustrated by the case of Colombia. Richani observes that narcotraffickers are 'economic liberals par excellence and agents of globalisation' who are able to exploit 'the free enterprise system, open markets [and] the cherished property rights laws, which ultimately protect their interests'.[26] For some, wartime environments offer vastly profitable opportunities that stem from an ability to exploit both the formal and informal economies and the ability to deftly move capital and labour between them.

The final, and most obvious, impact of civil war on economies comes in the form of damage: both physical and non-physical. The extent of physical damage may depend on the nature of the economy and the nature of the warfare. The extensive use of landmines, for example, may mean that vast tracts of land are no longer available for cultivation.[27] In the former Yugoslavia, the theft of agricultural equipment routinely followed ethnic cleansing and stripped families and communities from their opportunity to recover in the post-peace accord period. The only refugee returnees to many isolated villages in Bosnia-Herzegovina after the war were the elderly, with younger families remaining in towns or settled abroad. In the absence of a sustainable population and rural economy these villages will effectively die within 20 years.[28] War damage need not have a physical dimension and may take the form of the evaporation of investor confidence and the erosion of legitimacy from state financial and regulatory institutions. Crucial in this regard is the flight of human capital, not just in terms of potentially economically active individuals who flee during war, but also for the following generation who place emigration at the top of their list of career goals.[29] The chief point to make in relation to all of the abovementioned impacts of civil war on economies is their resistance to quick fixes. Many of these factors become structural (even psychocultural) and attempts to change behaviour and established norms often mean hardship and exclusion for certain sectors.

The reconstruction challenge

A fundamental and often overlooked question is reconstruction for what. There is a danger that post-war reconstruction efforts swing into action without reflecting on the essential purpose of the reconstruction. Mere reconstruction, or reconstituting the pre-war economy and infrastructure, misses the point. In many circumstances, the pre-war economy and the social relations it supported were profoundly dysfunctional and contributed to the outbreak of violent conflict. Many of the donor conferences held when a peace accord appears likely seem content with raising funds (real and pledged) without a critical interrogation of how the funds can be best utilised and whether the capacity to use them effectively is in place. It seems prudent that reconstruction is conducted in the service of the peace accord and the pacific management of conflict. As a result, reconstruction programmes and activities require targeting and calibration to deal with the sustainability of peace, inclusiveness and the repair of fractured relationships. In other words, reconstruction extends far beyond the bricks and mortar of infrastructure and buildings, and the putting in place of the conditions to speed economic recovery. Reconstruction in this view, therefore, becomes a key agent for the promotion of the social and political cohesion required for the success of a peace accord. Communities who perceive themselves as excluded from the benefits of a peace accord will be entirely rational in withholding support from that peace.

Susan Woodward identifies three sets of economic tasks crucial to the implementation of a peace accord: reviving the economy so as to inject public confidence in the peace process; funding specific commitments in the peace accord such as refugee repatriation and security sector reform and sustaining the peace by transforming the war economy into a successful civilian model.[30] Each of these tasks has the capacity to reinforce and expand the pro-peace accord constituency. Conversely, failure to deliver can lead to the attrition of public faith that a peace accord will make quality of life differences. All post-war reconstruction processes face three additional challenges: the extent to which the capacity for reconstruction can be synchronised with public aspirations; the extent to which a pro-peace balance can be struck between external actors and local participation in the reconstruction process and the extent to which reconstruction can facilitate rather than aggravate social and political cohesion.

The funding, capacity and expectation lag

The first of these challenges, the choreography of reconstruction aid with capabilities and popular expectations is complicated by the rush to reconstruct after a peace accord has been reached. Indeed, some international reconstruction conferences seem premature, based on the hope that peace can be secured rather than a cool-headed analysis of the actual prospects for peace. Admittedly, this is an easy criticism to make: potential donors may calculate that the promise of assistance will convince combatants to support a peace process or accord. Yet, there is strong evidence from a number of post-war environments (Afghanistan, Bosnia-Herzegovina, Iraq, Sri Lanka) of 'premature reconstruction' whereby monies are pledged or delivered and assistance rendered before the capacity for its effective use is in place. In the cases of Sri Lanka and Iraq, the persistence of violence and hostility meant that reconstruction and economic recovery were constrained. In Afghanistan, Bosnia-Herzegovina and elsewhere it rapidly became clear that the depredations of wartime had stripped governments of the legitimacy and administrative capacity required to implement effective reconstruction. Many government officials and NGO personnel had developed impressive skills in relief administration and distribution during the wartime, but were ill-equipped for the different skills sets required to initiate and sustain economic recovery. The relief-to-development step change proves a particularly daunting hurdle in societies that have experienced long-term conflict, such as Sudan, that may suddenly find themselves faced with the prospects of a peace accord and the need to implement significant economic change.[31]

Within weeks of the 1993 signing of the Israeli–Palestinian Declaration of Principles, donor states pledged $2 bn in development aid, with the figure eventually reaching $4 bn.[32] The fledgling Palestinian authority had few capacities to absorb and effectively use such funds. The story is not untypical of other cases of societies emerging from conflict, although the sums involved were rarely as large. There is usually only a brief window of opportunity of donor generosity that must be seized before the international issue agenda moves onto the next peace accord or natural disaster. Yet, at precisely the moment when recipient states have access to the most attention and funding, they have the least capacity. By the time they develop capacities through the training of personnel, the conduct of needs assessments and consultations, and the institution of administrative systems, donor interest may well have moved on. Barakat and Chard note how many post-war reconstruction interventions fail to grasp the profoundly dysfunctional nature of inter-group relations in post-peace accord societies:

> The fixed-term pre-planned project culture that characterises most donor-funded intervention is particularly unsuited to these circumstances, since it allows no space for solutions to evolve as people recover their confidence, understand their changed circumstances, identify possible courses of action, and thus become able to make choices about what they need to know and learn in order to pursue their goals. Usually the cart is put before the horse: organisational structures are imposed and skills training is delivered in measurable packages of "person hours" long before the real institutional and capacity building needs can be understood.[33]

Popular expectations of rapid and tangible change may peak just after a peace accord and fade as it becomes clear that the post-accord government is unable to deliver. Illustrated diagrammatically (Figure 6.1), we can see state capacity (C) reaching a peak just at the stage that donor funding (F) and public expectations tail off (E).

This suggests the need for the phased disbursement of donor aid in sequence with improving local capacities. Also crucial are the management of public expectations and the tempering of unrealistic prospects.

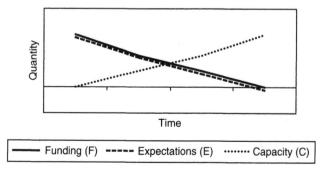

Figure 6.1 The post-war funding, capacity and expectation lag.

The balance between internal and external actors

The second key reconstruction challenge is the extent to which local and external actors can cooperate in the reconstruction process for mutual benefit and the embedding of a widely enjoyed peace. Arguments in favour of local participation in reconstruction and development are manifold: local actors may display an understanding of local needs and conditions, be motivated towards ensuring sustainability and can represent their fellow citizens as stakeholders in the development process. Local involvement in reconstruction (its planning, implementation and long-term development) can also act as a counterweight to 'donor psychosis' or the possibility that patron governments and bodies view local actors merely as passive recipients rather than active participants in the reconstruction.[34] Yet health warnings must accompany the role of internal actors in a post-peace accord reconstruction process. This is especially the case in deeply divided societies in which 'pork barrel politics' may have a sectarian or ethnonational hue. Often, an uneasy balance is struck between the distribution of reconstruction resources and opportunities for political purposes (to keep onboard rival groups favourable to the peace settlement) and the need for reconstruction activities to prioritise strict needs and efficiency. Thus, for example, reconstruction in post-Taliban Afghanistan has been driven as much by the need to preserve the inter-group balance as by a rational meeting of economic needs.

Makdisi's review of post-Taif Accord reconstruction and development in Lebanon notes how significant economic recovery was achieved, yet how the benefits of this reconstruction failed to become widespread. Key in this was a limited notion of 'public interest' in the polity. She points to:

> the continued inefficiency of the public sector and its total subjugation to political/sectarian patronage. All attempts at administrative reform have so far failed. Social inequities have increased. Natural resources and the security environment continue to suffer from lack of protection, if not systematic destruction. Urban and rural planning is inadequate. Corruption has increased.[35]

Clearly, the extent to which the reconstruction process can reflect and satisfy public needs is linked to the nature of the post-peace accord political system. While proponents of the liberal peace 'holy trinity' of open markets, democracy and peace have often sought to link reconstruction with democracy, the reality of post-war societies is that certain constituencies have to be kept on board. As Brynen observes, the 'politics of giving' must be viewed alongside the 'politics of getting'.[36] At times this might mean the consolidation of an imperfect regime, ministering to unsavoury (often militant) actors or sheltering some actors (perhaps with the capability to undermine the peace accord) from austerity measures. Media reports from Afghanistan have revealed how the United States and United Kingdom have paid cash bribes to warlords, many with appalling human rights records, in order to secure their support for the Karzai government. One observer noted though that, 'In any case, you do not buy warlords in Afghanistan: you "rent" them for a period.'[37] Although such financial co-option was crucial to ensure stability, it transmits a decidedly mixed message on the international priorities of reconstruction especially since infrastructure reconstruction was lagging behind its timetable because of funding shortages: security and order was to be valued ahead of more social and public categories of reconstruction.

Fundamentally, reconstruction and post-war development are costly long-term enterprises that can rarely be funded and managed using internal resources. The key issue is the management of reconstruction interventions by third parties. Caricatures depicting aggressive, insensitive and inappropriate interventions by NGOs, international organisations, IFIs and third party governments have become commonplace. The IMF and the World Bank in particular have provoked the ire of many commentators for their activities as agents of 'global capitalist expansion'[38] and their rigid, didactic and formulaic prescriptions. Many of these criticisms are entirely justified. In the mid-1990s, the World Bank was an unthinking cheerleader for template-style democratisation, while IMF structural adjustment programmes imposed massive social costs on the already vulnerable across a range of societies emerging from civil war. Both organisations were spectacularly obtuse in their insensitivity to local needs. One World Bank document aimed at the Middle East and North Africa noted:

no country is destined to be poor because of a bad endowment of natural resources, an isolated location, or a concentration on certain products. Production, finance, and trade have changed such that human talent is more important than natural endowment, agility more than location, and quality and innovation more than mass production. The implication is that countries can *choose*, through their policies, whether to be rich or poor.[39]

Doubtless this was comforting information to those emerging from their shelter to see the wreckage of Gaza following the latest missile strike.

Yet, for all of the crassness of the IFIs and how they enmesh post-war societies into iniquitous trading regimes, three points are worth making. The first is that both the World Bank and IMF have moderated the blunt neo-liberalism that was imposed on the post-communist transition societies in the early 1990s. There has been a modest lesson-learning exercise and a greater willingness to respect local needs. Thus, for example, the World Bank notes the importance of 'community-driven development' and the empowerment potential of poverty reduction, while statements from the Asian and African Development Banks are replete with a recognition of the need to consult and include local partners.[40] The second point is that reconstruction is incredibly costly, with the costs likely to last for generations. States have no choice but to look to external sources of regeneration finance, including the IFIs. The third (and related) point is that full membership of the World Bank and IMF is required in order to qualify for most forms of international economic assistance. Membership requires respect of the organisations' regulations including debt arrears.[41] The IMF and World Bank have become key players in the post-war reconstruction to the extent that they have been represented at peace negotiations in Guatemala and Bosnia-Herzegovina and have led the way in the trend towards the privatisation of post-war recovery.[42]

Many of the factors required for a sustainable peace are an antithesis to the canons of austerity, open markets and transparency beloved by the IFIs. Peacemaking and building require expensive and repeated interventions, often based on Keynesian principles of public sector employment and political rather than purely economic calculations. Massive public expenditure may be required to repair infrastructure, reconstruct administrative networks and fund essential services such as health and education. Post-peace accord governments may face strong redistributive pressures from groups overlooked in resource allocations under the previous political dispensation. Inter-group competition often persists despite the institution of a peace accord (as Northern Ireland and Lebanon testify) and groups are likely to jealously scrutinise budget allocations for evidence of discrimination. In such a context, post-war states may find themselves in the unenviable situation of attempting to satisfy the externally imposed strictures of small government and free markets, and internal pressures for expenditure to satisfy peace accord linked public expectations. Their ability to resist external pressure may be limited as donor aid may be linked to conditions.

Expressed bluntly, a completely open market is often the last thing needed by a society emerging from war needs. The benefits of an open economy, in the form of competitiveness and incentives for entrepreneurs, are often unable to contribute to the demands of an equitable and sustainable peace. A cushion is required to protect post-war economies from the immediate and uncontrolled ravages of the market. This is not to suggest proto-autarky or support for unsustainable nationalised mega-projects. Instead, it is merely to suggest that breathing space is found to help post-war societies attain productive capacity. Left to its own devices, the market quickly exploits already vulnerable economies, rendering them primarily consumption societies with little capacity for production. This breathing space could take the form of time-limited trade protection for certain products, currency controls and debt forgiveness to allow national governments greater control over their economy. Such suggestions may be deeply unfashionable and contradictory to the mores of IFIs and advanced industrial states, yet they may help reduce the risk of conflict recidivism.

One last point may be worth making in relation to the role of IFIs: the extent to which their interventions are premised on the existence of a formal and transparent economy in societies emerging from civil war. As Woodward notes, 'macroeconomic stabilization assumes ... that the economy is fully monetised when barter, informal economies and illegal trafficking actually predominate.'[43] A significant key to economic reform therefore is cultural rather than technical. One of the reasons that economic interventions are attractive to third parties is because they are relatively easy to plan and execute – certainly much easier than attempting to deal with affective or psychocultural issues such as reconciliation or trust. Yet, technocratic reform is only part of the equation. For many citizens in societies emerging from war, the informal economy is more convenient and less expensive than formal alternatives. Moreover, the formalisation of the economy is only likely to benefit a limited number of actors, many of them based overseas. While the language that accompanies formalisation is often innocuous (good governance, accountability and transparency etc.) its execution can have profound social and cultural impacts such as the destruction of traditional trading patterns and the politico-cultural balances they support.

Reconstruction for social and political cohesion

The third reconstruction challenge is to harness reconstruction and development efforts for social and political cohesion. The potential of economic transformation to create tensions and a sense of grievance has already been mentioned. Although ideas of a 'social pact' may be out of sync with the neo-liberal 'consensus', strategies for economic revival must pay attention to the need to create and sustain pro-peace social capital. Those directing reconstruction strategies are faced with a series of resource allocation choices and have the ability to exacerbate, contain or reverse inequality. Thus, decisions to prioritise certain regions or economic sectors, or to confront social cleavages directly through legislation or indirectly through trickle-down economics, can have enormous political repercussions. Take the example of Sudan following its 2005 peace accord between the north and south. The burden of the conflict has been disproportionately heavy on the south, though any reconstruction programme must take care to include as many sections of society as possible lest the peace accord be viewed as 'pro-south'.[44] While the exploitation of oil reserves has the potential to fund reconstruction, it also has the potential to spark grievances or the sense that one community is profiting disproportionately from the peace.[45] If properly designed and implemented, economic programmes can support pluralism, be sensitive to cultural aspirations and co-opt local communities as stakeholders in the reconstruction. But this relies on a post-peace political context mature enough to withstand actors willing to exploit apparent differentials in the peace dividend.

Virtuous reconstruction that contributes to social and political cohesion depends on the careful management of the switch between relief and development. In many cases, immediate basic needs relief is required in the aftermath of war, but there may come a point when such support is counter-productive and retards the indigenous development of sustainable livelihoods. In post-Taliban Afghanistan, for example, UN wheat handouts were much needed after years of drought and war-related dislocation. The continuation of mass scale World Food Programme wheat distribution after rains and excellent crops in 2003 was, in the eyes of one aid professional 'like keeping a patient in an intensive care bed long after an accident, when in reality they were ... ready to begin physiotherapy'.[46] In fact, continued food aid undercut the market for local farmers and made poppy cultivation a popular alternative. Different areas will have different needs and rates of recovery. This suggests the need for the regular review of relief and development programmes, and effort to prioritise sustainability and the importance of managing movement along the relief to development continuum so as to aid long-term social and political cohesion.

Reconstruction as a profitable activity?

In line with the privatisation of war and security, there has been an increasing trend towards the role of the private sector in post-war reconstruction.[47] Entrepreneurs have traditionally played a key role in reconstruction and recovery after war; often there was no alternative other than reliance on private resources. Yet, in the post-Second World War era, and particularly since the 1960s, organisations with the stated aim of maximising the public good have played an increasingly central role in post-war economic and social recovery. Whether states, third party governments, international organisations or NGOs, an international consensus developed that post-war reconstruction was often a task of such enormity that it should be conducted on a national scale, should be supported from the public purse and be free at the point of delivery. In many ways, the development of the norms of post-war reconstruction were linked to the development of the norms of modern humanitarian intervention as a moral duty. Such approaches were not without their problems, not least the implicit mindset that saw reconstruction as an essentially charitable endeavour to be ministered to passive 'victims' whose only role was to be grateful.

By the mid-1990s though the pendulum was swinging the other way. An increasing orthodoxy viewed the private sector as possessing many of the answers to the problems of post-war reconstruction. The case of Solidere, the Lebanese company at the forefront of the reconstruction of Beirut, was often trumpeted as an example of the potential of the private sector in powering economic and infrastructure recovery after war. More generally, the private sector was seen in some quarters as a legitimate 'partner' in multi-sectoral approaches to peacebuilding.[48] Although not (initially) a civil war situation, post-Saddam Iraq marked a highpoint in the privatisation of post-war reconstruction. In part, the prominent role afforded to the private sector reflected the fact that this was a US-led venture that was illegal under international war and that many states, international organisations and NGOs that were mainstays of other reconstruction efforts chose not to operate in such an insecure location. Indeed, US firms were openly favoured in the reconstruction tendering process.[49] But the Iraq case also marked a broadening of the intellectual support for the legitimacy of the private sector in reconstruction. Arguments in favour of such an approach were that the private sector could bring efficiencies and savings to the task of reconstruction that other operators could not. Since a key aim of the liberal democratic peace was the full introduction of the market, it seemed logical for the market to act as an agent of reconstruction.

In many ways, the NGO sector (or elements within it) has become complicit in this marketisation of reconstruction and peace support. In most cases, this has been borne of necessity as they have reacted to a changing operating environment. As governments and international organisations have increasingly contracted out their operations, NGOs have been invited to tender and bid for projects. At stake, very often, is the survival of the NGOs and these have been forced to adopt business plans and tailor their operations to suit the funding streams from governments and international organisations rather than their own strategic plans or – crucially – the actual needs of societies emerging from conflict. The nature of the programmes and projects supported under the increasingly prevalent rubric of marketised reconstruction and humanitarianism have reflected the neo-liberal mores of the IFIs and their leading member states. Thus, micro-credit schemes, income generation and community banking have become internalised as essential parts of the reconstruction process. Undoubtedly, such schemes have a role to play but there is a danger that they assume protected status, immune from criticism because of their closeness to the core principles of market-oriented post-war reconstruction.

What Klein calls 'predatory disaster capitalism', or the international business sector that profits from the opportunities arising from war and natural disaster, raises a series of ethical questions.[50] The seamless elision of destruction into reconstruction that marked the US–UK invasion of Iraq (and intervention in Afghanistan) seemed to re-brand war as a non-destructive activity capable of leaving a society in a better condition than before the onset of hostilities. The argument was that these were wars of reconstruction in which reconstruction was trailed as an essential part of the war itself. Under such circumstances, the Just War theory condition that ends must justify means was met.[51] Fundamentally though, the recasting of post-war reconstruction as a profitable activity threatened the humanitarian and duty-based compunctions that underpinned reconstruction efforts in other situations. The contradiction between the maximisation of private profits and the maximisation of pro-peace public goods and social capital seems insoluble. The profit margins from peace support and post-war reconstruction are necessarily made at the expense of someone: either taxpayers in a third country (in the case of reconstruction contracted out to the private sector by states or international organisations) or by citizens in the post-war society where their national resources (oil in the case of Iraq) are privatised or mortgaged to pay for 'aid' and assistance. None of the above is to suggest that the private sector has no useful role to play in post-war reconstruction. On the contrary, it should be one of the motors of a healthy economy, but it requires control. Yet, the interim or transitional years of a new post-peace accord administration may be precisely the time period when national capacities to resist external interference (in the form of technical assistance etc.) are at their lowest.

The drift towards the marketisation of post-war reconstruction brings with it a threat common to many other business environments: standardisation. The profit-seeking logic calls for a division of labour by agencies involved in reconstruction, the specialisation of their services and a set menu in terms of programmes and projects. Thus, recipient states are likely to receive the standard package of post-war 'aftercare' rather than a package based on local conditions and expensive needs assessments. Moreover, the 'marketplace' for post-war reconstruction is highly artificial. Created by leading states and international organisations, it reflects the ideological outlook at the heart of the liberal democratic peace and plays a crucial role in embedding the core elements of open markets, democracy and individual liberalism as orthodoxy.

Lessons from the Marshall Plan?

Despite professions of lesson learning by international organisations and IFIs, mistakes have been replicated across a range of post-war scenarios.[52] The post-Second World War Marshall Plan, the massive US-led recovery programme in Western Europe, contains a surprising number of lessons of contemporary relevance.[53] Clearly, the context in which the Plan was executed was unique: US power was 'artificially' inflated in the wake of the Second World War; international interest rates made lending possible on such an enormous scale; the sheer scale of reconstruction needs in the wake of truly global conflict made continent-wide initiatives a necessity and the political circumstances of a deepening Cold War made this a very political scheme.[54]

The Marshall Plan offers five perennial lessons to donors, administrators and recipients in contemporary post-war reconstruction schemes. In the first instance, the Plan crystallised the debate between donor altruism and self interest. After spilling so much blood and iron overseas during the Second World War there were understandable isolationist pressures in the United States to minister to domestic needs. Although predominantly in the form of loans rather than grants, the Plan involved a significant outlay of US resources by a society in the midst of donor fatigue following its heavy investments in Allied victory. Some cautioned against the folly of subsidising industrial reconstruction in Western Europe lest US investments be lost in the event of nationalisation or communist takeover. Against this, however, was a growing realisation that the collapse of European economies would have a severe impact on the US economy. By economically shoring up Europe, vital markets for US exports would be secured. The second lesson from the Marshall Plan was the central role afforded to recipients as stakeholders and participants in the recovery scheme. As General Marshall noted at the announcement of the European Recovery Program:

> It would be neither fitting nor efficacious for this government to undertake to draw up unilaterally and to promulgate formally on its own initiative a program designed to place Western Europe on its feet economically. This is the business of the Europeans. The formal initiative must come from Europe; and Europeans must bear the responsibility for it.[55]

Indeed, recipients of assistance were given remarkable freedom in how they could utilise the funds. Although very much elite-led and top-down in its organisation and execution, European states were invited to formulate a joint plan and submit it to the United States rather than engage in competitive bidding between states. As George Kennan noted, this would 'force the Europeans to begin to think like Europeans and not like nationalists'.[56] In other words (and the third lesson from the Plan), the Plan was very much part of a liberal democratic peace package, designed to encourage cooperation for mutual advantage between states. Free markets and currency convertibility were cornerstones of the Plan, as was a political orientation towards the United States.

The fourth lesson from the Marshall Plan was its comprehensive nature, of sufficient ambition and scale to tackle the enormity of the reconstruction challenge across all sectors of recovering economies and societies. The State Department warned that 'The program must contain reasonable assurance that if we support it, this will be the last such program we shall be asked to support in the foreseeable future.'[57] To this end, an emphasis was placed on sustainability so that Western European recovery would attain a 'financially self-supporting basis'.[58]

The fifth lesson from the Marshall Plan is one often overlooked in studies of post-war recovery: the psychological potential of international assistance. Kennan noted that the United States had 'let the economic situation slide for two years' but was then spurred into action by the combination of a developing Cold War and the danger of the United States slipping into recession. Revisionist historian John Lewis Gaddis observed that:

> The Marshall Plan worked by employing small amounts of economic assistance to produce large psychological effects: it restored self-confidence in Europe at just the point – some two to three years after the end of the war – at which it was sagging. What was critical was not so much the extent of the aid provided as its timing, its targeting, and its publicity; its purpose was to shift the expectations of its recipients from the belief that things could only get worse to the conviction that they would eventually get better.[59]

Many contemporary post-war societies are marked by a sense of hopelessness: that opportunities for economic recovery have been squandered through corruption or incompetence; that international attention has rapidly moved elsewhere; that macro-economic structures and dynamics preclude meaningful economic development and that peace may mean a hiatus in direct violence but brings little relief to structural inequalities and indignities.

The creation of a 'sense of the possible' or a generalised sense of optimism that a peace dividend can be generated and shared depends on many, often external, factors. Crucial in this is the strength of support for the peace accord as viable vehicle for long-term stability and conflict management. Even if created, any sense of optimism will be time-limited and conditional on delivery. Moreover, the level of expectations is unlikely to be evenly shared across all communities in a deeply divided society.

Concluding discussion

The issue of 'conditionality' in overseas aid has attracted negative commentary, especially whereby it disciplines and compels states to act in ways that are harmful to their long-term development.[60] Yet it seems unrealistic to expect that assistance will not come with either explicit or implicit conditions. There are strong arguments to build pro-peace and pro-plural incentives (conditions) into any externally funded reconstruction programme. Clearly, the precise definition of 'pro-peace' and 'pro-plural' incentives are likely to be contested in deeply divided societies, yet it seems feasible to construct linkages between levels of assistance and political stances. While basic humanitarian assistance should be exempt from such strictures, more advanced reconstruction packages can be calibrated to reward those who cooperate with a peace accord or engage in cooperative politics. This might mean rewarding certain areas that implement the disarmament provisions of a peace accord and withholding reconstruction aid for those who disrupt an accord. Such a strategy is not without its ethical questions, most fundamentally its acceptance of a particular peace process and accord as normatively good and a rejection of positions that may wish to question the accord.

There is a danger that reconstruction and economic recovery are regarded as a discrete element of the more general post-war rehabilitation in some way resembling technical issues that can be 'fixed' without reference to wider reconstruction challenges. Yet, reconstruction must be conducted in the service of the peace accord and the long-term management of the conflict. This suggests the need for an integration of the various strands of the post-war recovery process. It also suggests the importance of an overtly political dimension of the reconstruction in which linkages are made between its seemingly disparate elements. At the centre of this holistic approach to post-civil war reconstruction must be the reconstruction of fractured relationships. Exhortations to formally warring groups and constituencies to integrate and support a peace process and accord may be well-meaning, but they are likely to be fruitless if tangible benefits from peace remain elusive or iniquitously distributed.

In many ways, peace has the capacity to be a by-product of other integrative or cooperative social and economic processes. For example, communities in a post-peace accord society may have to cooperate to share or exploit resources, or support a joint economic venture. Through this endeavour, divisions and invidious social categorisations may erode and bridging social bonds may develop. Quite literally, in some cases, 'peace works' as individuals and communities get on with the business of earning livelihoods and a decline in hostilities follows. In the best case scenario, a virtuous circle develops, with communities calculating that any resumption of conflict would have unacceptable costs. Facilitating such initiatives and identifying their potential to produce positive social capital requires the careful targeting of post-war reconstruction aid. The distribution of resources in many societies emerging from civil war would not always facilitate the need for cooperation and sharing.

The Sri Lankan peace process provides a potentially encouraging example of the 'frontloading' of economic development into the peace process. The antagonists and supportive third parties held negotiations on reconstruction and economic development issues ahead of negotiations on more sensitive security and constitutional issues. Partly, this was a recognition of the potential of an impasse on security and constitutional issues to derail the peace process. But it also stemmed from a recognition of the need to reinforce and broaden the pro-peace constituency by delivering tangible reconstruction and economic development benefits. There was also a hope that Tamil–Sinhalese cooperation on economic development (at the local and elite levels) would pave the way for other forms of cooperation. The peace process has faced immense difficulties and shows little guarantee that it will deliver a comprehensive peace accord. Yet, the idea that economic development should be discussed and promoted as an integral part of the peace process, and certainly before a peace accord has been reached, has the capacity to reinforce a pro-peace constituency and provide a major bulwark against conflict recidivism.

7

Peace Prevented by External Actors

> We make our friends; we make
> our enemies; but God makes
> our next door neighbour.
>
> GK Chesterton

Introduction

Syrian involvement in post-Taif Accord Lebanon reveals the complexity of external involvement in post-peace accord societies. In one view, 'Taif's success is a function of the Syrian presence in Lebanon. Syria's stake in the stability of Lebanon provided the country with the requisites to weather a number of crises.'[1] While the costs of this external involvement came in the form of human rights abuses, stunted democracy and a lack of reconciliation, Syria provided the space for Lebanon to re-forge its national institutions, begin economic recovery and achieve the implementation of much of the Taif Accord. This 'Pax Syriana' continued until the 2005 Syrian military withdrawal.[2] In another view, Syria was 'an occupying force in Lebanon' that provided the most significant obstacle to the full implementation of the Taif Accord.[3] This negative view of Syrian involvement in Lebanon paints Syria as an exploitative power that used Lebanon as a pawn in its conflict with Israel, suppressed dissent with little regard for human rights and froze rather than confronted the sectarianism that lay at the root of Lebanon's civil war. That there are elements of truth in both the pro- and anti-Syrian views illustrates the difficulty of judging with any certainty the impact of external influences in post-peace accord societies.

It is becoming increasingly clear that the external environment is a key determinant for the success or failure of a peace accord. At the international level the essential variable would appear to be the 'willingness of international actors to provide resources and risk troops.'[4] This is dependent on whether major states and international organisations have substantial interests in overseeing a peace accord implementation process. States on the strategic margins with potentially costly and complex implementation programmes may expect little external peace-support intervention. At the 'neighbourhood' level, neighbouring states have the power to thwart a peace accord in the first place through their sponsorship of conflict parties or predation on a nearby war economy. Once an accord has been reached, they can hamper its implementation by hosting diaspora and spoiler groups or through excessive interference in the emergent post-civil war polity. Even if a propitious external environment exists for the implementation of a peace accord, third parties must have a political willingness to sustain their peace-support strategy. Barbara Walter stresses the importance of third parties acting as security guarantors of post-civil war settlements: 'the only type of peacekeeping that appears to help end a war is that which is backed up by a promise to use force.'[5] As the cases of Rwanda, Sebrenica and Darfur illustrate, robust third party peace support requires a commitment and capability that is often in short supply. Even where the political will to support pacific interventions has been present, the history of such interventions has been decidedly mixed.

This chapter focuses on interventions by third party states, international organisations, NGOs and private actors that have thwarted the implementation of peace accords or the fulfilment of a widely enjoyed peace. In some cases, these were deliberate attempts to spoil a peace, while in others they were well-meaning but counter-productive interventions. The chapter does not examine more generalised or structural external influences on post-peace accord societies in the form of trading regimes or neo-liberal economic norms. Nor does the chapter deny the very real contributions that external actors and influences have made in securing peace or providing humanitarian assistance in many post-peace accord societies. Instead, it questions the extent to which some peace-support interventions, often dressed in the verbiage of the liberal democratic peace, actually contribute to holistic and widely enjoyed peace. The chapter begins by examining the processes of legitimisation that have made external intervention into peace processes and post-peace accord societies increasingly acceptable for both external and internal actors. A second section records the pitfalls of external mediation and peace-support interventions. Three recurrent intervention pitfalls are highlighted: the failure of internationally supported peace initiatives and accords to make real connections with the inhabitants in post-war societies; the related tendency of peace accords and peace-support programmes to reflect donor rather than local concerns and the premature withdrawal of peace-support interventions. All three intervention pitfalls contribute to a key failing of the internationally supported liberal democratic peace model: inconclusive interventions before a holistic and sustainable peace has been instituted. While such interventions may minimise the conflict's violent impact, they also risk freezing and prolonging the conflict. In its third section, the chapter considers the potential of conflict 'spillover' factors from neighbouring states to derail a peace accord or harm the quality of peace. The tendency of civil wars to proliferate in regional clusters and the regularity with which post-civil war states have porous borders makes them peculiarly prone to the effects of conflict spillover. The chapter's final section considers interventions that can be described as 'malicious' or deliberately designed to thwart a peace accord or harm its implementation.

The legitimisation of external intervention in peace accords

The Cold War presented significant barriers to pacific external interventions in civil wars and peacemaking processes. The United Nations, the principal multilateral conflict resolution institution, was mandated to deal only with the maintenance of international security rather than civil wars, was largely respectful of state sovereignty and was prevented from adopting more interventionist strategies by East–West jealousies. The main peace-support tool at the UN's disposal, peacekeeping, was effective only under certain circumstances and often lacked the means to achieve more than an interdiction between antagonists.[6] This provided valuable relief for many at-risk civilian populations and space for the provision of humanitarian assistance, but it often resulted in 'frozen peace' or a 'controlled impasse' rather than an opportunity for conflict transformation in which the essential causes of a conflict were addressed.[7] The Cold War spread laterally, with parties in civil wars receiving superpower backing lest a rival superpower gain strategic advantage. The result was that many civil war sites were essentially the protectorates of one superpower or another, and the United States and the Soviet Union worked hard to thwart intervention from the other and from other third parties including multilateral organisations and NGOs. In a sense, much superpower intervention in civil wars was competitive, with an intervention race accompanying the arms race.

The Cold War lent sovereignty laws greater protection and many states were able to view secessionist conflicts as strictly 'internal matters' and beyond the purview of external scrutiny. While secessionist parties were often keen to internationalise the conflict, host states were resistant. Statements in the 1970s and 1980s by Britain on Northern Ireland, India on Kashmir, Russia on Afghanistan, Morocco on Western Sahara, Indonesia on East Timor, Spain on the Basque Country and China on Tibet had a certain sameness as each state claimed that the conflict was purely domestic and that international involvement, even if humanitarian or mediatory, would be inappropriate. The post-Cold War environment is significantly different, with a greater legitimacy associated with third party interventions, a greater assortment of intervening actors and a more extensive range of intervention activities. Crucially, external intervention has become a more generally accepted part of peacemaking processes and post-peace accord support. This acceptance is by no means universal, with for example, Burma fiercely resistant to external interest in its conflict with the Karen people. Nor are all types of external intervention welcome in all situations; some states may welcome humanitarian or reconstruction assistance but demur at more political interventions.

At least four factors explain the post-Cold War legitimisation of external intervention in peacemaking and post-peace accord support activities. First, the evaporation of Cold War patron–client relationships removed an insulating barrier whereby superpowers could protect their clients from external scrutiny and intervention. Second, while *de jure* state sovereignty remains largely wedded to Westphalian norms, state, multilateral, NGO and public attitudes towards sovereignty have undergone revision. The Cold War sanctity of sovereignty has given way to a more ambiguous recognition that rigid sovereignty may be overridden in certain circumstances. The context of globalisation, complex interdependence and humanitarian imperatives have all led to the erosion of sovereignty as an idea and practice, and contexts of state incapacitation through civil war or complex social emergencies lessen resistance to attempts to breach strict observance of sovereignty.[8] As Carment and James observe, 'Weak states riven by internal dissent attract the most third-party attention.'[9] A third explanation for the further legitimisation of external peace support activities in the post-Cold War era has been the increased willingness and ability of the 'newly liberated' United Nations to intervene in civil war situations.[10] The 1992 *Agenda for Peace* document outlined the ambition of the United Nations to widen its range of activities (from peacekeeping to peacemaking and peacebuilding) and to broaden its interventionist remit from the highpoint of violent conflict to other conflict stages including prevention and post-war reconstruction. Post-conflict peacebuilding was to include

> disarming the previously warring parties and the restoration of order, the custody and possible destruction of weapons, repatriating refugees, advisory and training support for security personnel, monitoring elections, advancing efforts to protect human rights, reforming or strengthening governmental institutions and promoting formal and informal processes of political participation.[11]

The United Nations' readiness to intervene waned somewhat as the 1990s progressed, but the organisation still retains its position as the premier international agent of pacific intervention. Many of its activities in post-peace accord societies are humanitarian, technical or development orientated rather than Political and quietly contribute towards opportunities for inhabitants in post-war environments to enjoy the benefits of peace. Along with the United Nations, a second tier of international organisations have become involved in conflict management activities, with the Organisation for Security and Cooperation in Europe (OSCE) massing greatest expertise and capability and other organisations, such as the African Union, aspiring to such capability.

The fourth explanation for the increased legitimacy attached to external involvement in peace accord support activities has been the explosion of the number and mandate of NGOs.[12] The growth in the number of NGOs in the post-Cold War period has been phenomenal (statistics for this vary enormously, but India alone is thought to have over one million NGOs and INGOs). Post-war zones commonly play host to a vast mix of indigenous and international NGOs many of which play acutely political roles in the form of democratisation, institutional reform and reconciliation programmes. While NGOs may have traditionally performed roles that could be termed as auxiliary to the main actors and dynamics in a peacemaking process, in many cases their roles have been enhanced to the point that they are core actors in a peace process and post-accord implementation.[13] Specialist Conflict Transformation Agencies (CTAs) have undertaken sensitive mediation tasks, in some cases attaining the trust of the conflicting parties because of their lack of state attachment.[14] Much of this is due to contracting out by international organisations.[15] In the increasingly marketised NGO operating environment, NGOs must pursue opportunities and 'compete for what might be crudely termed implementation "market share" '.[16]

Many NGOs have become agents of the liberal democratic peace and act in a near proxy capacity for leading states and international organisations. For NGOs, the cost may come in terms of their independence, but the benefits, particularly in terms of the boost to their legitimacy, are considerable.

To summarise, peace-support and peace accord implementation have become accepted and cardinal parts of international activities by states, international organisations and international NGOs. The ability of combatants to resist such interventions has declined in the post-Cold War era. Simultaneously, combatants' opposition to external peace-support interventions has also declined in some cases. This may be in recognition both of the overwhelming power of some of the intervening actors and the ability of intervening actors to extend and withhold resources in the form of reconstruction and development aid. The growing acceptance of third party intervention in support of peace processes and accords also has an ideological dimension. To a large extent, peace has been reinvented after the Cold War. Peace made in the context of the Cold War often reflected the superpower jealousies and strategic realities characteristic of that period. The label 'peace process' was rediscovered to refer to a number of highly visible attempts to reach accommodations in civil wars. Various factors, including attempts by multilateral organisations to foster best practice in their interventions and the tendency towards standardisation of policy and procedure common in most large institutions, meant that many peace processes and interventions contained standardised components that reflected prevailing ideological mores of leading western states. Thus, the 'new peace' of the 1990s and beyond reflected the increasing orthodoxy of the liberal democratic peace as both a type of peace and the means through which this peace was to be attained. Proponents of the liberal democratic peace regarded this version of peace a universal and unproblematic good. Its (western) components of electoral democracy, individual rights, good governance and free markets were regarded as ripe for export and essential for the management of conflict and the reconstruction of war-torn areas. Thus, third parties were tempted to view their interventions as acts of kindness or charity, guiding societies emerging from civil war towards the celestial delights of liberal enlightenment. In more extreme cases, and particularly in the context of the 'war on terror' and the consequent emphasis on order and stability, third parties viewed their interventions in a more messianic light – as a duty and responsibility. In the midst of the 2001 US assault on Afghanistan, one highly respected

British commentator noted,

> This war belongs within the much larger spectrum of a far older conflict between settled, creative productive Westerners and predatory, destructive Orientals. It is no good pretending that the peoples of the desert and the empty spaces exist on the same level of civilisation as those who farm and manufacture. They do not. Their attitude to the West has always been that it is a world that is ripe for picking.[17]

The danger, of course, is that peace-support and security interventions collapse into one generalised category of intervention and that the recipients of intervention take an increasingly jaundiced view of the motives of third parties.

A final point to make in relation to the legitimacy associated with peace-support intervention stems from the enormous moral energy and interest peace processes and accords are capable of generating. In the post-Cold War period there was a greater tendency among a widening constituency to regard 'peace' as a good thing rather than a Cold War compromise. This positive aura surrounding the peace following civil wars was, in many cases, independent of the quality of that peace. Thus, the term 'peace' was applied to a range of post-civil war situations that fell far short of notions of holistic peace. Some third parties were also attracted by the reflected glory from peace 'successes' or opportunities to 'showboat' or gain kudos from their involvement in a peace process or peace accord. While Norway, for example, has expended much effort on patient and effective mediation in the Middle East, Sri Lanka and the Philippines, it is not above publicising its 'peace diplomacy' as an indicator of Norway's model international citizenship.[18]

Intervention pitfalls

India's intervention in Sri Lanka from 1987–1990 can be described as a 'worst case scenario' in which a poorly conceived and executed intervention in support of a partial peace accord fuelled the conflict to reach a further level of intensity.[19] India dispatched a peacekeeping force to the north and east of Sri Lanka in support of the 1987 Indo-Sri Lanka Peace Agreement. Many Tamils were initially welcoming of the Indian troops in that they offered relief from the Sinhalese state and its heavy-handed approach to security. Given India's position as the regional hegemon, the Sri Lankan government had little choice other than to resignedly accept Indian intervention. The Liberation Tigers of Tamil Eelam (LTTE) or Tamil Tigers had been uninvolved in negotiations leading to the peace accord and unsurprisingly refused to abide by its provisions that they disarm. Tensions between the Indian Peace Keeping Force (IPKF) and the LTTE escalated rapidly, and the peace accord, with its ill-thought through plans for a transitional administration and devolution, quickly became moribund.

Full-scale conflict between the LTTE and IPKF erupted by late 1987 and was to continue for two years. The consequences were devastating for all parties involved. Rather than a peacekeeping force, many Tamils came to regard the Indians as an army of occupation. India's reputation as a regional power was severely dented as it became mired in a Vietnam-type struggle in which its troops performed poorly and with little regard to human rights. New Delhi's relations with the Tamil community in India (predominantly in Tamil Nadu) were also damaged.[20] Ultimately, the episode cost Prime Minister Rajiv Gandhi his life. The LTTE received a massive psychological boost and was re-energised to continue its struggle against the Sinhalese state. The Tamil people, however, suffered dreadfully in the conflict. Intra-Sinhalese politics were radicalised by the Indian intervention, with the People's Liberation Front (JVP) portraying Indian interference as a surrender by the Sri Lankan government.[21] A JVP insurgency cost up to 10,000 lives and changed the shape of Sinhalese politics, effectively acting as a brake on peace initiatives and reconciliation between the Tamils and Sinhalese.[22] Needless to say, the 1987 peace accord was irretrievably lost, and the very notion of third party intervention became so discredited that Tamils and Sinhalese were wary of outside interference for many years.

In short, it was an anti-textbook case of external intervention in support of a peace accord. Key ethical and practical issues central to mediation and third party intervention were overlooked.[23] The intervention was uninvited, with the LTTE excluded from negotiations and the Sri Lankan government acquiescing to the peace accord because of Indian power preponderance. The intervening party failed to convince either side that it was sufficiently impartial to act in a disinterested way. It was clear that domestic politics formed a strong motivating factor behind India's actions and India suffered from a 'strong hubris syndrome', believing that it had the power to implement the peace accord regardless of local opposition or opinion.[24] The intervention plan was hampered by a lack of an exit strategy and the peace accord amounted to little more than a ceasefire with a series of vague aspirations on constitutional and security issues. Fundamentally, the peace accord failed to address the core grievances and aspirations of both sides, rendering the Indian intervention a wasted and counter-productive exercise.

The Sri Lankan case provides signal lessons on the pitfalls of external intervention in support of a peace accord. The decade following the end of the Cold War has witnessed an upsurge of external support for the peace accords reached in the aftermath of civil wars. As the first section of this chapter outlined, intervention in support of peace accords attracted much greater legitimacy in the post-Cold War era, the intervention capabilities of multilateral institutions were enhanced and the range of interventionist activities undertaken was broadened. Many of these interventions have been successful and where peace accords have collapsed, or failed to meet expectations, the blame often lies with the combatants rather than the intervening parties. Three intervention pitfalls have been repeated in a number of societies emerging from civil conflict and are worthy of elaboration. All three pitfalls are characteristic of the liberal democratic peace, or the western-inspired peacemaking process and ethos that underlines many internationally supported contemporary peace interventions. Furthermore, all three have the capacity to seriously jeopardise the quality of peace offered through contemporary peace accords and restrict that peace to certain groups.

Lack of local ownership

The first recurrent peace-support intervention pitfall is the lack of ownership that many inhabitants in a post-peace accord society feel towards the peace accord and the political dispensation charged with its implementation. This may also be true in largely indigenous peace accords whereby local elites effectively exclude wider constituencies from influencing the peace accord or its implementation. The lack of connection between the peace accord and its ostensible recipients and beneficiaries may stem from the restriction of the negotiation and implementation of the accord to elites (whether internal or external), the external coercion of combatants to sign a peace accord or the terminology and direction of the peace accord. An accord may fail to address the core conflict causation and maintenance grievances, may fall short of cultural expectations of peacemaking and reconciliation, and may employ language and conceptualisations alien to local understandings of peace. The implementation programmes in support of peace accords often target specific sectors in the post-war society (combatants, government employees, civil society or the inhabitants of a certain locality) and fail to make meaningful connections with significant sections of society. In many cases, those charged with implementation are outsiders or a small coterie of the local civil society. The urban bias attendant in many development programmes is also evident in many post-war reconstruction efforts. The overall impression that the inhabitants of many post-war societies may have is that peace is something done unto them with minimal, if any, local participation.

Serbia's experience of 'peacemaking' illustrates some of the pitfalls of exclusion from the peacemaking process. The prelude to the 1995 Dayton Peace Accord came in the form of a US-supported Croatian military offensive against Serbian military forces, UN sanctions against the rump Yugoslav state and NATO bombing and tomahawk missile strikes on Bosnian Serb positions.[25] There can be few illusions that Bosnian Serb representatives were willing participants in the peace negotiations. The pattern of external preponderance and compulsion continued throughout the implementation of the accords with the 'peace' of Dayton accompanied by a massive international security apparatus, civilian administration and democratic engineering in the form of the disbarring of nationalist election candidates and the insertion of EU governors to run cities. The sense of disconnection that some communities can experience in a post-peace accord situation was summed up by one Serb community leader as the world focused on a commemoration of the dead of the Serb-perpetrated Sebrenica massacre: 'For every memorial to Serb war victims there are 10 for the Muslims; for every grant to help us, there are ten for them; for every one Muslim sent to The Hague, 10 Serbs are extradited.'[26] For many Serbs, it was peace by imposition, something to be sullenly endured rather than enjoyed. With the peace came the labels of pariah and perpetrator and little opportunity for local ownership of the peace.[27]

Reflects external rather than internal concerns

The second potential intervention pitfall associated with the externally led implementation of peace accords arises from the tendency of accords to reflect external rather than internal concerns. Local priorities may be subordinated to international concerns, with international priorities following the template set down through the liberal democratic peace rather than a case-specific consideration of needs. The unrolling of formulaic peace interventions may reflect the skills and capabilities of third parties rather than the actual needs of the civil war society; in other words, intervention may be supply-led rather than demand-led. A key example of the prioritisation of international concerns over local needs and demands comes in the form of international support for electoral processes to validate a peace accord or post-accord political dispensation.

Democratisation programmes have played central (often positive) roles in many cases of peace accord implementation and have been the recipient of enormous funds and energy. International organisations, western governments and western publics are keen to regard democratisation schemes – and particularly elections – as the chief indicator of a successful transition. For citizens in a society emerging from a civil war however, an election may be a luxury rather than a necessity.[28] This is not to deny the possible advantages accruing from post-peace accord elections, nor the popularity of elections with certain sectors. Instead, it points towards the priorities of communities in post-peace accord societies who may attach greater urgency to the servicing of basic needs such as security, rights or livelihoods. The UN Stabilisation Mission in Haiti, for example, was charged with assisting the Transitional Government 'in its efforts to organize, monitor, and carry out free and fair municipal, parliamentary and presidential elections'.[29] By the end of its first year (2004), the Transitional Government and United Nations had managed to encourage less than 5 per cent of the electorate to register to vote.[30] Doubtless very real security fears contributed to the low voter registration, but the low take-up rate also underlines the local perception that electoral processes are superfluous to their immediate needs. The key point is the tendency of many internationally led peace-support activities to reflect the mores and priorities of external constituencies rather than the needs of the 'peace-kept' or the 'peace supported'.

Premature withdrawal of external support

The third persistent failing of international efforts to shore up the implementation of peace accords comes in the form of premature withdrawal, whereby international peace-support activities are wound down before the peace accord and its components become self-sustaining. The post-peace accord period of conflict can be incredibly delicate, and rather than signalling time for international withdrawal, a peace accord may demand long-term international peace support. As Stedman notes,

> The two worst humanitarian emergencies of the 1990s – Angola in 1993 and Rwanda in 1994 – followed the failure of international actors to implement peace agreements. In those countries, far more people died in the aftermath of failed peace implementation than died from the preceding years of civil war.[31]

That states, international organisations and NGOs wish to limit their peace-support activities should come as no surprise given resource pressures, security concerns, a shifting issue environment and limited attention spans. In a number of cases though, the withdrawal of international peace accord support institutions and activities was pre-cipitous. The United Nations Transitional Authority in Cambodia (UNTAC), for example, was in operation for a little over eighteen months (1992–1993), thereafter passing responsibility to a power-sharing government and other UN agencies. Although hampered by a weak mandate, UNTAC facilitated immensely valuable humanitarian work and pulled off a Herculean feat in organising elections in May 1993.[32] The conclusion of the election, however, marked a signal for the wind-ing down of the UN operation, well before many peacebuilding tasks had been undertaken. Key combatant groups remained intact, the power-sharing government proved to be a precarious lesson in mistrust and many development issues were left unaddressed.[33]

The UN's \$2bn investment in securing peace in Cambodia can be considered poor value for money; UNTAC's role of managing *transition* was not fulfilled.[34] As this and other cases make clear, securing peace is a long-term and expensive endeavour, likely to outlast programme and project cycles of a few years. The long-term and structural nature of many civil wars results in the almost total degradation of infrastructure, government institutions and service provision, and inter-group rela-tions. Despite the chronic nature of ethnonational conflict, many inter-national peace-support activities focus on the proximate effects of civil war: refugees, physical war damage and the mobilisation of young men into armed groups. This ameliorative work is important, but is often lim-ited to the short- to medium-term and can be driven by quantitative tar-gets (numbers of refugees returned or combatants demobilised etc.) rather than more qualitative considerations such as the impact of the peace-support activities on broadening the pro-peace constituency. Many third parties intervening in support of peace accords have cor-rectly cautioned against fostering a dependency culture in post-civil war societies whereby governments, communities and individuals develop learned helplessness. The rationale is clear: while third parties can use-fully provide security, conflict relief and development assistance, for peace to develop beyond a grudging ceasefire, it must acquire organic and self-sustaining qualities. The essential aims of many third party interventions in support of peace accords are threefold: to stabilise a del-icate post-civil war situation, to ameliorate the effects of war and to devolve responsibility to local actors. In other words, an exit-strategy is built into most peace-support activities. In a number of cases though, this exit has been premature and occurred before peace became embedded or sustainable. Third parties may even be tempted to exploit the need to handover responsibility to local actors and use narratives of local 'ownership' and 'participation' to justify their early exit.

The three intervention pitfalls considered thus far (a failure to make local connections, reflect local concerns and to remain committed to the peace support project for the long-haul) contribute to a wider problem that can be labelled as 'inconclusive interventions'. Through inconclusive interventions, third parties may unwittingly prolong a conflict by shoring up or insulating antagonists from circumstances that may force them to sue for accommodation.

Inconclusive interventions

A key feature of international interventions in support of the liberal democratic peace is their ability to dampen or freeze conflicts rather than extinguish them. This is not to deny the benefits of interventions that separate warring parties and spare populations from the dislocation and misery stemming from violent conflict. Instead, it is to point to the problems connected with the prolongation of conflict through international peace-support operations. In many cases, the most obvious forms of direct violence are staunched (war between organised groups) but less visible direct violence (localised attacks) and indirect violence (intergroup tension and intimidation) can continue indefinitely. In a provocative but convincing argument, Edward Luttwak notes how wars, if left unchecked, usually reach a 'natural' conclusion through the forceful supremacy of one side over the other, the exhaustion of the protagonists or a political transformation that addresses grievances. He notes that:

> Since 1945 wars among lesser powers have rarely been allowed to follow their natural course. Instead, they have typically been interrupted very early, long before they could exhaust and destroy the energies of war to establish the preconditions of peace ... Unless directly followed by successful peace negotiations, armistices perpetuate the state of war indefinitely because they shield the weaker side from the consequences of refusing the concessions needed for peace ... An armistice is not ... half a peace or a halfway station to peace, but merely a frozen war.[35]

In one reading, Luttwak's assessment may seem callous in the extreme and condemn the weaker party in any conflict to the annihilation of a Carthaginian peace.[36] His argument is very much in the vein of the 'new barbarism' literature that urges selectivity with regard to third party intervention in conflict. Yet Luttwak, reflecting on international interventions into the ethnonational wars of the early and mid-1990s, noted how 'ceasefires and armistices imposed on lesser powers *systematically* prevent the transformation of war into peace.'[37] His insight guides us towards a powerful critique of contemporary multilateral peace-support interventions in which the international community (or elements thereof) are motivated to intervene to staunch civil wars but not effect fundamental conflict transformation. Risk averse multilateral military interventions (aided by equally risk shy political direction and public support) separate antagonists and provide some level of civilian protection but are rarely prepared to take on the militarily stronger force in the civil war society. The neutral ethos of many NGOs, in this view, means that they minister to – and shield – all sides including antagonists. Where political transformation is attempted and peace accords are reached, these may concentrate on codifying an armistice between armed groups and on technocratic solutions in the form of institutional reform, infrastructure reconstruction and quantifiable demobilisation and disarmament schemes. Armed groups may find themselves elevated to the status of negotiating partners in an internationally sponsored peace process, regardless of their actual popularity or claims to be the true or sole representative of a certain community. Thus, NATO ordained the Kosovo Liberation Army (KLA) as the legitimate representatives of the Kosovo people in the 1999 Rambouiltet negotiations with the Yugoslav state, a move with long-term repercussions on the politics of Kosovo. Although well-intentioned, many third party interventions risk having counterproductive outcomes and, as Luttwak points out, their interruption of military dynamics suspends the conflict into perpetual conflict.

The nature of the liberal democratic peace may mean that some civil war societies experience a mass of interventions from a range of actors on a range of actors. Thus, high profile diplomatic visits, peace accord signing ceremonies, donor conferences, reconciliations events and a mass of prosaic initiatives may characterise many societies with an advanced peace process. Yet, it is important not to confuse activity with effectiveness in conflict transformation. Many core activities associated with liberal democratic peace interventions may not actually address core conflict causation and maintenance grievances. Instead, they may legitimise antagonists and their negotiating positions, freeze battlefield gains and make permanent interim measures.

While Luttwak's commentary is provocative and useful in probing the essential outcome (frozen peace) of many multilateral interventions in support of peace initiatives and accords, his attachment to 'the transformative effects of both decisive victories and exhaustion' is open to criticism.[38] Decisive victories and fights to exhaustion entail obvious human costs. Even if mutual exhaustion encourages antagonists to reach a hurting stalemate and more actively review non-violent alternatives, there are few guarantees on the nature of the peace that will follow.

Conflict spillover

In a number of cases, civil wars occur in regional clusters and show little respect for the strictures of political cartography. Thus, a peace process or peace accord in one state may be prone to a spillover effect from a neighbouring state. The main spillover of factors retaining potential to thwart the implementation of a peace accord or the wide enjoyment of peace are people, ideas, arms and resources. Common to all of these spillover factors is state incapacitation particularly in relation to poor border control. Civil wars often result in the degradation of state capacities or the withdrawal of state agents from certain functions or areas. There may be a considerable lag between a peace accord and the (re-)extension of state capacities. For example, border policing may be dependent on wider processes of security sector reform or ethnic geography may mean that state forces may have difficulty operating in areas in which minority groups form a majority along a border with a neighbouring state. Porous and poorly policed borders thus become laxly controlled gateways to the post-peace accord society and may facilitate the entry of spillover factors that can threaten the peace.

The spillover of people is a function of mismatch between people and territory so common in ethnonational conflicts. Groups that claim a common heritage, identity or grievance may be scattered across a number of states. The displacement and possible boundary changes associated with civil wars are likely to exacerbate the dissonance between people and territory. 'Demographic engineering' or the state-directed movement of ethnic groups has long been a feature of conflict regulation (and indeed inflammation).[39] This section is primarily interested in the movement of people after a peace accord has been reached, particularly in the potential of such flows to destabilise delicate population balances in and place resources under pressure. Refugee repatriation has been a common feature of contemporary peace accords, and in some cases, sophisticated repatriation mechanisms have been put in place to provide for minority protection and the livelihoods and public goods needs of returnees. Such schemes have played a major part in realising the quality of life ambitions of peace accords and are essential first steps in wider processes of post-war reconciliation and inter-communal peacebuilding. In other cases, however, international organisations and other bodies are not in place to manage refugee return with the result that refugees repatriate themselves. Often this voluntary and self-administered refugee return is unproblematic. It can, however, be destabilising to host communities who harbour concerns on the resource implications of the return and the impact of unregulated return on the ethnic mix of their locality. The *ad hoc* and unrecorded nature of such refugee flows means that rumour and conjecture can attach malign intent to such movements.

The spillover of (former) combatants can also be potentially destabilising in a post-peace accord environment. While former combatants may be legitimately contained within refugee populations, out-group members may regard their presence as potentially threatening and it may influence their view of the refugees. Rather than civilian returnees, out-group members may see the refugees as primarily a cover for the return of former combatants against whom they still harbour fear and suspicion. Neighbouring states may also provide bases or areas of support for combatants who are opposed to, or excluded from, a peace accord. With their passage across the border unchecked, they may be able to engage in spoiling activity or stir up dissent and disillusionment with a peace accord. It could be, of course, that groups have good reason to feel dissatisfied with a peace process or peace accord, but deeply divided societies with newly minted peace accords remain peculiarly susceptible to the destabilising potential of ethnic entrepreneurs.

The movement of people across borders can play a major role in the transmission of ideas, especially ideas of disenchantment or opposition to peace initiatives that can puncture the public euphoria or relief that might accompany a peace accord. In a number of conflicts, diaspora communities have been more radical than their cousins in the conflict zone. From a distance, they can provide an articulate rationale for the rejection of a peace accord and the continuation of 'the struggle'. The third spillover factor with the potential to destabilise a post-peace accord environment, the flow of arms, is especially prevalent in regions that have witnessed a number of conflicts.[40] The multiple conflicts in the Horn of Africa or in the Great Lakes region mean that weapons may be available from many sources as the violent phase of different conflicts reach negotiated conclusions. DDR programmes may face severe difficulty if a conflict in a neighbouring state provides a ready market for arms (and indeed combatants).

A final conflict inflaming spillover factor with the potential to destabilise post-peace accord societies is the transnational flow of resources, mainly in the form of illegal and unregulated trade. The extent of the shadow economy can seriously undermine attempts to rejuvenate the formal economy, particularly by depriving the public purse of tax revenue. Illegal trade, particularly smuggling and the narcotics industry, can create massive public insecurity through the formation of private armies to organise and protect the trade from state (or international) attempts to disrupt it. Post-war states can also easily acquire reputations as corrupt economic environments thus deterring inward investment.

Bad neighbours

Related to the issue of conflict spillover are 'bad neighbours'. Most third party peace-support interventions by international organisations, states and NGOs are well-meaning. Even if patently self-interested (the stabilisation of a region lest a conflict spills over or an intervention to gain international kudos) most peace-support interventions contain significant elements directed (notionally at least) towards the alleviation of human suffering and the effects of war. Despite its many faults, the liberal democratic peace is capable of delivering stability, the disarmament of combatants, electoral representation and economic development. Although such benefits are often unevenly distributed, there can be little doubting their pacific potential. Some interventions though are deliberately designed to thwart peace initiatives, undermine peace accords or destabilise the post-peace accord society. Although more common during the Cold War when superpower jealousies inflamed civil wars, such subversive interventions persist in the post-Cold War era and stem from 'bad' neighbours or (aspirant) regional hegemons who regard the peace as antithetical to their interests.[41] Examples include Israeli and Syrian interference in post-Taif Lebanon, the US strategy of undermining PLO leader Yasser Arafat and Ethiopian undermining of attempts to broker peace between Somali warlords.

The Ethiopian–Somali example reveals how a peaceful and strong Somalia has the potential to jeopardise a united Ethiopia and its designs of 'regional dominance'.[42] Enmity between the two states has a long history, stemming from disputed borders, clashes between ethnic groups and competition over resources. The 1977–1978 Ogaden war caused massive displacement and cost up to 30,000 lives. The 1991 collapse of the Somali government, and the absence of capable government ever since, has meant that Somalia has been a site of conflict, displacement and instability threatening an already fragile region. Ethiopia, the region's largest military power, has maintained an interventionist stance in its neighbour's affairs. Fears of a 'Greater Somalia' with irredentist ambitions towards Ethiopia have meant that Ethiopia has, at times, pursued a 'divide and conquer' strategy of backing some Somali clans in the hope that they can undermine others. Refugee flows, warlord activities within its borders and anxiety at the possibility of Sudanese-backed Islamic groups destabilising inter-group relations in Ethiopia have all resulted in Ethiopian interference. An added dimension came with 1993 Eritrean independence which rendered Ethiopia landlocked and in need of port access. The result has been the Ethiopian courting of the unrecognised state of Somaliland. A Transitional National Government (TNG) established in 2000, following mediation by the regional Inter-Governmental Authority on Development (IGAD), accused Ethiopia (an IGAD member) of undermining it by backing warlords who had been excluded from the TNG.[43] Ethiopia's opposition to the TNG continued until its favoured warlord assumed control of the Transnational Federal Government established in October 2004.[44]

Bad neighbours though are atypical. The advantages of a stable neighbouring state and harmonious regional relationships are obvious. It is also noticeable that a number of regional powers (for example, Nigeria, South Africa, Malaysia and Australia) are assuming peace-support role that in previous decades were left to the United Nations. There may be elements of self-interest in such peace support, perhaps to stem refugee flows or to reinforce a claim to be the regional top dog, but such actions have stabilised a number of conflict situations. The intra-regional nature of such peace-support interventions has an advantage in that the intervening parties are more likely to be aware of the cultural perspectives of the antagonists and have an awareness of the conflict history.

Concluding discussion

It would be misleading to paint a picture of external factors constantly fouling up peace accords or stymieing peace processes to the point where they become empty vessels that freeze or exacerbate tension rather than address conflict-causing or conflict-maintaining grievances. External factors can make the crucial difference that propel peace initiatives into fully fledged peace processes. They may also encourage (or coerce) antagonists to reach a peace accord and provide the funding, security and technical assistance required to realise that accord. The experiences of other peace processes, and the personnel involved in them, may offer inspiration and lessons to antagonists. In a number of long-running civil wars, local resources are so denuded (particularly in public health and infrastructure) that external parties are the only actors able to inject sufficient resources into the society to provide any sort of dividend. In the absence of such third party intervention or inspiration, local antagonists may remain locked in a stalemate or unable to transform a respite in conflict into tangible benefits.

Ultimately though, peace needs to be made and maintained locally. To be sustained and widely enjoyed it must have voluntary and local elements to complement external inputs. In a significant number of cases, international actors have displayed more enthusiasm for peace than local actors: they have cajoled and coerced local actors to the negotiating table; identified and ordained legitimate negotiating partners; labelled and excluded illegitimate political actors; chivvied parties to meet negotiation deadlines and persuaded parties to reach a peace accord. Once agreed, international actors may assume the role of policing the accord, ensuring its implementation and delivering and distributing relief and development assistance to support the accord. The accord may be more popular in European and North American capitals, and in the western liberal press, than in the post civil war society itself. Such is the lack of local enthusiasm for internationally driven peace accords that external parties may be compelled to commit long-term and substantial investments of energy and resources just to ensure that the accord survives. While local actors may have to enact the letter of the accord, they may have little respect for its spirit.

Such 'peace processes under sufferance' can deliver distinct advantages, not least if they engineer a reduction in direct violence or facilitate relief or development assistance. In many ways, the spirit of liberal optimism and the logic of the liberal democratic peace are interventionist, and peace-support interventions are to be expected. Yet, in a significant number of cases, international actors have over-estimated local support for peace initiatives. The result has been internationally led peace processes with a 'long tail' of reluctant local followers who owe little allegiance to the peace process and retain an involvement in it to monitor their opponents or avoid international opprobrium lest they are blamed for its collapse. Local actors may have begun their involvement in the peace process with enthusiasm, but this may dissipate as the compromises and disappointments inherent in peace processes become clear. In many cases, internationally led peace processes have resulted in frozen peace, whereby the conflict is ossified and essential conflict causes are left unaddressed. In less benign cases, extensive international pressure in driving the peace process may jeopardise future pacific third party interventions.

Conclusion: What Works?

Peace is a process.

Sydney Bailey

Evaluating the liberal democratic peace

The liberal democratic peace is best described as a confluence of behaviour, attitudes and structural factors that encourage a particular type of peace and peacemaking. It can be identified through its possession of five core elements:

- means or methodology;
- core components (distinctive forms of liberalism and democracy);
- nature of its principal actors and sponsors;
- ideological perspective;
- type of peace effected.

The first core element of the liberal democratic peace is its methodology or the means through which it is pursued. A western business negotiation model is often prioritised, the aim of which is 'the deal', or the peace accord which takes the form of a solemn compact followed by constitutional or legal reform. The emphasis is often on deal-making or striking a bargain rather than a review of the strained relationships that shape the conflict. This peacemaking model often follows a preset sequence of events: pre-negotiations to test the seriousness of antagonists to pursue peace initiatives, followed by negotiations, an accord, an implementation phase and institutionalisation. The liberal democratic peace methodology favours technocratic approaches with the result that traditional or indigenous approaches to peacemaking, which may draw on custom and cultural practice, are ignored or marginalised.

The second key element of the liberal democratic peace comes in the form of its core components: liberalism and democracy. A peculiarly western variant of liberalism lies at the heart of the liberal democratic peace; one that prioritises the individual over the group and attaches immense moral and practical significance to the pacific and regenerative powers of the market. Complementing this brand of liberalism is a highly specialised form of democracy that emphasises electoral contests (rather than other, more traditional, forms of representation), western notions of civil society and good governance. The good governance agenda usually brings with it a series of administrative and government reforms with far-reaching consequences for the organisation of the post-civil war state and its interaction with citizens. Uniting the forms of liberalism and democracy deployed is an absolute belief of the superiority of these ideals and a concomitant belief in the inferiority of alternative bases for peacemaking.

The liberal democratic peace model's third key element is the nature of the actors and sponsors involved in the peacemaking process. While this peacemaking model is tolerant of a wide range of actors, it is clear that it favours engaging with certain types of local actors in war-torn societies: well-defined groups such as governments, political parties or militant groups with clear-cut hierarchies. Important sectors in many 'new wars', such as loosely structured gangs of marginalised youths, many find themselves with few opportunities for representation or engagement within the rubric of the liberal democratic peace. Many programmes and projects enacted as part of peace processes or peace accord implementation schemes are geared towards engagement with specific sectors such as organised groups of former combatants, local civil society or the English-speaking metropolitan elite. In terms of the sponsors of the liberal democratic peace, the key actors are leading western governments, a select group of international organisations and IFIs. Some actors will have more influence, resolve and capability than others, and the array of leading advocates of the liberal democratic peace is open to change. A second tier of advocates comes in the form of the governments of smaller western states, NGOs and private businesses. Huge swathes of the NGO sector have been co-opted into the liberal democratic peace framework: at times due to a genuine belief that their efforts are capable of effecting real change and, at others, because funding streams require compliance with the mores of the liberal democratic peace.

A distinctive ideological outlook comprises the fourth core characteristic of the liberal democratic peace. Liberal optimism, or a belief in the perfectibility of society, lies at the heart of this ideological perspective. By its very nature, this perspective is interventionist, believing that individual, group and state sovereignty can be overridden if the end will result in improved social relations. It is believed that the dissemination of liberal and democratic values and practices will reduce the likelihood of tension and conflict at both the inter- and intra-state levels.

The final core characteristic of the liberal democratic peace is the type of peace delivered. While each society emerging from civil war will experience its own version of peace (and indeed, individuals and groups within this society will have their own radically different experiences of this peace) it is possible to identify common traits in internationally-sponsored peace processes and peace accords in the post-Cold War period. The regularity with which the same external actors (UN, EU, NATO, US, UK, Nigeria, World Bank, IMF and major NGOs etc.) intervene in civil war and post-civil war situations and the almost customary and formulaic nature of the tasks conducted as part of these interventions combine to mean that many liberal democratic peace interventions have a certain sameness. While all interventions must be tailored to suit local circumstances, the liberal democratic peace model also encourages an 'off the rack' approach with external peace-support actors drawing on a set repertoire.

It is the argument of this book that the peace accruing from the liberal democratic peace model is often flawed; a negative rather than a positive peace. The regularity with which peace enacted through the liberal democratic rubric is prefaced with terms such as 'tense' or 'fragile' is in part due to the agents and structure that implement this type of peace. Yet, any evaluation of the liberal democratic peace must recognise the positive difference that such interventions have made in civil war and post-civil war situations. The interdiction of peacekeepers between antagonists, the encouragement of antagonists to investigate peace initiatives, the calling and maintaining of ceasefires, the sponsorship of peace talks, the institution of security, government, constitutional and resource allocation reforms, and the introduction of relief, development and reconstruction assistance have all made enormous differences to many societies during their war to peace transitions. The liberal democratic peace has saved and improved millions of lives. All peace is a compromise, especially given the complexity of intra-state war, and to quibble with the quality of peace resulting from liberal democratic peace interventions may seem querulous or thankless. A heavily compromised peace may be by far the best possibility available. Yet, with a remarkable regularity, the liberal democratic peace delivers a partial peace that freezes conflict rather than addresses its essential causation and maintenance factors. Liberal democratic peace support interventions have had success in arresting conflict, but often fail to effect more profound change. The dangers of this inconclusive peacemaking are manifold: conflict may be placed in cold storage to be re-energised by later generations; violence (often informal) can seep into the interregnum of a stalled peace process; public optimism is eroded by a lack of progress; the civil war society becomes dependent on international support; antagonists (some marginal in terms of size and importance) may be legitimised through the peace process and the economy may be stabilised but reform renders it incapable of autonomous development.

The advantages of the liberal democratic peace are often restricted to the short-term: brokering ceasefires, chairing or mediating negotiations and pump-priming reconstruction. Longer-term goals that would constitute transformative peace (e.g., functional inter-group relations or reconciliation) usually lie beyond the scope of the liberal democratic peace or internationally approved peace interventions.

Three significant features of the liberal democratic peace are worthy of elaboration: its essential conservatism, the manner in which it allows its international sponsors to absolve themselves of blame for the shortcomings of this version of peace and its relative instability. First, in some respects, peace processes managed under the aegis of the liberal democratic peace are capable of promoting radical change through regime change, new constitutions or more prosaic modifications in the organisation of the post-civil war society such as land reform or the provision of security to traditionally harassed minorities. In other respects, however, the liberal democratic peace model has conservative biases that often maintain and replicate social, economic and political relations. While the initial stages of the peace process and the peace accord may herald significant change, a key aim of the liberal democratic peace is the introduction of stability, regularity and order into deeply divided societies. The benefits of this strategy are obvious, especially for war-torn contexts, yet after initial change and relief, the liberal democratic peace model risks freezing antagonism in the conflict society. The peace accord may be awarded an exalted status and suggestions that it is outdated or requires revision may be interpreted as a rejection of the peace. Civil war antagonists may be reaffirmed as the legitimate representatives of the post-civil war society, thus retarding the development of non-nationalist politics. The first power-holders in the post-peace accord dispensation may use the peace accord implementation phase to entrench themselves in power, limiting the possibility of future political transitions. A key source of conservatism in this peacemaking model is its emphasis on state-building: notions of state sovereignty and the nature of formal state-based administrative culture all militate against the radical change than can facilitate the transformation from negative to positive peace. In the context of the war on terror, 'stabilisation' (a Trojan horse for securitisation) has become a core aim of US and UK interventions in societies emerging from conflict. Stabilisation allows little room for anything other than controlled change, with the key controlling actors usually being external.

Second, the liberal democratic peace model has a remarkable ability to defer and transfer responsibility for its own shortcomings. Such chameleon-like quality complicates the task of evaluation. This peacemaking model often depicts itself as a neutral, non-partisan and non-ideological intervention in civil wars. It often uses the language of 'common sense' and humanitarianism, offering to intervene in a dispassionate manner. Yet, in a socially constructed world, all actors and actions are political, more so in the highly contested context of a deeply divided society. Setbacks in a peace process or peace accord implementation can easily be blamed on the antagonists, whose naked self-interest stands in stark contrast to external peace-support interventions advertised and justified as worthy and selfless mediation. In many cases, local antagonists are indeed to blame for peace process difficulties, and it is disingenuous to place the blame for all of the ailments with peacemaking at the door of the liberal democratic peace. Yet, this model of peacemaking is peculiarly insulated against criticism since international actors paint themselves as saintly referees endeavouring to keep apart the 'warring natives'.

Third, one of the most remarkable features of the liberal democratic peace, as the primary 'operating system' that underpins many contemporary peace accords and peacemaking processes, is its relative invisibility. In some respects this may seem an odd statement since the liberal democratic peace model has left behind a hefty footprint in many societies emerging from civil war. Yet, many attempts to conceptualise and describe internationally supported peace processes and peace accords do so at the individual case study level and neglect to identify trends and commonalities across peacemaking processes. Other studies concentrate on particular elements of peacemaking processes such as security sector reform or reconciliation and fail to make connections between the various components of the peace process. This work differs from many studies of peacemaking by its identification of seemingly disparate peace processes and peace accord situations as falling within the rubric of the liberal democratic peace. The use of the term liberal democratic peace, rather than plain 'peace', identifies this as a peculiar version of peace. There are limits on the extent to which peace processes can be systematised under the liberal democratic peace mantle, particularly given the variety local circumstances. Yet, the liberal democratic peace paradigm provides a useful organising device for the conceptualisation and interrogation of contemporary peacemaking.

The most fundamental advantage offered by the liberal democratic peace lens is its compatibility with a critical perspective which encourages an analysis of the quality of peace resulting from contemporary peace processes. In the uncritical view, conflict is a dysfunction to be 'fixed'. Uncritical studies tend to pursue technocratic 'problem-solving' approaches that neglect inquiry into underlying conflict causation and maintenance factors, many of which may be structural. Thus, making peace or perfecting a stalled peace accord is reduced to a series of technical tasks, for example, identifying better mechanisms for the reintegration of former combatants or the more efficient collection of weapons, rather than considering the underlying perceptual factors that make membership of armed groups and the retention of weapons rational choices. The intentions of many studies maintaining an uncritical perspective on peacemaking are undoubtedly benign, but they risk regarding negative peace as an adequate substitute for more holistic, sustainable and widely enjoyed varieties of peace.

It is important not to conceive of the liberal democratic peace as a vast Machiavellian plot foisted on societies emerging from civil war by a handful of scheming foreign ministries, IFIs and tame international organisations and NGOs in their pay. Nor should the liberal democratic peace be viewed as omnipresent and all-embracing; it has been implemented and advocated with varying degrees of intensity. In other words, we should conceive of a 'variable geometry' of liberal democratic peace, with different post-civil war societies enjoying (or enduring) different aspects of this version of peace applied with varying degrees of enthusiasm. Some societies emerging from conflict are deemed too remote or strategically peripheral to receive anything but a cursory version of the liberal democratic peace. Other post-civil war societies are within the geo-political realm of regional hegemons (Russia in the case of Moldova) and so the version of liberal democratic peace they experience has a regional flavour. Caution is also required in that by adopting the liberal democratic peace lens, and thus concentrating on the internationally sponsored and influenced aspects of peacemaking, observers may overestimate the significance of exogenous factors and underestimate the ability of local actors to resist, negotiate and mould external peace-making influences.

What works?

The significant number of peace processes and peace accords over the past two decades means that it is possible to identify relative success, and relative and complete failure, in peacemaking initiatives. Yet, local variations in civil war situations mean that extreme caution is required in recommending peace-enhancing strategies that can be transferred between conflict situations. 'Best practice' from one location may be culturally inappropriate in another, or could even inflame conflict. Each situation requires a thorough conflict analysis or critical peace assessment to examine local needs and the feasibility of peace initiatives. Where inspiration or guidance is taken from another location, it will require modification so as to suit the new area of application. This work concludes by identifying ten propositions designed to help prevent peace processes and peace accords from stalling to, rejuvenate peace processes or peace accords once they have stalled and to help transform negative peace into a more positive peace.

Having identified the failings of orthodox approaches to peacemaking throughout this book, it is important that this study does not conclude by prescribing precisely those peacemaking strategies that have been found wanting in earlier chapters. The book advocates a radical rethink of many of the assumptions and practices underpinning contemporary peacemaking. Yet, the infrastructure and norms of orthodox peacemaking are difficult to avoid. Propositions must be mindful of the possible. Not all of the following propositions are appropriate to all stalled peace process and accord situations. Yet, if applied with prudence they offer opportunities to revive becalmed peacemaking processes, to inject greater levels of public participation, to move beyond the froth and tinsel of superficial peace deals and to tackle the genuine reconciliation required for any sustained and holistic peace. All of the propositions constitute a challenge to the currently dominant and internationally supported methods of peacemaking and peacebuilding.

Proposition one
Review mechanisms need to be integral parts of
peace processes and peace accords

Once a long-running civil war is interrupted by a peace initiative it is understandable if some key local and international actors attach immense value to the initiative. The peace process or accord may herald a respite from conflict, it may encapsulate the hopes of many for deliverance from conflict and it may acquire immense symbolic importance. Under the liberal democratic peace rubric, international actors may strongly back the peace process or accord regardless of local opposition. In such circumstances, to criticise the peace process or settlement may be interpreted as being 'against peace'. Yet circumstances change, particularly in cases of societies emerging from civil war. An end to violent conflict may bring unexpected consequences, for example, the return of large numbers of refugees or an increase in crime. Public enthusiasm that may have accompanied a peace accord may wane as the promised peace dividend materialises in a halting or apparently inequitable way. While one community in a deeply divided society may regard the peace accord as a just settlement, another community may see it as biased.

To guard against the consequences of an over-rigid peace process or accord, flexibility needs to be built into both. As important as review mechanisms, or built-in reassessment devices, is the internalisation among peace process participants, observers and recipients of the need to allow reviews. In other words, flexibility in attitudes to the peace process and accord is as important as 'technical solutions' in the form of review mechanisms in a peacemaking process. This does not mean that a peace process should be a scene of eternal re-negotiation and impermanence; negotiations require ground rules and accords require respect (especially if publicly endorsed). Yet, it is worth moving away from the notion of a peace 'settlement' or a final resolution of a conflict. The management of conflict is a process, involves constantly evolving relationships and must retain the agility to deal with both new and recurring grievances. Consequently, peace processes and accords must be open to constant reappraisal, and in doing so may be able to anticipate and obviate some of the issues that commonly lead to the stalling of peacemaking processes.

Proposition two

Issues of trust need to be addressed in a
peace process and peace accord

Many peace processes and accords have had remarkable success in devising and instituting technical means for bringing antagonists together in talks, forging an agreement and dealing with potentially difficult issues such as prisoners, weapons, combatants, territory and the sharing of power and other resources. Yet, a recurring source of the collapse or freezing of peace processes is an absence of trust between antagonists. The technocratic approach to peacemaking means that antagonists can engage in a wide range of activities without actually developing substantial levels of mutual trust. This is especially the case if these technical activities (e.g., disarmament, demobilisation and reintegration), are overseen by external third parties. Antagonists may trust the peace process as guaranteed by third parties but may not trust each other. The ostensible reasons for the collapse or freezing of a peace process or accord often mask a deeper malaise: a chronic lack of trust between antagonists at both the elite and communal levels. The reason given for the collapse of the Israeli–Palestinian Oslo process is often summarised as the failure of the Palestinian Authority to rein in militant spoilers. In the case of Northern Ireland, the repeated suspension of the post-Belfast Agreement devolved power-sharing government is often blamed on the failure of the IRA to decommission its weapons and cease its militant activities. In southern Sudan, the repeated failure of peace initiatives in the late 1990s was often attributed as the failure of the Government and the Sudanese People's Liberation Army to cease violence despite undertakings to do so. In all of these cases, and in many more, a key factor in the collapse or effective stalling of the peace process or accord was mistrust between antagonists.

To a certain extent, the nature of the liberal democratic peacemaking model is unable to foster sufficient trust between antagonists. Its emphasis on technocratic responses to conflict and its tendency to view peace as an event rather than a process retards the ability of a peace process to enhance trust. That antagonists emerging from a civil war mistrust each other is unsurprising. It may be entirely rational to doubt the *bona fides* and good intentions of opponents and to respect or implement those parts of an accord likely to bring advantages to the in-group. Yet, to be sustained and widely shared and enjoyed, a peace must have mutual and voluntary aspects. Trust building is very much a long-term process, requiring organic development based on experience and observed evidence. While some members of elites may be able to develop trust through cooperation in the peace process, it may be more difficult to encourage more widespread trust. Trust often develops as a by-product of other social processes such as cooperation over economic issues or reconstruction efforts.

Proposition three

Peace process participants need to anticipate the
dangers of a stalled peace

A stalled peace process or peace accord holds many advantages, particularly if antagonists opt to hold the peace process in suspended animation rather than return to violent conflict. Its chief advantage is a respite from violence and the attendant dislocation. A stalled peace can be comfortable: communities can return to some sort of normality, relief and reconstruction assistance can make appreciable differences to lives and many of the advantages gained during the peace process can be maintained. Yet, there is a very real danger that the respite offered by a stalled peace is mistaken for a more positive and sustainable version of peace. In a sense, the advantages of a negative peace may offer antagonists disincentives to pursue a positive peace.

While the negative peace of a stalled peace accord may offer stability, it may not facilitate reconciliation between formerly warring communities or address the grievances contributing to the conflict. A stalled peace may affirm battlefield gains and losses, and freeze the physical separation of communities. Behind the dividing lines, unflattering myths of the out-group may be perpetuated, invented or embellished, thus prolonging conflict. The lack of momentum and political activity associated with a stalled peace process or peace accord is also likely to help dispel public optimism that the peace process is a vehicle capable of delivering real change. In other words, a stalled peace process can lower the bar of what elites and publics think is possible and condemn the peace process to permanent impermanence. Violence may also seep into the vacuum of political inactivity in frozen peace situations. This was certainly the case in Kosovo and Northern Ireland in which the political agenda was driven by security issues and crises in the absence of political momentum. The result was a sapping of public confidence in the peace. It may be the case that international actors can play a useful role in alerting local elites and communities to the dangers of a frozen peace and the policy stances that lead to a frozen peace. This might involve encouraging antagonists and their support communities out of the comfort zone of a stalled peace and creating incentives for the investigation of transformative peace.

Proposition four

It is important to interrogate the concept of peace during peace processes

At first glance conceptualising peace may seem like a luxury open only to those far-removed from the immediacy of war-torn societies. It may seem naïve to recommend 'navel-gazing' at a time of crisis. Yet, if peace is reduced to a series of technical, and at times ephemeral, tasks then it risks delivering a technocratic peace that fails to deal with many of the perceptual and affective issues that underlie conflict. By conceptualising peace beyond the proximate goals of surviving, achieving a victory over the enemy or implementing the provisions of the peace accord, antagonists and inhabitants in a war-torn society may be encouraged to envisage peace as a more holistic process that has a life beyond the immediate crisis. The critical peace assessment methodology outlined in Chapter 4 proposes 'imagining peace' as a key part of any peace process and the rejuvenation of a stalled or dysfunctional peace accord.

Stalled peace processes and peace accords encourage the view that negative peace equates to peace. The acculturation of antagonists and inhabitants in post-civil war societies to the pacific stalemate of a stalled peace accord lowers the bar of optimism on what is achievable via the peace process. Imagining peace encourages peace process participants to see peace in its own right rather than as a commodity that can only be viewed in the context of the conflict or the latest crisis to befall the peace accord. It may also encourage inhabitants in a war-torn society to make connections between peace and their social and economic conditions, thus enhancing the concept of peace beyond purely political, constitutional or security issues. The entreaty to interrogate the concept of peace also serves to challenge the hegemonic ambitions of western peacemaking models. By reflecting on the nature of peace – as an idea and practice – recipients of peace processes may be able to identify and remedy the shortcomings of the liberal democratic peace template approach.

Proposition five

Public expectations require careful management

A recurring feature of many peace processes and post-peace accord situations has been the dissipation of public faith in the ability of the process or accord to deliver meaningful or lasting change. Initial public optimism is understandable and often reflects relief from violence and the deprivations of war. In some cases, a peace process or peace accord may offer the partial or full achievement of a long-standing political goal: for example, the formal recognition of a group or state as legitimate, or the granting of independence or autonomy. In other cases, a peace process or accord may facilitate the return of prisoners, the free movement of people, the resumption of trade and the reconstruction of war-damaged infrastructure, all of which may raise public morale. Many such benefits may be concentrated in the early phase of the peace process or come into effect soon after a peace accord is agreed. Such momentum may be difficult to sustain. The encountering of difficulties is to be expected in a peace process, but these may have a cumulative quality, building up to a sense that the peace accord demands concessions but delivers little.

Important in the management of public expectations is the reining in of extravagant promises by political leaders. This applies both within and without the conflict society. Political leaders may emphasise the prospects of peace initiatives in order to maximise public and political support for that initiative. If electoral processes are involved in the peace process or accord, political leaders may be tempted to inflate the potential of peace. The result of such exaggerations may be a precipitous decline in support for the peace process or accord when it becomes evident that it is incapable of delivering rapid or widespread benefits. Post-peace accord situations are likely to include winners and losers, with 'power-holders' and their constituencies having to make concessions (whether tangible or symbolic) as a price to end violence by 'power-seekers'. To sell any peace process or peace accord as a cost-free endeavour is folly. More sensibly, political leaders can alert constituents to potential pitfalls and compromises but place these in a context of overall gain. A key problem lies in the perceptual differential between the compromises made by each side. While one side may see its own concessions as major and painful, these may be interpreted with less generosity by the other side. Political leaders, and international actors, can play a key role in moderating expectations and alerting all parties to mutually shared costs and benefits.

Proposition six

Post-war economies require protection

Such a proposal goes against the grain of the neo-liberal 'consensus' in which marketisation is a key part of post-war reconstruction. Moreover, the benefits of the market, allied with liberalism, are presumed to offer protection against slippage back into civil war whereby rational actors are loathe to trade the benefits of economic growth for a return to war. Yet, peace processes and peace accords have regularly heralded a decline in living standards, employment and economic growth. While some post-civil war societies do experience a peace dividend, the benefits are rarely perceived to be shared equitably. Third party donors and IFIs often lay down tough market reform conditions in return for economic assistance. The result may be the formalisation of the economy where the informal market had reigned, the sacking of government employees as part of austerity packages and the penetration of the post-war economy by external suppliers before local suppliers can reconstruct their capacity. Many inhabitants in post-war societies may experience a peace deficit and associate peace with a decline in their standard of living. While post-war economies may receive an initial boost in the form of aid and loans, they will not be insulated from the predations of the global economy in which capital follows the path of greatest reward.

In order to support peace and bolster the confidence of the pro-peace accord constituency, post-war economies require respite from the full effects of the open market. This may come in the form of time-limited trade protection, import controls and debt relief and forgiveness. Post-war reconstruction is expensive, time-consuming and often relies on the public direction of funding. Thus, it is firmly out of sympathy with dominant economic doctrine. The IMF, World Bank and their principal backers have thus far failed to understand fully the impact of the market in the erosion of the bridging social capital required to hold post-civil war societies together. Neo-autarky is not possible, yet the economic and social costs of the Washington 'consensus' impose intolerable burdens on post-civil war states. The most realistic means to secure economic protection is through bilateral and multilateral agreements with supportive states. There is also an urgent need to review the *ad hoc* nature of international economic responses to peace accords. Some contexts are greeted with donor conferences and relatively generous reconstruction packages. Other post-civil war contexts receive little. A twenty-first century rolling Marshall Plan for post-war societies could attempt to guarantee a minimum level of aid, investment and protection for *all* societies emerging from civil war. Massive aid differentials whereby Bosnia or Northern Ireland received immensely more reconstruction aid (per capita) than Rwanda or Liberia are indefensible.

A fundamental issue is the need for post-war reconstruction and economic activity to be conducted in the service of peace. The fixation on positive economic indicators shown by IFIs may be of limited value if communal tensions are left unaddressed or if conflict-contributing underdevelopment persists. Because of its context, post-civil war economic recovery is often archly political (e.g., involving the co-option of recalcitrant elements via economic incentives) and thus requires market-distorting incentives.

Proposition seven

Third party interventions require sensitivity to traditional and indigenous conceptions of peace and methods of peacemaking

The liberal democratic peace model encourages a template or conveyor belt approach to peacemaking in which similar peacemaking methods are employed in different locations. In many cases, this reflects 'best practice' or efforts by international sponsors of peace processes and accords to replicate success in one location. There is a danger, however, that the standardisation of peacemaking squeezes the space for traditional or indigenous approaches to peacemaking. The technocratic approach to peacemaking may overlook that many societies in the midst of civil wars have long traditions of indigenous peacemaking embedded in cultural practice. Although such peacemaking methods may have broken down, they often emphasise sustainability, ecological balance and the importance of relationships. Their emphasis on ritual and tradition may mean that they sit uncomfortably with the more technocratic approach to peacemaking often found in internationally sponsored peace initiatives.

Traditional or indigenous approaches to peacemaking may be inappropriate for complex conflicts involving multiple sets of antagonists and in which dislocation has been so extensive as to erode respect for the culture that sustains traditional peacemaking. Yet, in many post-peace accord situations, there is a profound and debilitating disconnection between the national and elite levels. A peace that has been agreed at the elite level may seem remote at the local level. One way of bridging this gap is for the accommodation of local and traditional approaches to peacemaking within the liberal democratic peacemaking framework. Thus, a nationally agreed peace accord could have the flexibility to acknowledge and encourage local variations on some issues and traditional rituals and practices to be involved in the implementation process.

Traditional peacemaking can perhaps make its greatest contribution at the affective level, a key blind spot in more technocratic versions of peace. Traditional reconciliation ceremonies (such as the *agaweed* in Darfur or the *mato oput* in northern Uganda) may address the building of inter-group relationships needed to sustain and deepen a peace. Western-sponsored or inspired peace processes and accords may be unable to connect with local belief systems, language and practice. The deeply embedded, almost intuitive, nature of much cultural practice means that it may not always be obvious to third parties. As a result, third parties must tread with care and be prepared to deviate from the western script.

Proposition eight

Peace needs to be broadly owned

As the last proposition noted, many peace processes and accords are creatures of national and international elites. Local constituencies may feel little ownership of the peace process or accord. This is often a function of the secrecy required to foster peace initiatives, the technical skills required when discussing certain issues and the need to restrict any talks process to manageable proportions. Yet, if there is a disconnection between the elite guardians and supposed recipients of the peace accord, then there is a real danger that peace will wither. Widespread ownership of a peace process or accord cannot be created. Instead, incentive structures are required to encourage and sustain wider involvement in peacemaking through, for example, referendums, consultation processes, public participation in reconstruction activities and serious attempts to broaden the chief advocates of peace beyond the established civil society and metropolitan elites. The January 2005 Sudanese peace accord between the government and the Sudanese People's Liberation Movement points towards possible best practice in that both sides engaged in an extensive post-accord 'education programme' to appraise constituents of the implications of the accord.

A key problem in deeply divided societies emerging from civil war is a differential connection to the peace accord, with different communities holding widely varying interpretations of the same accord. While one community may interpret the accord as 'fair' and distributing benefits and concessions evenly, others may see it as a train of concessions (e.g., Kosovo or Northern Ireland). This may require a revision of the peace accord so that the balance of gains and concessions is more evenly distributed or may require preparatory work by political and local leaders to manage perceptions and interpretations of the accord.

Proposition nine

Peace accords have more chance of delivering success if external third parties act as servants rather than masters of the peace

There can be little doubt of the added value that third parties have brought to some peace processes and accords. Third parties have provided the security, assistance and inspiration which have allowed peace initiatives to blossom into peace processes and accords capable of delivering real change. Yet, there is a key difference between an internationally led and an internationally supported peace process and accord. In the former, the third party or parties may be overbearing, directing rather than encouraging the peace process. Under such circumstances, individuals and groups in the post-civil war society may have difficulty in making any meaningful connection with the peace accord.

Third parties can have different influences at different stages of the peacemaking process. It may be that their inspiration, technical expertise or resources are called for at some moments more than others. This points to the need for sensitivity in third party intervention: a need to guard against learned helplessness or dependency on the part of local peace process participants; a need to recognise that all post-civil war states do not need to be recreated in the mould of western states and an acknowledgement that the more a peace process is driven by external parties then the less likely it is to owned by local parties.

Proposition ten

Antagonists and their constituents have the right to reject a bad peace

In many peace processes (e.g., Bosnia-Herzegovina, Angola, Sudan and Northern Ireland), third parties have used their full repertoire of coercion to browbeat antagonists into engaging with a peace initiative or endorsing a peace accord. In most cases, the motivations of the third parties are benign. They depend, however, on entirely uncritical views of peace. Such is the strength of the pro-peace international hegemony in many cases that parties who question or oppose the peace initiative or accord are painted as anti-peace or pro-war. Yet local antagonists may have very good reasons for rejecting a peace process or accord more popular in London, New York or Washington than in the society attempting to extricate itself from civil war. While external coercion can nudge reluctant parties towards the negotiating table, a peace stemming from coercion or imposition is unlikely to be enjoyed. Peace under duress and peace that leads to a lowering of living standards is unlikely to be self-sustaining or long-lasting. For such a proposition to become realisable, it requires key elements in the international community to internalise the fallibility of their approach to peacemaking.

Concluding discussion

The starting point for the vast majority of academic works on peace is conflict. This work differs from many other studies of contemporary peacemaking by identifying peace as its point of departure. Serious thinking on the nature and meaning of peace is the ghost at the academic banquet of contemporary peace and conflict studies. In the policy world, serious thinking on peace is not even afforded a spectral presence. Yet, the political, economic, institutional and moral energy expended in the name of peace is enormous. This book has defined peace as the facilitation of non-exploitative, sustainable and inclusive social relationships free from direct and indirect violence and the threat of such violence. Such a situation and state of mind is far-removed from the grudging co-existence that passes for peace in many societies experiencing stalled peace processes and peace accords. Not only is such a holistic peace not present (as has been argued throughout this book), the very structure of the liberal democratic peace means that the chances of inclusive and sustainable peace are remote. The main flaws in the currently dominant 'problem-solving' approach to peacemaking are systemic. The identification of the liberal democratic peace as the chief organising idea and operating system behind internationally supported peace interventions is crucial to our understanding of the nature and failings of contemporary peacemaking. Once the liberal democratic peace has been identified and its increasing dominance noted, observers can move on to chart trends in this method of peacemaking, note variations in its intensity and application, and develop strategies to engage with it and challenge its more predatory and harmful features.

Importantly, this work has no ambitions to be an unremitting counsel of doom. The post-Cold War period has witnessed significant levels of peace-support activities. Some of these activities have exacerbated problems, while others have been of dubious relevance. Many others, however, have made positive differences to the quality of life of millions of people in societies emerging from civil war. They have provided security and certainty, facilitated social and physical reconstruction, and have helped institute liberating reforms. While much of this added value is due to orthodox peace-support interventions, much of it is also due to coping and survival mechanisms in war-torn societies and to non-orthodox peace-support activities (often employing traditional and indigenous approaches to peacemaking). As such, this latter category of activities is often overlooked or dismissed as being local and small scale. Yet, it is at the local level that war and peace are experienced. One of the key inabilities of the liberal democratic peace model is to translate its society-wide pacific ambitions to the local level. This provides enormous opportunities to local actors to construct and manage their own versions of peace and inter-group cooperation.

The key concluding point to make is to underline the importance of adopting a critical approach in relation to contemporary peacemaking. The opening quotation from Chapter 1 (The Romans brought devastation, but they called it peace) reminds us that the banner of peace can cover a multitude of sins. The regularity with which contemporary peace accords and peacemaking processes result in situations that fall far short of the inclusive or holistic peace that deals with direct and indirect violence demands that we reappraise the meaning that we attach to the word 'peace'. More specifically, there is room for the peace studies community to assume a more assertive role in the appropriation and application of the term. This assertiveness does not have to restrict itself to university campuses, nor should it linger with the conceit of purely theoretical debate. The meaning and use of the term peace has direct application and relevance to policy debates. The onus is on the peace studies community to alert the policymaking community to that application and relevance.

Notes

Introduction

1. 'Students protest over death, tension in Jaffna', www. tamilnet.com (4 March 2005) and author observations of the militarism in May 2005; 'Suicide and other bombing attacks in Israel since the signing of the Declaration of Principles (Sept 1993)', Israel Ministry of Foreign Affairs website, *www.mfa.gov.il/MFA*; 'Protestant family insist they won't be forced out of home', *News Letter* (14 July 2005) and 'Living as prisoners in their own homes', *Irish Times* (17 June 2005); Oxfam Community Aid Abroad, *Two Years On … What Future for anIndependent East Timor?* (Victoria: Oxfam Community Aid Abroad, 2004), p. 6 and 'The road to recovery', *Guardian* (28 December 2004).
2. P. du Toit, *South Africa's Brittle Peace: The Problem of Post-settlement Violence* (Basingstoke: Palgrave, 2001); T. Debiel and A. Klein, *Fragile Peace: State Failure, Violence and Development in Crisis Regions* (New York: Zed Books, 2002); C. Crocker, F.O. Hampson and P. Aall (eds) *Turbulent Peace: The Challenges of Managing International Conflict* (Washington, DC: United States Institute of Peace Press, 2001); B. Rowan, *The Armed Peace: Life and Death after the Ceasefires* (Edinburgh: Mainstream Publishing, 2004); D. McKittrick, *The Nervous Peace* (Belfast: Blackstaff, 1996).
3. H. Schmid, 'Peace Research and Politics', *Journal of Peace Research*, 5, 3 (1968) pp. 217–32.
4. S. Stedman, 'Policy Implications', in S. Stedman, D. Rothchild and E. Cousens (eds) *Ending Civil Wars: The Implementation of Peace Agreements* (Boulder, CO: Lynne Rienner, 2002) pp. 633–71 at p. 664.
5. Emphasis added. R. Cooper and M. Berdal, 'Outside Intervention in Ethnic Conflict', in M. Brown (ed.) *Ethnic Conflict and International Security* (Princeton, NJ: Princeton University Press, 1993) pp. 181–205 at p. 181.

1 Peace

1. Testifying to the value of peace as a commercial brand, a software package (a customer information system for the utility industry) has been named after peace: www.peace.com.
2. For example, the weighty and very useful *Turbulent Peace* compendium from the United States Institute of Peace has contributions from over fifty authors, yet none of them conceptualise peace. C.A. Crocker, F.O. Hampson and P. Aall (eds) *Turbulent Peace: The Challenges of Managing International Conflict* (Washington, DC: United States Institute of Peace Press, 2001).
3. Accounts of the Israeli–Palestinian peace process can be found in E. Said, *The End of the Peace Process: Oslo and After* (London: Granta, 2002); G. Usher, *Dispatches from Palestine: The Rise and Fall of the Oslo Peace Process* (London: Pluto, 1999) and

G.R. Watson, *The Oslo Accords: International law and the Israeli-Palestinian Peace Agreements* (Oxford: Oxford University Press, 2000).

4. G. Sartori, 'Concept misinformation in comparative politics', *American Political Science Review*, 64, 4 (1970), pp. 1033–53 at p. 1035.

5. H. Schmid, 'Peace research and politics', *Journal of Peace Research*, 5, 3 (1968), pp. 217–232.

6. Q. Skinner, 'Meaning and understanding in the history of ideas', *History and Theory: Studies in the Philosophy of History*, 8, 1 (1969), pp. 3–53 at p. 52.

7. *Ibid.*, pp. 52–3.

8. E. Luttwak, 'The curse of inconclusive intervention', in Crocker, Hampson and Aall (eds) *op. cit.*, pp. 265–72 at p. 265.

9. 'Al Qaeda issues new threat', www. cnn.com (18 November 2002).

10. P. Bourdieu, *Language and Symbolic Power* (Cambridge: Polity, 1992) p. 105.

11. S. Bailey, *Peace is a Process* (London: Quaker Home Service, 1993) and E. Adler, 'Condition(s) of peace', *Review of International Studies*, 24 (1998) pp. 165–91 at p. 168.

12. Many authors are careful to distinguish between conflict resolution and conflict transformation, with the latter paying greater attention to unjust social relationships in addition to direct violence. See, H. Miall, O. Ramsbotham and T. Woodhouse, *Contemporary Conflict Resolution: The Prevention, Management and Transformation of Deadly Conflicts* (Cambridge: Polity, 2000) p. 21.

13. M. Gopin, 'What do I need to know about religion and conflict?', in J.P. Lederach and J.M. Jenner (eds) *A Handbook of International Peacebuilding* (San Francisco, CA: Jossey Bass, 2002) pp. 107–13 at pp. 110–11.

14. R.S. Appleby, *The Ambivalence of the Sacred: Religion, Violence and Reconciliation* (Lanham, MD: Rowman & Littlefield, 2000) p. 284.

15. *Ibid.*, pp. 207–44. See also C. Mitchell, 'Mennonite Approaches to Peace and Conflict Resolution', in C. Sampson and J.P. Lederach (eds) *From the Ground Up: Mennonite Contributions to International Peacebuilding* (Oxford: Oxford University Press, 2000) pp. 218–32.

16. C. McKeogh, *Innocent Civilians: The Morality of Killing in War* (Basingstoke: Palgrave, 2002) p. 5. H. Slim questions the idea of the civilian in 'Why protect civilians? Innocence, immunity and enmity in war', *International Affairs*, 79, 3 (2003) pp. 481–501.

17. Matter of fact accounts of humans killing other humans retain a shock value on account of their lack of empathy. See, for example, the diary extract from a Gestapo officer, Felix Landau, detailed to execute Polish civilians during the Second World War, 'Diary of Blutordenstrager Felix Landau, 12 July 1941', in R.J. Aldrich (ed.) *Witness to War: Diaries of the Second World War in Europe and the Middle East* (London: Corgi, 2005) pp. 315–16.

18. See US Defense Secretary D. Rumsfeld's references to the Geneva Convention when US troops were captured by Iraqi forces in March 2003. Transcript of 'Secretary Rumsfeld interview with Bob Schieffer and David Martin', CBS *Face the Nation* (23 March 2003) www. defenselink.mil.

19. J.H. Yoder, *When War is Unjust: Being Honest in Just War Thinking* (New York: Orbis, 1996) pp. 8–11 and M. Howard, *War in European History* (Oxford: Oxford University Press, 1976) p. 5.

20. R.W. Dyson, *Aquinas: Political writings* (Cambridge: Cambridge University Press, 2002) pp. xxxii–xxxiv.

21. I.L. Horowitz, *War and Peace in Contemporary Social and Philosophical Theory* 2nd edn. (London: Souvenir Press, 1973) p. 24. See also M. Howard, *War and the Liberal Conscience* (London: Temple Smith, 1978) p. 16.

22. The notions of negative peace (a mere cessation of direct violence) and positive peace (a more holistic version of peace cognisant of equity, justice and the need to deal with both direct and indirect violence) are associated with Johan Galtung.

23. Background on civil war in the Democratic Republic of Congo can be found in T. Trefon (ed.) *Reinventing Order in the Congo: How People Respond to State Failure in Kinshasa* (London: Zed Books, 2004) and G. Prunier, *From Genocide to Continental War: The Congo Conflict and the Crisis of Contemporary Africa* (London: Hurst, 2005).

24. D. Anand discusses the social construction of 'the other' in 'The violence of security: Hindu nationalism and the politics of representing "the Muslim" as a danger', *The Round Table: The Commonwealth Journal of International Affairs*, 94, 379 (2005) pp. 203–15.

25. See J. Baudrillard's marvellously caustic *The Gulf War Did Not Take Place* (Indianapolis, IN: Indiana University Press, 1995) pp. 29–59. See also, J. Der Derain, 'Virtuous war/virtual theory', *International Affairs*, 76, 4 (2000) pp. 771–88.

26. R. McNamara in the documentary movie *Fog of War*, directed by E. Morris (Los Angeles: Sony, 2004).

27. On peacemaking in traditional societies see A.P. Vayada, *War in Ecological Perspective: Persistence, Change and Adaptive Processes in Three Oceanian Societies* (New York: Plenum Press, 1976) and R.M. Keesing, *Custom and Confrontation: The Kwaio Struggle for Cultural Autonomy* (Chicago, IL: University of Chicago Press, 1992).

28. R.G. O'Connor, 'Victory in modern war', *Journal of Peace Research*, 6, 4 (1969) pp. 367–84 at p. 380.

29. See A.P. Vayada, *Maori Warfare* (Wellington: Reed, 1960) and J. Evans (ed.) *Elsdon Best: Notes on the Art of War* (Auckland: Reed, 2001).

30. See, for example, speeches by President G.W. Bush commending US troops in their efforts to 'promote peace', 'Speech by President George Bush, Fort Bragg, North Carolina' (26 May 2005) and 'Remarks by the President to Military Personnel at Macdill Air Force Base, Tampa, Florida', (16 June 2004) both from www.whitehouse.gov.

31. Adler, *op. cit.*, p. 165.

32. U. Heyn, *Peacemaking in Medieval Europe: A Historical and Bibliographical Guide* (Claremont, CA: Regina Books, 1997) p. 17.

33. The persistent ethical dilemmas associated with war, sovereignty and humanitarianism mean that Just War theory is served by an excellent and constantly updated literature. Modern classics on the subject include: M. Walzer, *Just and Unjust Wars: A Moral Argument with Historical Illustrations* (New York: Basic Books, 1992); J.B. Elsthtain (ed.) *Just War Theory* (Oxford: Blackwell, 1992) and Y. Melzer, *Concepts of Just War* (Leyden: A.W. Sijthoff, 1975).

34. Howard, *op. cit.*, p. 5.

35. *Ibid.*

36. See, for example, N. Hunter, 'Rethinking pacifism: the Quakers' dilemma in a time of war', *The American Prospect*, 12, 21 (2001), online edition, no

pagination; M. Evans (ed.) *Just War Theory: A Reappraisal* (Edinburgh: Edinburgh University Press) and P. Lawler, 'The "good war" after September 11', *Government and Opposition*, 37, 2 (2002) pp. 151–72.

37. K. Boulding, *Stable Peace* (Austin, TX: University of Texas Press, 1978) p. 19.
38. D. Scott, *Ask that Mountain: The Story of Parihaka* (Auckland: Reed/Southern Cross, 1994).
39. For earlier schemes for pacific unions see V. Vaněček, *The Universal Peace Organization of King George of Bohemia: A Fifteenth Century Plan for World Peace 1462–1464* (Prague: Publishing House of the Czechoslovak Academy of Sciences, 1964), Eméric Crucé's 1623 proposal for a universal arbitration system (mentioned in M. Howard, *op. cit.*, p. 19) and of course Immanuel Kant's, *Perpetual Peace* (New York: Macmillan, 1957).
40. Schmid, *op. cit.*, p. 217.
41. *Ibid.*, p. 229.

2   Liberal democratic peace

1. Bellamy and colleagues stress how the 'liberal-democratic peace' has shaped contemporary UN peacekeeping, A. Bellamy, P. Williams and S. Griffin, *Understanding Peacekeeping* (Cambridge: Polity, 2001) pp. 26–31.
2. R. Muggah, 'No magic bullet: a critical perspective on disarmament, demobilization and reintegration (DDR) and weapons reduction in post-conflict contexts', *The Round Table: The Commonwealth Journal of International Affairs*, 94, 379 (2005) pp. 239–52 at p. 242.
3. J. Darby, 'Borrowing and lending in peace processes' in J. Darby and R. Mac Ginty (eds) *Contemporary Peacemaking: Conflict, Violence and Peace Processes* (Basingstoke: Palgrave Macmillan, 2003) pp. 245–55 and A. Guelke, 'The Politics of Imitation: The Role of Comparison in Peace Processes', in A. Guelke (ed.) *Democracy and Ethnic Conflict: Advancing Peace in a Deeply Divided Society* (Basingstoke: Palgrave Macmillan, 2004) pp. 168–84.
4. The term 'the invention of peace' comes from M. Howard, *The Invention of Peace: Reflections on War and International Order* (New Haven, CT: Yale University Press, 2000).
5. M. Ignatieff, *Empire Lite: Nation-building in Bosnia, Kosovo and Afghanistan* (London: Vintage, 2003) p. 7.
6. Oliver Richmond uses the term 'liberal peace' in his excellent *The Transformation of Peace: Peace as Governance in Contemporary Conflict Endings* (Basingstoke: Palgrave, 2006).
7. Amy Chua describes the US view of democracy in *World on Fire: How Exporting Free Market Democracy Breeds Ethnic Hatred and Global Instability* (London: Heinemann, 2004) pp. 274–5.
8. The rarity of international war can be tracked in Wallenstein and colleague's annual conflict survey contributions to the *Journal of Peace Research*.
9. For critical views of international peace-support intervention in Bosnia-Herzegovina, see D. Chandler, *Bosnia: Faking Democracy after Dayton* (London: Pluto, 1999) and E.M. Cousens, 'From Missed Opportunities to Over-Compensation: implementing the Dayton Agreement in Bosnia', in S.J. Stedman, D. Rothchild and E.M. Cousens (eds) *Ending Civil Wars: The*

Implementation of Peace Agreements (Boulder, CO: Lynne Rienner, 2002) pp. 531–66.

10. M. Howard, *War in European History* (Oxford: Oxford University Press, 1976) pp. 5–19.

11. U. Heyn, *Peacemaking in Medieval Europe: A Historical and Bibliographical Guide* (Claremont, CA: Regina Books, 1997) p. 22.

12. Howard, *op. cit.*, p. 6.

13. K. Petkov, *The Kiss of Peace: Ritual, Self, and Society in the High and Late Medieval West* (Leiden: Brill, 2003) p. 25.

14. Although venerated by some commentators, others were less complimentary to Wilson. Harold Nicolson referred to the 'slowness of the President's own mental processes' at the Versailles peace talks in H. Nicolson, *Peacemaking 1919* (London: Constable, 1944) p. 72. A more sympathetic portrait is provided by E.J. Dillon, *The Inside Story of the Peace Conference* (New York: Harper, 1920) pp. 89–116. See also R. Paris, 'Wilson's Ghost: The Faulty Assumptions of Postconflict Peacebuilding', in C.A. Crocker, F.O. Hampson and P. Aall (eds) *Turbulent Peace: The Challenges of Managing International Conflict* (Washington, DC: United States Institute of Peace Press, 2001) pp. 765–84.

15. Discussion of Wilson's vision and reactions to it can be found in A. Williams, *Failed Imagination? New World Orders of The Twentieth Century* (Manchester: Manchester University Press, 1998) pp. 19–78.

16. Speech delivered by President Woodrow Wilson to a Joint Session of Congress 8 January 1918. Point 14.

17. *Ibid.*

18. *Ibid.*, Point 3.

19. Address by President Woodrow Wilson to Sixty-Fifth Congress, 1st Session, Senate Document No. 5, 2 April 1917.

20. H. Kissinger, *Diplomacy* (New York: Simon & Schuster, 1994) p. 226–7.

21. A. Williams, 'Post-war reconstruction before World War Two', paper presented at the Department of Politics seminar series, University of York (14 November 2003).

22. For commentary on pessimistic accounts of the League's capability to deal with international crises, see D. Birn, *The League of Nations Union, 1918–1945* (Oxford: Clarendon, 1981) pp. 226–9.

23. S. Marks, *The Illusion of Peace: International Relations in Europe 1918–1933* (London: Macmillan, 1976).

24. The text of the Atlantic Charter can be accessed at www.usinfo.state.gov.

25. Preamble of the Charter of the United Nations.

26. Winston Churchill intended that the Atlantic Charter would only apply to western European states, leaving Eastern and Central Europe to a Soviet fate.

27. Extract from the 'Truman Doctrine' cited in D. Acheson, *Present at the Creation: My Years in the State Department* (New York: W.W. Norton, 1969) p. 222.

28. State of the Union Address by President Ronald Reagan to a Joint Session of Congress (4 February 1986).

29. Cited in the movie *Muhammad Ali – When We Were Kings* (Los Angeles, CA: Universal Pictures, 2001). For similar sentiments see '*The Black Scholar* interviews Muhammad Ali', in G. Early (ed.) *The Muhammad Ali Reader* (New York: Rob Weisbach Books, 1998) pp. 83–89.

30. M. Cox, 'Rethinking the end of the Cold War', *Review of International Studies*, 20 (1994), pp. 187–200.

31. M. Mandelbaum, *The Ideas that Conquered the World: Peace, Democracy and Free Markets in the Twenty-First Century* (New York: PublicAffairs, 2002) p. 11.

32. *Ibid.*, p. 40.

33. F. Fukuyama, 'The end of history?' *The National Interest*, (Summer 1989) pp. 3–18 at p. 4. See also, J.L. Gaddis, *The United States and the End of the Cold War: Implications, Reconsiderations, Provocations* (Oxford: Oxford University Press, 1992) pp. 168–92 and Mandelbaum, *op. cit.*, p. 47.

34. M. Doyle, 'Liberalism and world politics', *American Political Science Review*, 80, 4 (1980) pp. 1151–69.

35. Typical of this genre are K. DeRouen and S. Goldfinch, 'Putting the numbers to work: Implications for violence prevention', *Journal of Peace Research*, 41, 1 (2005) pp. 27–45 and M. Benson, 'Dyadic hostility and the ties that bind: state-to-state versus state-to-system security and economic relationships', *Journal of Peace Research*, 41, 6 (2004) pp. 659–76.

36. E.A. Henderson, *Democracy and War: The End of an Illusion?* (Boulder, CO: Lynne Rienner, 2002) p. 2.

37. B. Boutros-Ghali, *An Agenda for Peace: Preventive Diplomacy, Peacemaking and Peace-Keeping* (New York: United Nations, 1992) p. 35.

38. S.M. Lynne Jones, 'Preface', in M.E. Brown, O.R. Coté, S.M. Lynne Jones and S.E. Miller (eds) *Debating the Democratic Peace* (Cambridge, MA: MIT Press, 1996) pp. ix–xxxiii.

39. J.M. Owen, 'How liberalism produces democratic peace', in M.E. Brown, O.R. Coté Jr., S.M. Lynn Jones and S.E. Miller (eds) *Debating the Democratic Peace* (Cambridge, MA: MIT Press, 1996) pp. 116–54 at p. 117.

40. *Ibid.*, p. 124.

41. J. Rawls, *The Law of Peoples* (Cambridge, MA: Harvard University Press, 1999) pp. 44–5.

42. Owen, *op. cit.*, p. 138.

43. Henderson, *op. cit.*, p. 146.

44. See M. Cox, G.J. Ikenberry and T. Inoguchi (eds) *American Democracy Promotion: Impulses, Strategies and Impacts* (New York: Oxford University Press, 2000).

45. A. Mack, 'Civil war: academic research and the policy community', *Journal of Peace Research*, 39, 5 (2002) pp. 515–25 at p. 516.

46. R. Smith, 'The unfinished tasks of liberalism', in B. Yack (ed.) *Liberalism without Illusions: Essays on Liberal Theory and The Political Vision of Judith N. Shklar* (Chicago, IL: Chicago University Press, 1996) pp. 241–62 at pp. 241–2.

47. W. Kymlicka provides an excellent discussion of the tension between rights for the individual and the group in *Multicultural Citizenship* (Oxford: Clarendon Press, 1995) pp. 39–48.

48. J. MacMillan, *On Liberal Peace: Democracy, War and the International Order* (London: I.B. Taurus, 1998) p. 13.

49. Owen, *op. cit.*, p. 117.

50. Mandelbaum, *op. cit.*, p. 11. Mandelbaum's argument that the legitimacy of the market has never been so widely accepted is contested by opponents of globalisation. See, for example, A. Callinicos, *Against the Third Way* (Cambridge: Polity, 2001) pp. 28–43.

51. Mandelbaum, *op cit.*, p. 265.
52. *Ibid.*, p. 295.
53. *Ibid.*, p. 297.
54. R. Falk, 'Global Civil Society and the Democratic Prospect', in B. Holden (ed.) *Global Democracy: Key Debates* (London: Routledge, 2000) pp. 162–78 at p. 171.
55. R. Sandbrook, *Closing the Circle: Democratization and Development in Africa* (London: Zed Books, 2000) p. 11.
56. G. Soros, *The Bubble of American Supremacy: Correcting the Misuses of American Power* (London: Weidenfeld & Nicolson, 2004) p. 10.
57. This was certainly the author's impression during observation of UN sponsored women's empowerment schemes in Jordan, December 2004.
58. R. England, 'Market forces can help fight AIDS', *Financial Times*, 12 July 2004.
59. K. Good, *The Liberal Model and Africa* (Basingstoke: Palgrave, 2002) p. 71.
60. *Ibid.*, pp. 75–88.
61. See examples in G. Kemp and D. Fry (eds) *Keeping the Peace: Conflict Resolution and Peaceful Societies around the World* (New York: Routledge, 2004).
62. Chua, *op. cit.*
63. A. Karatnycky, 'Freedom in the world 2003: Liberty's expansion in a turbulent world – thirty years of the survey of freedom', www.freedomhouse.org.
64. Sandbrook, *op. cit.*, p. 6.
65. Burnell provides an account of the expansion of democracy assistance in the 1990s in P. Burnell, 'Democracy Assistance: Origins and Organizations', in P. Burnell (ed.) *Democracy Assistance: International Cooperation for Democratization* (London: Frank Cass, 2000) pp. 34–64 at pp. 39–44.
66. T. D. Sisk, 'Elections – Conflict Management in Africa: Conclusions and Recommendations', in T.D. Sisk and A. Reynolds, *Elections and Conflict Management in Africa* (Washington, DC: United States Institute of Peace Press, 1998) p. 147.
67. M. Bratton, 'Second Elections in Africa', in L. Diamond and M.F. Plattner (eds) *Democratization in Africa* (Baltimore, MD: The Johns Hopkins University Press, 1999) pp. 18–33 at p. 19.
68. S. Bastian and R. Luckham, 'Introduction: Can Democracy be Designed?', in Bastian and Luckham (eds) *Can Democracy be Designed? The Politics of Institutional Choice in Conflict-Torn Societies* (London: Zed Books, 2003) pp. 1–13 at p. 1.
69. F. B. Adamson, 'International Democracy Assistance in Uzbekistan and Kyrgyzstan', in S.E. Mendelson and J.K. Glenn (eds) *The Power and Limits of NGOs: A Critical Look at Building Democracy in Eastern Europe and Eurasia* (New York: Columbia University Press, 2002) pp. 177–206 at p. 178.
70. *Ibid.*, p. 178.
71. M.A.M. Salih, *African Democracies and African Politics* (London: Pluto, 2001) p. 3.
72. For conceptual and case study coverage of this issue see D. Rapport and L. Weinberg (eds) *The Democratic Experience and Political Violence* (London: Frank Cass, 2001). See also A. Mack, S. Gates and K. Strøm, 'Democratic institutions: governance and civil war', concept paper for Democratic Institutions Workshop, 7–9 June 2004, Bellagio, Italy.
73. B. Reilly, 'Electoral systems for divided societies', *Journal of Democracy*, 13, 2 (2002) pp. 156–70 and L. Garber and K. Kumar, 'What have we learned

about post-conflict elections?', *New England Journal of Public Policy*, 14, 1 (1998) pp. 25–43.

74. J. Haynes, *Democracy in the Developing World: Africa, Asia, Latin America and the Middle East* (Cambridge: Polity, 2001) pp. 43–5.

75. Adamson, *op. cit.*, p. 200.

76. V.P. Gagnon Jr, 'International NGOs in Bosnia-Herzegovina: Attempting to Build Civil Society', in Mendelson and Glenn (eds) *op. cit.*, pp. 207–31 at p. 223–4.

77. S. Barakat and M. Chard, 'Theories, rhetoric and practice: recovering the capacities of war-torn societies', *Third World Quarterly*, 23, 5 (2002) pp. 817–35 at p. 823.

78. In 2003, the US GDP was larger than the *combined* totals of Japan, Germany, the United Kingdom and France (Source: the World Bank). In 2003, the United States spent US$417.4 bn on its military. The *combined* total of military expenditure for the next 14 highest military spenders was $316.5 bn. Figures are in constant 2000 dollars and calculated according to SIPRI data: http://web.sipri. org/contents/milap/milex/mex_major_spenders.pdf (2004). On the strategic capability of the United States see R. Kagan, *Paradise and Power: America and Europe in the New World Order* (London: Atlantic Books, 2003) p. 26.

79. R. Khaldi, *Resurrecting Empire: Western Footprints and America's Perilous Path in the Middle East* (London: IB Tauris, 2004) p. 153.

80. Ignatieff, *op. cit.*, p. 2.

81. *Ibid.*, p. 112.

82. G.J. Ikenberry, 'American power and the empire of capitalist democracy', *Review of International Studies*, 27, (2001), pp. 191–212 at p. 192. It is worth noting that Ikenberry denies that the United States is an empire. M. Kaldor also questions whether the United States is 'truly an empire' in 'American Power: from "compellance" to cosmopolitanism', *International Affairs*, 79, 1 (2003) pp. 1–22.

83. G.J. Ikenberry, 'Democracy, Institutions, and American Restraint' in G.J. Ikenberry (ed.) *America Unrivalled: The Future of the Balance of Power* (Ithaca, NY: Cornell University Press, 2002) pp. 213–238 at p. 215.

84. *Ibid.*, p. 217.

85. Mandelbaum, *op. cit.*, p. 36.

86. Falk, *op. cit.*, p. 171.

87. MacMillan, *op. cit.*, p. 125.

3 Conflict

1. E. Conteh-Morgan, *Collective Political Violence: An Introduction to the Theories and Cases of Violent Conflicts* (New York: Routledge, 2004) p. 1.

2. J. Darby, *What's Wrong with Conflict?* (Centre for the Study of Conflict, Coleraine: University of Ulster, 1995) p. 1.

3. See 'Seeking shelter for the night: Uganda's "night commuter" children', www.msf.org (23 March 2004) and 'Flood of "night commuter" children rises in northern Uganda', www.tearfund.org (17 June 2004) accessed on 1 March 2005. See also Meera Selva, 'The mystic and his brutal army of child soldiers', *The Independent* (30 July 2004).

4. Women's Commission for Refugee Women and Children, *Against All Odds: Promoting the Protection and Capacity of Ugandan and Sudanese Adolescents in Northern Uganda – Participatory Research Study with Adolescents in Northern Uganda May–July 2001* (New York: Women's Commission for Refugee Women and Children, 2001) pp. 42–3.

5. Datasets include those maintained by the Department of Peace and Conflict Research at the University of Uppsala, the Correlates of War dataset at the University of Michigan, and the now defunct PIOOM (Interdisciplinary Research Programme on the Root Causes of Human Rights Violations).

6. M. Eriksson, P. Wallenstein and M. Sollenberg, 'Armed conflict, 1989–2002', *Journal of Peace Research*, 40, 5 (2003), pp. 593–607.

7. T. Gurr and B. Harff, *Ethnic Conflict in World Politics* (Boulder, CO: Westview, 1994) p. 13.

8. P. Wallenstein and M. Sollenberg, 'Armed Conflicts, Conflict Termination and Peace Agreements, 1989–96', in M. Sollenberg (ed.), *States in Armed Conflict 1996* (Uppsala: Department of Peace and Conflict Research, Uppsala University, 1997), pp. 7–12 at p. 7.

9. Eriksson, Wallenstein and Sollenberg, *op. cit.*, p. 593.

10. R. Brubaker and D.D. Laitin, 'Ethnic and nationalist violence', *Annual Review of Sociology*, 24 (1998) pp. 423–54 at p. 424.

11. T. Gurr identifies 275 substantial ethnic or communal minorities at risk in his *People Versus States: Minorities at Risk in the New Century* (Washington, DC: United States Institute of Peace Press, 2000) p. 8.

12. T. Gurr, 'Ethnic warfare on the wane', *Foreign Affairs*, 79, 3 (May/June 2000) pp. 52–64.

13. Two influential works in this regard were D.P. Moynihan, *Pandaemonium: Ethnicity in International Politics* (New York: Oxford University Press, 1993) and M. Kaldor, *New and Old Wars: Organized Violence in a Global Era* (Cambridge: Polity Press, 1999).

14. D.L. Horowitz, *Ethnic Groups in Conflict* (Berkeley, CA: University of California Press, 1983) p. xi. S. Huntington's 'The clash of civilizations?' essay was seminal in popularising ethnic explanations, *Foreign Affairs*, 72 (1993) pp. 22–49. For a more cautious view of the term 'ethnic conflict' see J.R. Bowen, 'The myth of global ethnic conflict', *Journal of Democracy*, 7, 4 (1996) pp. 3–14.

15. N.P. Gleditsch, P. Wallenstein, M. Eriksson, M. Sollenberg and H. Strand, 'Armed conflict 1946–2001: a new dataset', *Journal of Peace Research*, 39, 5 (2002) pp. 615–37 at p. 619.

16. Eriksson, Wallenstein and Sollenberg, *op. cit.*, p. 593.

17. P.B. Spiegel, M. Sheik, B.A. Woodruff and G. Burnham, 'The accuracy of mortality reporting in displaced persons camps during the post-emergency phase', *Disasters*, 25, 2 (2001) pp. 172–80.

18. A.J. Jongman, 'The world conflict and human rights map 2000: the PIOOM Experience with mapping dimensions of contemporary conflicts and human rights violations', paper prepared for the Uppsala Conference on Conflict Data, 7–10 June 2001 and *www.freedomhouse.org*.

19. 'US aim in Iraq: "Lightning action" ', *USA Today* (27 September 2002).

20. This issue, and suggested corrective measures, are discussed in P.B. Spiegel, M. Sheik, B.A. Woodruff and G. Burnham, *op. cit.*

21. A good background account of the war in Nepal can be found in M. Hutt (ed. *Himalayan 'People's War': Nepal's Maoist Rebellion* (London: Hurst, 2004).
22. The complexity of Nepalese constitutional politics is explained in M. Chadda, *Building Democracy in South Asia: India, Nepal, Pakistan* (Boulder, CO: Lynne Rienner, 2000) pp. 111–42.
23. See, for example, 'Nepalese Maoists may accept monarchy', *BBC News Online* (23 January 2004).
24. Communist Party of Nepal (Maoist), Central Committee, 'Press Statement' (25 March 2004).
25. 'Statement by Comrade Prachanda, Communist Party of Nepal (Maoist) 27 August 2003', Revolutionary Worker/Obrero Revolucionario website.
26. 'Interview with Chairman Prachanda, leader of the Communist Party of Nepal (Maoist), 28 May 2001', *A World To Win*, 27 (2001).
27. R. Bevacqua, 'Nepal and the "War on Terror"', Japan Policy Research Institute Working Paper, 100 (May 2004). See also 'Nepal Timeline', *BBC News Online*, (2 June 2004) and 'US deplores unleashing of violence by Maoists', *Gorkhapatra Daily* (13 September 2003).
28. P. Collier, 'Economic causes of civil conflict and their implications for policy', World Bank Policy Paper (15 June 2000) p. 2.
29. W. Reno, 'War, markets, and the reconfiguration of West Africa's weak states', *Comparative Politics*, 29, 4 (1997) pp. 493–510 and W. Reno, 'African weak states and commercial alliances', *African Affairs*, 96 (1997) pp. 165–85.
30. Collier, *op. cit.*
31. For critiques see D. Lemke, 'African lessons for international relations research', *World Politics*, 56 (October 2003) pp. 114–38 and R. Mac Ginty 'Looting in the context of violent conflict: a conceptualisation and typology', *Third World Quarterly*, 25, 5 (2004) pp. 857–70 at p. 858. For a discussion of how quantitative peace research can be made more accessible, see R.P. Smith, 'Quantitative methods in peace research', *Journal of Peace Research*, 35, 4 (1998) pp. 418–27.
32. Paul Collier, the author most closely associated with the greed thesis, is Research Director at the World Bank. See his *Breaking the Conflict Trap: Civil War and Development Policy* (Washington, DC and New York: World Bank and Oxford University Press, 2003).
33. C. Young, 'Explaining the Conflict Potential of Ethnicity', in J. Darby and R. Mac Ginty (eds.) *Contemporary Peacemaking: Conflict, Violence and Peace Processes* (Basingstoke: Palgrave Macmillan, 2003) pp. 9–18 at p. 14.
34. A.D. Smith, 'Interpretations of National Identity', in A. Dieckhoff and N. Gutiérrez (eds.) *Modern Roots: Studies of National Identity* (Aldershot: Ashgate, 2001) pp. 21–43 at p. 37.
35. W. Connor, *Ethnonationalism: The Quest for Understanding* (Princeton, NJ: Princeton University Press, 1994) p. 204.
36. *Ibid.*
37. *Ibid.*, pp. 205–6.
38. C. Mitchell, 'Necessitous Man and Conflict Resolution: More Basic Questions about Basic Human Needs Theory', in J. Burton (ed.) *Conflict: Human Needs Theory* (Basingstoke: Macmillan, 1990) pp. 149–76 at p. 153.
39. A.H. Maslow, *Motivation and Personality*, 3rd edn (New York: Harper Collins, 1987).

40. J. Burton, *Violence Explained* (Manchester: Manchester University Press, 1997) p. 38.
41. P. Sites, 'Legitimacy and Human Needs', in J. Burton and F. Dukes (eds.) *Conflict: Readings in Management and Resolution* (Basingstoke: Macmillan, 1990) pp. 117–44 at p. 136.
42. E.E. Azar, *The Management of Protracted Social Conflict: Theory and Cases* (Aldershot: Dartmouth Publishing, 1990) p. 9.
43. C. Tilly, 'Violent and Non-Violent Trajectories in Contentious Politics', in K. Worcester, S. Bermanzohn and M. Ungar (eds.) *Violence and Politics: Globalization's Paradox* (New York: Routledge, 2002) pp. 13–31 at p. 21.
44. Azar, *op. cit.*, p. 9.
45. H. Tajfel, 'Social Categorization, Social Identity and Social Comparison', in H. Tajfel (ed.) *Differentiation between Social Groups: Studies in the Social Psychology of Intergroup Relations* (London: Academic Press, 1978) pp. 61–76.
46. See J.C. Turner, M. Hogg, P. Oakes, S. Reicher and M. Wetherell, *Rediscovering the Social Group: A Self-categorization Theory* (Oxford: Blackwell, 1987).
47. L. Wells and G. Marwell, *Self-esteem: Its Conceptualisation and Measurement* (London: Sage, 1976) p. 67.
48. J. Macrae, M. Bradbury, S. Jaspers, D. Johnson and M. Duffield, 'Conflict, the continuum and chronic emergencies: a critical analysis of the scope for linking relief, rehabilitation and development planning in Sudan', *Disasters*, 21, 3 (1997) pp. 223–43.
49. See list of characteristics of 'Chronically Vulnerable Areas', in D. Maxwell, 'Programmes in Chronically Vulnerable Areas: Challenges and Lessons Learned', *Disasters*, 23, 4 (1999) pp. 373–84 at p. 376.
50. S. Moeller, *Compassion Fatigue: How the Media Sells Disease, Famine, War and Death* (New York: Routledge, 1999).
51. J. Macrae, M. Bradbury, S. Jaspers, D. Johnson and M. Duffield, *op. cit.*
52. For a discussion of the Israeli-backed South Lebanon Army see R. Brynen, 'Palestinian-Lebanese Relations: A Political Analysis', in D. Collings (eds.) *Peace for Lebanon? From War to Reconstruction* (Boulder, CO Lynne Rienner, 1994) pp. 83–96.

4   Critical peace assessment

1. Sophisticated conflict assessment models have been pioneered by government donors such as DFID and USAID, and NGOs such as International Alert. See, Department for International Development (DFID), *Conducting Conflict Assessments: Guidance Notes* (London: DFID, 2002); USAID Office of Conflict Management and Mitigation, 'Conducting a conflict assessment: a framework for analysis and program development', (9 May 2004); P. Ardon, N. Karuru, M. Lionhardt and A. Sherriff, *PCIA as a Peacebuilding Tool* (London: International Alert, 2002) http://www.international-alert.org/pdf/pubdev/pcia.pdf accessed on 13 January 2005. See also, C. Roche, *Impact Assessment for Development Agencies: Learning to Value Change* (Oxford: Oxfam, 1999). For a more education- specific conflict assessment model see, Canadian International Development Agency, 'Education, Conflict and Peacebuilding: A diagnostic tool', www.acdi-cida.gc.ca.

2. N. Dodds, 'Only we can deliver a deal', *Guardian* (17 August 2005).
3. See, for example, S. Bose, *Bosnia after Dayton: Nationalist Partition and International Intervention* (London: Hurst, 2002).
4. UNHCR Press Release, 'One millionth returnee goes home in Bosnia and Herzegovina' (21 September 2004) www.unhcr.ch.
5. USAID, *op. cit.*, p. 12.
6. *Ibid.*
7. For discussion of Guatemala's post-accord experiences, see C. Moser and C. McIlwaine, *Violence in a Post-conflict Context: Urban Poor Perceptions from Guatemala* (Washington, DC: World Bank, 2001).
8. See, for example, M. Sommers, *Urbanization, War, and Africa's Youth at Risk* (Washington, DC: USAID and Basic Education Policy Support, 2003) and Women's Commission for Refugee Women and Children, *Untapped Potential: Adolescents Affected by Armed Conflict – A Review of Programs and Policies* (New York: WCRWC, 2000).
9. D. Lemke, 'African lessons for international relations research', *World Politics*, 56 (October 2003) pp. 114–38 at p. 115.
10. H. Kline, *State Building and Conflict Resolution in Colombia, 1986–1994* (Tuscaloosa, AL: University of Alabama Press, 2001) pp. 85–118.
11. See B.F. Walter, 'Designing transitions from civil war: demobilization, democratization and commitments to peace', *International Security*, 24, 1 (Summer 1999) pp. 127–55.
12. J. Darby, *The Effects of Violence on Peace Processes* (Washington, DC: United States Institute of Peace Press, 2001) pp. 47–8.
13. Perhaps the seminal contribution to the 'new barbarism' corpus came with R. Kaplan's 'The coming anarchy', *Elmwood Quarterly* (1994) pp. 11–24. For a commentary on the likening of contemporary warfare to medieval wars see N. Winn (ed.) *Neo-medievalism and Civil Wars* (London: Frank Cass, 2004).
14. Indeed, development aid is increasingly targeted at those states deemed the most capable, 'US to direct its aid only to best governed countries', *Financial Times* (18 February 2005).
15. This has certainly been the impression gained by the author following numerous research trips to the former Yugoslavia and Northern Ireland.
16. Excellent consideration of methodological and ethnographic research requirements in deeply divided societies can be found in M. Smyth and G. Robinson (eds) *Researching Violently Divided Societies: Ethical and Methodological Issues* (London and Tokyo: Pluto and United Nations University Press, 2001). See also, R. Lee and E. Stank (eds) *Researching Violence: Essays on Methodology and Measurement* (London: Routledge, 2001).
17. The devolution-monitoring programme in Northern Ireland, for example, is conducted by academics and NGOs and its updates are eagerly awaited as non-partisan assessments of the performance of devolved governance in the wake of the peace accord.
18. N.D. White provides a very useful review of UN observation and monitoring missions 1947–92 in *Keeping the Peace: The United Nations and the Maintenance of International Peace and Security* (Manchester: Manchester University Press, 1993) pp. 215–30. See also S. Hill and S. Malik, *Peacekeeping and the United Nations* (Aldershot: Dartmouth, 1996).

19. N.D.White, *Keeping the Peace: The United Nations and the Maintenance of International Peace and Security* (Manchester: Manchester University Press, 1993), p. 215.

20. *Ibid.*, p. 219.

21. 'Monitoring Committee for Cotabato peace zones to be formed', *Minda News*, III, 18 (11 June 2004) and 'Peace Agreement Between the Government of Liberia (GOL), The Liberians United for Reconciliation and Democracy (LURD), The Movement for Democracy in Liberia (MODEL) and the Political Parties', Accra, Ghana (18 August 2003).

22. Protocol concerning the Peace Monitoring Group made pursuant to (and amending) the Agreement between Australia, Papua New Guinea, Fiji, New Zealand and Vanuatu concerning the Neutral Peace Truce Monitoring Group for Bougainville of 5 December 1997, Australia Treaty Series (1998) no. 12, Article 4.

23. See, for example, 'IMC report lacks credibility', Sinn Féin press release, *www.sinnfein.ie* (24 April 2004) accessed on 6 May 2005.

24. For a critical examination of evaluation in a developing world context see B.E. Cracknell, *Evaluating Development Aid: Issues, Problems and Solutions* (Thousand Oaks, CA: Sage, 2000) and J. Becker, 'Making sustainable development evaluations work', *Sustainable Development*, 12, 4 (2004) pp. 200–11.

25. S. Barakat, M. Chard, T. Jacoby and W. Lume, 'The composite approach: research design in the context of war and armed conflict', *Third World Quarterly*, 23, 5 (2002) pp. 991–1003 at p. 991.

26. The concept of 'ethnic censuses' is explored in D. Kertzer and D. Ariel (eds) *Census and Identity: The Politics of Race, Ethnicity and Language in National Censuses* (Cambridge: Cambridge University Press, 2002).

27. See R. Chambers, 'The origins and practice of Participatory Rural Appraisal', *World Development*, 22, 7 (1994) pp. 953–69 and R. Chambers, 'Participatory Rural Appraisal (PRA): Analysis of experience', *World Development*, 22, 9 (1994)– pp. 1253–68.

28. W. Cooke and U. Kothari (eds) *Participation: The New Tyranny* (London: Zed Books, 2002).

29. The pitfalls of referendums in deeply divided societies are recounted in R. Mac Ginty, 'Constitutional referendums and ethnonational conflict: the case of Northern Ireland', *Nationalism and Ethnic Conflict*, 9, 2 (2003) pp. 1–22; J. Haskell, *Direct Democracy or Representative Government? Dispelling the Populist Myth* (Boulder, CO: Westview, 2001) and B. Reilly, 'Democratic validation' in J. Darby and R. Mac Ginty (eds) *Contemporary Peacemaking: Conflict, Violence and Peace Processes* (Basingstoke: Palgrave Macmillan, 2003) pp. 174–83.

30. S. Hickey and G. Moran, 'Participation: from tyranny to transformation?', briefing paper presented to the 'Bridging Research and Policy' Development Studies Association Conference, London (12 November 2004).

31. DFID, *op. cit.*, p. 5.

32. *Ibid.*, p. 6.

33. *Ibid.*

34. *Ibid.*, pp. 15–16.

35. *Ibid.*, pp. 25–29.

36. USAID, *op. cit.*, p. 26.

37. *Ibid.*, p. 31.

38. M.E. Brown, 'The Causes of Internal Conflicts: An Overview', in M.E. Brown, O.R. Coté Jr., S.M. Lynn-Jones and S.E. Miller (eds), *Nationalism and Ethnic Conflict* (Cambridge, M.A.: MIT Press, 1997) pp. 3–25 at p. 15.
39. USAID, *op. cit.*, p. 2.
40. S.J. Stedman, 'Policy Implications', in S.J. Stedman, D. Rothchild and E.M. Cousens (eds) *Ending Civil Wars: The Implementation of Peace Agreements* (Boulder, CO: Lynne Rienner, 2002) pp. 663–71.

5   Peace accords thwarted by violence

1. Background on the Kosovo war and its aftermath can be found in W. O'Neill, *Kosovo: An Unfinished Peace* (Boulder, CO: Lynne Rienner, 2002) and T. Judah, *Kosovo: War and Revenge* (New Haven, CT and London: Yale University Press, 2000).
2. For accounts of the violence see 'Kosovo rioters burn Serb churches' (18 March 2004) and 'NATO troops tackle Kosovo discord' (20 March 2004) both from *BBC News Online*, www.news.bbc.co.uk; Human Rights Watch, 'Failure to Protect: Anti-minority violence in Kosovo, March 2004', *www.hr.org*; United Nations Mission in Kosovo, 'Condemning violence in Kosovo, Security Council demands return to rule of law', *UNMIK Online* (18 March 2004) *www.unmikonline.org* accessed on 2 February 2005.
3. 'No evidence over Kosovo drowning', *BBC News Online* (28 April 2004) www.news.bbc.co.uk.
4. Those attempting to defend a peace accord may wish to re-brand continuing or mutating violence as a 'security' issue, thus simultaneously making the points that there has been a qualitative change in the conflict (from civil war between groups to a criminal assault on a new political dispensation) and staking a claim to the righteousness of the pro-peace accord position. But such terminological deftness cannot mask the persistence of violence.
5. N. Ball, 'The Challenge of Rebuilding War-Torn Societies', in C.A. Crocker, F.O. Hampson and P. Aall (eds), *Turbulent Peace: The Challenges of Managing International Conflict* (Washington, DC: USIP Press, 2001) pp. 719–36 at p. 721. See also a similar list of factors that complicate the ending of civil wars in S.J. Stedman, 'Implementing peace agreements in civil wars: lessons and recommendations for policymakers', IPA Policy Paper on Peace Implementation (New York: International Peace Academy, May 2001).
6. Hence the tendency in some peace processes to locate negotiations away from the conflict area. For example, negotiations between the Government of Sri Lanka and the Tamil Tigers took place in Thailand (September 2002), Norway (December 2002), Berlin (February 2003) and London (June 2003). The first meeting of Israeli Prime Minister Ariel Sharon and Palestinian leader Mahmoud Abbas took place in the Dead Sea resort of Sharm al-Sheikh, Egypt in February 2005. J. Egeland describes another set of overseas peace talks in 'The Oslo Accord: Multiparty Facilitation through the Norwegian Channel', in C.A. Crocker, F.O. Hampson and P. Aall (eds), *Herding Cats: Multiparty Mediation in a Complex World* (Washington, DC: United States Institute of Peace Press, 1999) pp. 529–46.

7. R. Licklider, 'Obstacles to Peace Settlements', in C.A. Crocker, F.O. Hampson and P. Aall (eds),, *Herding Cats: Multiparty Mediation in a Complex World* (Washington, DC: United States Institute of Peace Press, 1999) pp. 697–718 at p. 703.

8. See, for example, the furore following the December 2004 robbery of the Northern Bank in Northern Ireland. Although thought to be the largest bank robbery in European history, it was not a particularly violent incident by the standards of the violent conflict that preceded it.

9. S.J. Stedman, 'Spoiler problems in peace processes', *International Security*, 22, 2 (Fall 1997), pp. 5–53 at p. 5. For a reprise of his argument, including a defence against criticism, see S.J. Stedman, 'Peace Processes and the Challenges of Violence', in J. Darby and R. Mac Ginty (eds), *Contemporary Peacemaking: Conflict, Violence and Peace Processes* (Basingstoke: Palgrave Macmillan, 2003) pp. 103–113.

10. Stedman (1997), 'Spoiler problems in peace processes', *International Security*, 22, 2 (Fall 1997) p. 10.

11. *Ibid.*, p. 11.

12. *Ibid.*, pp. 10–11.

13. *Ibid.*, pp. 8–12.

14. *Ibid.*, p. 6.

15. J. Darby, *The Effects of Violence on Peace Processes* (Washington, DC: United States Institute of Peace Press, 2001) pp. 120–1.

16. M.J. Zahar, 'Reframing the spoiler debate in peace processes' in J. Darby and R. Mac Ginty eds., *op. cit.*, pp. 114–24.

17. For example, the first Irish government made a point of calling anti-Treaty Irish Republican Army forces 'Irregulars'. See, M. Hopkinson, *Green Against Green: The Irish Civil War* (Dublin: Gill & Macmillan, 2004) p. 180.

18. See, for example, 'Anti-Iraqi forces fire on marines from mosque' or 'IEDS brings prison terms for anti-Iraqi forces' both United States Central Command News Release, (19 April 2004) and (16 August 2004) respectively.

19. See, for example, 'Anti-Iraqi forces over the weekend', *New York Jewish Times* (31 August 2004); 'US soldier killed; Dozens of anti-Iraqi fighters captured', *Tri-State News* (30 July 2004).

20. P. Richards, *Fighting for the Rain Forest: War, Youth and Resources in Sierra Leone* (London and Oxford: The International African Institute and James Currey, 2002) p. xvi.

21. Quotations from A. Nüsse, *Muslim Palestine: The Ideology of Hamas* (Amsterdam: Harwood Academic Publishers, 1998) pp. 146–9.

22. E. Said, *The End of the Peace Process: Oslo and After*, 2nd edition (London: Granta Books, 2002).

23. *Ibid.*, p. 19.

24. The was a key finding of a United Nations University research seminar on spoiler violence in peace processes, Bruges, 16–17 December 2003.

25. G. Stephanopoulos, *All Too Human: A Political Education* (London: Hutchinson, 1999), p. 190.

26. 'Palestinians arrest Jihad activists after bombing', www.cnn.com (7 November 1998).

27. J. Darby, *op. cit.*, pp. 46–50.

28. *Ibid.*, p. 48.

29. J. Darby, *op. cit.*, p. 49.
30. Stedman (1997) uses the examples of Angola in 1992 (300,000 dead) and Rwanda in 1994 (1 million dead) to illustrate the costs when spoilers prevail, *op. cit.*, p. 5.
31. Ceasefire observance was by no means total or universal, but the main militant organisations generally ceased their attacks on the state and each other, while the state toned down its overt security responses.
32. 'Sharp rise in intimidation', *BBC News Online* (23 September 2004) www.news.bbc.co.uk accessed on 12 February 2005 and 'Violence in Ulster drives 1,240 people from homes', *Guardian* (24 September 2004).
33. 'JVP says Ranil's MOU with Prabhakaran unconstitutional and call it a surrender of the country to LTTE terrorists', www.Lankaweb.com (undated) accessed on 13 February 2005.
34. R. Mac Ginty, 'Unionist political attitudes after the Belfast Agreement', *Irish Political Studies*, 19, 1 (2004) pp. 87–99.
35. R. Mac Ginty, 'Constitutional referendums and ethnonational conflict: the case of Northern Ireland', *Nationalism and Ethnic Politics*, 9, 2 (2003) pp. 1–22.
36. Cited in 'Kosovo residents still on edge', *BBC News Online* (23 March 2004) http://www.news.bbc.co.uk accessed on 2 February 2005.
37. Full results from the Northern Ireland Life and Times survey of political attitudes (1998–2003) can be found online: http://www.ark.ac.uk/nilt/results/polatt.html accessed on 15 April 2005.
38. R. Gould crystallises feuds in terms of group versus individual tensions in 'Collective violence and group solidarity: evidence from a feuding society', *American Sociological Review*, 64 (1999) pp. 356–80.
39. Darby, *op. cit.*, p. 46.
40. See, for example, C. Steenkamp, 'The legacy of war: conceptualizing a "culture of violence" to explain violence after peace accords', *The Round Table: The Commonwealth Journal of International Affairs*, 94, 379, (2005) pp. 253–67.
41. See, T. German, *Russia's Chechen War* (London: Routledge Curzon, 2003) and J.B. Dunlop, *Russia Confronts Chechnya: Roots of a Separatist Conflict* (Cambridge: Cambridge University Press, 1998).
42. A. Lieven, *Chechnya: Tombstone of Russian Power* (New Haven, CT and London: Yale University Press, 1999) p. 351.
43. A. Matveeva, 'Chechnya: Drive for Independence or Hotbed for Islamic Terrorism?', in P. van Tongeren, H. van de Veen and J. Verhoeven (eds), *Searching for Peace in Europe and Eurasia: An Overview of Conflict Prevention and Peacebuilding Activities* (Boulder, CO: Lynne Rienner, 2002) pp. 354–73.
44. Cited in Ian Traynor, 'Russia rebuffs Chechen peace overture', *Guardian* (12 October 1999).
45. 'Russians "paid Maskhadov bounty" ', *BBC News Online* (15 March 2005) http://www.news.bbc.co.uk.
46. Namibia, for example, has not mirrored South Africa's dramatic rise in crime rates.
47. T. Farer, 'Introduction', in T. Farer (ed.) *Transnational Crime in the Americas* (New York: Routledge, 1999) pp. xiii–xvi.
48. Human Rights Watch reported 48 deaths from lynching in Guatemala in 1999 and 22 instances of lynching or attempted lynching in the first half of 2000. See 'Guatemala: Human Rights Developments' in *Human Rights Watch*

World Report 2001 available at *www.hrw.org/wr2k1/americas/guatemala.html* accessed on 22 March 2005.

49. J. Brewer, B. Lockhart and P. Rodgers 'Informal social control and crime management in Belfast', *British Journal of Sociology*, 49, 4 (1998) pp. 570–85.
50. These factors are more fully explained in R. Mac Ginty, 'Crime after Peace Accords', in J. Darby (ed.) *Violence and Reconstruction* (South Bend, IN: University of Notre Dame Press, 2006).
51. See the 'Culture of Violence' typology in Steenkamp, *op. cit.*, p. 256.
52. C. Tilly, *op. cit.* at p. 21.
53. A. Özerdem, 'Vocational training of former Kosovo Liberation Army combatants: For what purpose and end?' *Conflict, Security and Development*, 3, 3 (2003) pp. 383–405.
54. W. Reno, 'War, markets, and the reconfiguration of West Africa's weak states', *Comparative Politics*, 29, 4 (1997) pp. 493–510 at p. 495.
55. M. Masiiwa, 'The fast track resettlement programme in Zimbabwe: disparity between policy design and implementation', *The Round Table: The Commonwealth Journal of International Affairs*, 94, 379 (2005) pp. 217–24 and N.H. Thomas, 'Land reform in Zimbabwe', *Third World Quarterly*, 24, 4 (2003) pp. 691–712 at p. 700. It is worth noting that many of the so-called veterans engaged in land disputes around 2000 were not literally war veterans from the war of the national liberation in the 1970s. The adoption of the label veterans, however, is revealing.
56. It was estimated that there were 4 million illegal firearms in South Africa by the end of 1997, P. du Toit, *South Africa's Brittle Peace: The Problems of Post-Settlement Violence* (Basingstoke: Palgrave, 2001) p. 50.
57. M. Knight and A. Özerdem provide an excellent critical appraisal of the complexity of DDR in 'Guns, camps and cash: disarmament, demobilization and reinsertion of former combatants in transitions from war to peace', *Journal of Peace Research*, 41, 4 (2004) pp. 499–516.
58. The impact of crime on investment is discussed in E. Glaeser, *An Overview of Crime and Punishment* (Washington, DC: World Bank, 1999).
59. An excellent description of the conflict is provided in S. Dinnen, 'Winners and losers: politics and disorder in the Solomon Islands 2000–2002', *Journal of Pacific History*, 37, 3 (2002) pp. 285–98. See also, R. Liloqula and A. Aruhe'eta Pollard, 'Understanding conflict in Solomon Islands: a practical means to peacemaking', Discussion Paper 7 (Canberra: Australian National University, 2000).
60. *Ibid.*
61. C. Call, 'Crime and peace: why do successful peace processes produce the world's most violent countries', paper presented at the Annual Conference of the International Studies Association, Washington, DC (February 1999), p. 1.
62. J. Schirmer provides a fascinating overview of the civil-military overlap in 'The Guatemalan Politico-Military Project: legacies of the violent peace', *Latin American Perspectives*, 26, 2 (1999) pp. 92–107.

6 The elusive peace dividend

1. R. Brynen, *A Very Political Economy: Peacebuilding and Foreign Aid in the West Bank and Gaza* (Washington, DC: United States Institute of Peace Press, 2000) p. 4.

2. K. Gonachar and T. Roetger, 'Assisting conversion and company restructuring in Moldova', Bonn International Center for Conversion, Brief 19 (October 2001) p. 13.
3. S. Makdisi, *The Lessons of Lebanon: The Economics of War and Development* (London: I.B. Tauris, 2004) p. 150.
4. B. Kamphuis, 'Economic Policy for Building Peace', in G. Junne and W. Verkoren (eds), *Postconflict Development: Meeting New Challenges* (Boulder, CO: Lynne Reinner, 2005) pp. 185–210 at p. 191.
5. T. Addison, A.R. Chowdhury and S.M. Murshed, 'The Fiscal Dimensions of Conflict and Reconstruction', in T. Addison and A. Roe (eds), *Fiscal Policy for Development, Poverty, Reconstruction and Growth* (Basingstoke: Palgrave Macmillan, 2004) pp. 260–73 at p. 254.
6. An example of rendering post-war societies fit for consumption rather than production can be seen in Rory Carroll's 'Cola wars as Coke moves on Baghdad', *Guardian* (5 July 2005).
7. S.L. Woodward, 'Economic priorities for successful peace implementation', in S. Stedman, D. Rothchild and E. Cousins (eds), *Ending Civil Wars: The Implementation of Peace Agreements* (Boulder, CO: Lynne Rienner, 2002) pp. 183–214 at p. 184.
8. See, for example, the intertwining of peace with prosperity in 'Remarks by the President to the Corporate Council on Africa's U.S.–Africa Business Summit', Washington, DC (26 June 2003).
9. K. Hartley, *Economic Aspects of Disarmament: Disarmament as an investment process* (New York: United Nations, 1993) pp. 67–8.
10. D. Braddon, *Exploding the Myth? The Peace Dividend, Regions and Market Adjustment* (Amsterdam: Harwood Academic Publishers, 2000) p. 182.
11. Annual Human Development Reports can be found at www.undp.org.
12. P. Collier, 'Development and security', 12th Bradford Development Lecture, University of Bradford (11 November 2004).
13. *Ibid.*
14. S. Kaufman, *Modern Hatreds: The Symbolic Politics of Ethnic War* (Ithaca, NY: Cornell University Press, 2001) pp. 7–9.
15. See C. Moyroud and J. Katunga, 'Coltan exploitation in the Eastern Democratic Republic of Congo', P. Goldsmith, L. Abura and J. Switzer, 'Oil and Water in Sudan' and F. Flintan and I. Tamrat, 'Spilling blood over water? The case of Ethiopia', in J. Lind and K. Sturman (eds), *Scarcity and Surfeit: The Ecology of Africa's Conflicts* (Pretoria: Institute for Security Studies, 2002) pp. 159–85, 187–241 and 243–319. Coltan, or columbite-tantalite is a metal ore used in the manufacture of mobile phone circuit boards.
16. See MILF website at http://www.luwaran.com/ accessed on 28 March 2005.
17. UNDP Human Development Indicators (2004) p. 205.
18. T. Brück, 'The Economics of Civil War in Mozambique', in J. Brauer and K. Hartley (eds), *The Economics of Regional Security: NATO: The Mediterranean and Southern Africa* (Amsterdam: Harwood Academic Publishers, 2000) pp. 191–215 at p. 208.
19. R. Brynen, *op. cit.*, p. 25.
20. N.J. Colletta and M.L. Cullen, *Violent Conflict and the Transformation of Social Capital: Lessons from Cambodia, Rwanda, Guatemala and Somalia* (Washington, DC: World Bank, 2000) p. 109.

21. C. Nordstrom, *Shadows of War: Violence, Power, and International Profiteering in the Twenty-First Century* (Berkeley, CA: University of California Press, 2004).
22. *Ibid.*
23. For a critical approach to the concept of corruption see E. Brown, J. Cloke and M. Sohail, 'Key myths about corruption', A briefing paper for a workshop on corruption and development', Development Studies Association Annual Conference, Westminster, London (6 November 2004).
24. Discussion of the definition of corruption can be found in P. Le Billon, 'Buying peace or fuelling war: the role of corruption in armed conflict', *Journal of International Development*, 15 (2003) pp. 413–26.
25. Nordstrom, *op. cit.*, pp. 98–9 and 108.
26. N. Richani, *Systems of Violence: The Political Economy of War and Peace in Colombia* (Albany, NY: State University of New York Press, 2002) p. 101.
27. It was estimated that 35 per cent of land in Cambodia was rendered unusable as a result of landmines. Kamphuis, *op. cit.*, p. 192.
28. Author field observations, Bosnia-Herzegovina (December 2000).
29. *Ibid.* It was noticeable how many children in Bosnia-Herzegovina regarded travelling to Denmark or Germany as their main aim in leaving school.
30. Woodward, *op. cit.* pp. 185–8.
31. J. Abbink, 'Reconstructing Southern Sudan in the post-war era: Challenges and prospects of "Quick Impact Programmes" ', Leiden, African Studies Centre Working Paper 55 (2004).
32. Brynen, *op. cit.*, p. 3.
33. S. Barakat and M. Chard, 'Theories, rhetoric and practice: recovering the capacities of war-torn societies', *Third World Quarterly*, 23, 5 (2002) pp. 817–35 at pp. 826–7.
34. C. Bundegaard, 'The Battalion State: Securitization and Nation-Building in Eritrea', Geneva, Programme for Strategic and International Security Studies Occasional Paper 2 (2004) p. 42.
35. Makdisi, *op. cit.*, p. 91–2.
36. Brynen, *op. cit.*, p. 25.
37. Cited in Jason Burke and Peter Beaumont, 'West pays warlords to stay in line', *Observer* (21 July 2002) and S. Hersh, 'The other war', *The New Yorker* (5 April 2002).
38. C. Obi, 'Economic Adjustment and the Deepening Environmental Conflict in Africa', in L.A. Jinadu (ed.) *The Political Economy of Peace and Security in Africa* (Harare: ANPS Books, 2000) pp. 131–47 at p. 139.
39. Emphasis added. The World Bank, *Claiming the Future: Choosing Prosperity in the Middle East and North Africa* (Washington, DC: The World Bank, 1995) p. 63.
40. See the World Bank's 'Strategic Direction' outlined at *www.worldbank.org* accessed on 16 April 2005.
41. Woodward, *op. cit.*, p. 188.
42. *Ibid.*, p. 185.
43. Woodward, *op. cit.*, p. 192.
44. See J. Abbink, *op. cit.*
45. E. Rogier, 'Designing an integrated strategy for peace, security and development in post-Agreement Sudan', The Hague, Netherlands Institute of International Relations, Conflict Research Unit, 2005, pp. 55–8.

46. D. Nutt, 'Against the grain', *Guardian* (11 September 2003).

47. G. Olsen, 'Neo-medievalism in Africa: Whither Government-to-government Relations between Africa and the European Union?', in N. Winn (ed.) *Neo-medievalism and Civil Wars* (London: Frank Cass, 2004) pp. 94–120 at. pp. 101–3.

48. J. Nelson, *The Business of Peace: The Private Sector as a Partner in Conflict Prevention and Resolution* (London: International Alert, 2000) p. 15.

49. R. Mac Ginty, 'The pre-war reconstruction of post-war Iraq', *Third World Quarterly*, 24, 4 (2003) pp. 601–17.

50. N. Klein, 'Allure of the blank state', *Guardian* (18 April 2005).

51. Mac Ginty, *op. cit.*, pp. 613–5.

52. R. Ahmed, M. Kulessa and K. Malik (eds), *Lessons Learned from Crises and Post-conflict Situations: The Role of the UNDP in Reintegration and Reconstruction Programmes* (New York: United Nations Development Programme, 2002).

53. Commentators and political leaders are fond of calling for 'a new Marshall Plan' in the wake of complex emergencies. See, for example, 'Annan's "Marshall Plan" for AIDS', *BBC News Online* (27 April 2001) *http://www.news.bbc.co.uk* accessed on 12 April 2005; 'Brown takes "Marshall Plan" to US', *BBC News Online* (17 December 2001) http://www.bbc.co.uk accessed on 12 April 2005 and David Osborne, 'America urged to devise "Marshall Plan" for Asia', *Independent*, (3 January 2005).

    Perhaps the most authoritative account of the Plan is M. Hogan, *The Marshall Plan: America, Britain, and the Reconstruction of Western Europe, 1947–1952* (Cambridge: Cambridge University Press, 1987). For a more critical account that is circumspect on the real impact of the Plan see A. Milward, *The European Rescue of the Nation-State* (London: Routledge, 1992).

54. On US ascendancy see P. Kennedy, *The Rise and Fall of the Great Powers: Economic Change and Military Conflict from 1500 to 2000* (London: Fontana, 1989). For an excellent discussion of pre-Second World War international attempts at post-war reconstruction see A. Williams, *Failed Imagination? New World Orders of the Twentieth Century* (Manchester: Manchester University Press, 1998).

55. Cited in G.F. Kennan, *Memoirs 1925 – 1950* (London: Hutchinson, 1968) pp. 336.

56. *Ibid.*, p. 337.

57. State Department Planning Staff Paper sent to Secretary Marshall (23 May 1947) cited in Kennan, *ibid.*, p. 337.

58. *Ibid.*

59. J.L. Gaddis, *The United States and the End of the Cold War: Implications, Reconsiderations, Provocations* (Oxford: Oxford University Press, 1992) p. 210.

60. See J. Boyce, *Investing in Peace: Aid and Conditionality after Civil Wars* (Oxford: Oxford University Press and Institute of Strategic Studies, 2002); N. Leader and J. Macrae (eds), *Terms of Engagement: Conditions and Conditionality in Humanitarian Action* (London: Overseas Development Institute, 2000) and G. Crawford, 'Foreign aid and political conditionality: issues of effectiveness and consistency', *Democratization*, 4, 3 (1997) pp. 69–108.

7 Peace prevented by external actors

1. M.J. Zahar, 'Peace by Unconventional Means: Lebanon's Taif Agreement', in S.J. Stedman, D. Rothchild and E.M. Cousens (eds), *Ending Civil Wars: The*

Implementation of Peace Agreements (Boulder, CO: Lynne Rienner, 2002) pp. 567–97 at 567.

2. R. Cooper and M. Berdal, 'Outside Intervention in Ethnic Conflict', in M. Brown (ed.) *Ethnic Conflict and International Security* (Princeton, NJ: Princeton University Press, 1993) pp. 181–205 at p. 190.

3. 'President's Radio Address', *White House Press Release* (5 March 2005). See also, 'White House Fact Sheet: Implementing the Syria Accountability and Lebanese Sovereignty Restoration Act of 2003', www.whitehouse.gov (11 May 2004) accessed on 12 May 2005.

4. S.J. Stedman, 'Policy Implications', in Stedman, Rothchild and Cousens (eds), *op. cit.*, pp. 663–71.

5. B.F. Walter, 'The critical barrier to civil war settlement', *International Organization*, 51, 3 (1997) pp. 335–64 at p. 361.

6. An excellent overview of UN interventions, especially the transition from peacekeeping to peace enforcement and peace support, can be found in A. Bellamy, P. Williams and S. Griffin, *Understanding Peacekeeping* (Cambridge: Polity, 2004) esp. pp. 93–186.

7. S. Ryan, *The United Nations and International Politics* (New York: St Martin's Press, 2000) p. 163.

8. An excellent treatise on post-Cold War sovereignty can be found in R. Falk, 'State of siege: will globalization win out?' *International Affairs*, 73, 1 (1997) pp. 123–36.

9. D. Carment and P. James, 'Ethnic Conflict at the International Level: An Appraisal of Theories and Evidence', in D. Carment and P. James (eds), *Wars in the Midst of Peace: The International Politics of Ethnic Conflict* (Pittsburgh, PA: University of Pittsburgh Press, 1997) pp. 252–63 at p. 254.

10. A. Mack, 'Plus ca change ...', *Security Dialogue*, 34, 3 (2003) pp. 363–67.

11. B. Boutros-Ghali, *An Agenda for Peace: Preventive Diplomacy, Peacemaking and Peacekeeping* (New York: United Nations, 1992) p. 32.

12. See, A. Natsios, 'An NGO Perspective', in I. Zartman and J. Rasmussen (eds), *Peacemaking in International Conflict: Methods and Techniques* (Washington, DC: United States Institute of Peace Press, 1997) pp. 337–61.

13. H. Slim, 'The continuing metamorphosis of the humanitarian practitioner: Some new colours for an endangered chameleon', *Disasters*, 19, 2 (1995) pp. 110–26.

14. S. Barakat, D. Connolly and J. Large, 'Winning and losing in Aceh: five key dilemmas in third-party intervention', *Civil Wars*, 5, 4 (2002) pp. 1–29.

15. L. Gordenker and T. Weiss, 'Devolving Responsibilities: A Framework for Analysing NGOs and Services', in T. Weiss (ed.) *Beyond UN Subcontracting: Task-sharing with Regional Security Arrangements and Service-providing NGOs* (Basingstoke: Macmillan, 1998) pp. 30–45.

16. E.M. Cousens, 'From Missed Opportunities to Over-compensation: Implementing the Dayton Agreement in Bosnia', in S.J. Stedman, D. Rothchild and E. Cousens (eds), *op. cit.*, pp. 531–66 at p. 544.

17. J. Keegan, 'In this war of civilisations, the West will prevail', *Daily Telegraph*, (8 October 2001).

18. See, for example, the addresses by Norwegian Foreign Minister, J. Petersen, 'Norwegian perspectives on peaceful conflict resolution', Moscow State Institute for International Affairs, (7 April 2005) and 'Norwegian perspectives

on international peace and security', China Institute of International Studies Forum, Beijing, (29 March 2005).

19. An excellent account of the episode is provided by S. Bose, 'Flawed Mediation, Chaotic Implementation: The 1987 Indo-Sri Lanka Peace Agreement' in S.J. Stedman, D. Rothchild and E. Cousens (eds), *op. cit.*, pp. 631–59. See also, B. Matthews, 'Sri Lanka in 1989 – peril and good luck', *Asia Survey*, 30, 2 (1990) pp. 144–9 and M. Singer, 'Sri Lanka in 1990 – the ethnic strife continues', *Asia Survey*, 31, 2 (1991) pp. 140–5.

20. J. Dixit, 'Indian Involvement in Sri Lanka and the Indo-Sri Lanka Agreement of 1987: A Retrospective Evaluation', in K. Rupesinghe (ed.) *Negotiating Peace in Sri Lanka: Efforts, Failures and Lessons* (London: International Alert, 1998) pp. 31–45 at p. 43.

21. T. Gunasekara, 'Insurrectionary violence in Sri Lanka: the Janatha Vimukthi Peramuna insurgencies of 1971 and 1987–1989', *Ethnic Studies Report*, xvii, 1 (1999) pp. 66–88.

22. Uppsala Conflict Database, www.pcr.uu.se/database accessed on 6 January 2005.

23. Chris Mitchell gives a good account of ethical and practical considerations associated with mediation in 'Mediation and Ending Conflicts', in J. Darby and R. Mac Ginty (eds.) *Contemporary Peacemaking: Conflict, Violence and Peace Processes* (Basingstoke: Palgrave Macmillan, 2003) pp. 77–86.

24. Bose, *op. cit.*, p. 654.

25. M. Glenny, *The Fall of Yugoslavia* (London: Penguin, 1996) pp. 283–89.

26. Serb community leader Vinko Lale cited in 'Serbs hold memorial for their own war dead', *Irish Times* (13 July 2005).

27. For an excellent account of Serbian attitudes after Dayton see L.H. Wong, 'An analysis of the influence of the media on the Serbian people's perception towards collective guilt', MA dissertation submitted at the University of York, 2003.

28. This expression was used by an Afghan student in one of the author's MA classes in 2004.

29. Mandate of the United Nations Stabilisation Mission in Haiti (MINUSTAH) (1 June 2004), www.un.org.

30. 'UN troops storm Haiti shanty town', *BBC News Online* (6 July 2005).

31. Stedman, *op. cit.*, pp. 663–71 at pp. 668–9.

32. 'Cambodia – UNTAC: Summary', www.un.org accessed 22 February 2005.

33. W. Verkoren, 'Bringing It All Together: A Case Study of Cambodia' in G. Junne and W. Verkoren eds., *Postconflict Development: Meeting New Challenges* (Boulder, CO: Lynne Rienner, 2005) pp. 289–306.

34. J. Rasmussen, 'Peacemaking in the Twenty-First Century: New rules, New Roles and New Actors', in Zartman and Rasmussen (eds), *op. cit.*, pp. 23–50 at p. 29.

35. E. Luttwak, 'The Curse of Inconclusive Intervention', in C. Crocker, F.O. Hampson and P. Aall (eds), *Turbulent Peace: The Challenges of Managing International Conflict* (Washington, DC: United States Institute of Peace Press, 2001) pp. 265–72 at pp. 267–8.

36. The term 'Carthaginian peace' stems from the conclusion of the Third Punic war between Rome and Carthage in which Rome's recipe for peace was the destruction of Carthage.

37. Emphasis in original. Luttwak, *op. cit.*, p. 268.
38. Luttwak, *op. cit.*, p. 272.
39. J. McGarry, ' "Demographic engineering": the state-directed movement of ethnic groups as a technique of conflict regulation', *Ethnic and Racial Studies*, 21, 4 (1998) pp. 613–38.
40. Bonn International Center for Conversion, 'Reasonable measures: addressing the excessive accumulation and unlawful use of small arms', BICC Briefing Paper 11, (1998) p. 9.
41. An example of superpower 'peace interference' during the Cold War was the US opposition to the 1987 Central American Peace Plan. See 'President Reagan's address to the people of Nicaragua, August 22 1987', US Department of Statement Bulletin.
42. S. Grosse-Kettler, 'External actors in stateless Somalia: A war economy and its promoters', BICC Briefing Paper 39 (2004), p. 26.
43. 'Somalia peace talks open', *BBC News Online*, 16 October 2002, *http://www.news.bbc.co.uk* accessed on 7 May 2005. See also, 'Background note: Somalia:', US Department of State, undated, *www.state.gov* accessed on 7 May 2005.
44. 'Is Peace Possible in Somalia', Reuters, www.alertnet.org, 21 October 2004 accessed on 7 May 2005.

Bibliography

Reports

Ahmed, R., M. Kulessa and K. Malik (eds) *Lessons Learned from Crises and Post-conflict Situations: The Role of the UNDP in Reintegration and Reconstruction Programmes* (New York: United Nations Development Programme, 2002).

Ardon, P., N. Karuru, M. Lionhardt and A. Sherriff, *PCIA as a Peacebuilding Tool*, (London: International Alert, 2002) available at http://www.internationalalert. org/accessed on 9 December 2005.

Department for International Development, *Conducting Conflict Assessments: Guidance Notes* (London: DFID, 2002).

Gonachar K. and T. Roetger, 'Assisting conversion and company restructuring in Moldova', Bonn International Center for Conversion, Briefing Paper 19 (October 2001).

Grosse-Kettler, S., 'External actors in stateless Somalia: a war economy and its promoters', Bonn International Center for Conversion, Briefing Paper 39 (2004).

Hartley, K., *Economic Aspects of Disarmament: Disarmament as an Investment Process* (New York: United Nations, 1993).

Karatnycky, A., 'Freedom in the world 2003: liberty's expansion in a turbulent world – thirty years of the survey of freedom', www.freedomhouse.org (2003) accessed on 7 April 2005.

Nelson, J., *The Business of Peace: The Private Sector as a Partner in Conflict Prevention and Resolution* (London: International Alert, 2000).

Oxfam Community Aid Abroad, *Two Years On ... What Future for An Independent East Timor?* (Victoria: Oxfam Community Aid Abroad, 2004).

SIPRI, http://web.sipri.org/contents/milap/milex/mex_major_spenders.pdf (2004) accessed on 17 April 2005.

Sommers, M., *Urbanization, War, and Africa's Youth at Risk* (Washington, DC: USAID and Basic Education Policy Support, 2003).

USAID Office of Conflict Management and Mitigation, 'Conducting a conflict assessment: a framework for analysis and program development' (9 May 2004).

Women's Commission for Refugee Women and Children, *Untapped Potential: Adolescents Affected by Armed Conflict –A Review of Programs and Policies* (New York: WCRWC, 2000).

Women's Commission for Refugee Women and Children, *Against All Odds: Promoting the Protection and Capacity of Ugandan and Sudanese Adolescents in Northern Uganda – Participatory Research Study with Adolescents in Northern Uganda May–July 2001* (New York: WCRWC, 2001).

World Bank, *Claiming the Future: Choosing Prosperity in the Middle East and North Africa* (Washington, DC: The World Bank, 1995).

Conference proceedings, conference papers and occasional papers

Abbink, J., 'Reconstructing Southern Sudan in the post-war era: challenges and prospects of "Quick Impact Programmes" ', Leiden, African Studies Centre Working Paper 55 (2004).

Bevacqua, R., 'Nepal and the "War on Terror" ', Japan Policy Research Institute Working Paper 100 (May 2004).

Brown, E., J. Cloke and M. Sohail, 'Key myths about corruption', A briefing paper for a workshop on corruption and development, Development Studies Association Annual Conference, Westminster, London (6 November 2004).

Bundegaard, C., 'The battalion state: securitization and nation-building in Eritrea', Geneva, Programme for Strategic and International Security Studies, Occasional Paper 2 (2004).

Call, C., 'Crime and peace: why do successful peace processes produce the world's most violent countries', paper presented at the Annual Conference of the International Studies Association, Washington, DC (16–20 February 1999).

Collier, P., 'Economic causes of civil conflict and their implications for policy', World Bank Policy Paper (15 June 2000).

Collier, P., 'Development and security', 12th Bradford Development Lecture, University of Bradford (11 November 2004).

Darby, J., *What's Wrong with Conflict?* (Centre for the Study of Conflict, Coleraine: University of Ulster, 1995).

Hickey, S. and G. Moran, 'Participation: from tyranny to transformation?', briefing paper presented to the 'Bridging Research and Policy' Development Studies Association Conference, London (12 November 2004).

Jongman, A.J., 'The world conflict and human rights map 2000: the PIOOM experience with mapping dimensions of contemporary conflicts and human rights violations', paper prepared for the Uppsala Conference on Conflict Data (7–10 June 2001).

Liloqula R. and A. Aruhe'eta Pollard, 'Understanding conflict in Solomon Islands: a practical means to peacemaking' Discussion Paper 7 (Canberra: Australian National University, 2000).

Mack, A., S. Gates and K. Strøm, 'Democratic institutions: governance and civil war', Concept Paper for Democratic Institutions Workshop, Bellagio, Italy (7–9 June 2004).

Rogier, E., 'Designing an integrated strategy for peace, security and development in post-agreement Sudan', The Hague, Netherlands Institute of International Relations, Conflict Research Unit (2005).

Stedman, S.J., 'Implementing peace agreements in civil wars: lessons and recommendations for policymakers', IPA Policy Paper on Peace Implementation (New York: International Peace Academy, May 2001).

Williams, A., 'Post-war reconstruction before World War Two', paper presented at the Department of Politics seminar series, University of York (14 November 2003).

Wong, L.H., 'An analysis of the influence of the media on the Serbian people's perception towards collective guilt', MA dissertation submitted at the University of York (2003).

Journal articles

Adler, E., 'Condition(s) of peace', *Review of International Studies*, 24 (1998) pp. 165–91.

Anand, D., 'The violence of security: Hindu nationalism and the politics of representing "the Muslim" as a danger', *The Round Table: The Commonwealth Journal of International Affairs*, 94, 379 (2005) pp. 203–15.

Barakat, S. and M. Chard, 'Theories, rhetoric and practice: recovering the capacities of war-torn societies', *Third World Quarterly* 23, 5 (2002) pp. 817–35.

Barakat, S., M. Chard, T. Jacoby and W. Lume, 'The composite approach: research design in the context of war and armed conflict', *Third World Quarterly*, 23, 5 (2002) pp. 991–1003.

Barakat, S., D. Connolly and J. Large, 'Winning and losing in Aceh: five key dilemmas in third-party intervention', *Civil Wars*, 5, 4 (2002) pp. 1–29.

Becker, J., 'Making sustainable development evaluations work', *Sustainable Development*, 12, 4 (2004) pp. 200–11.

Benson, M., 'Dyadic hostility and the ties that bind: state-to-state versus state-to-system security and economic relationships', *Journal of Peace Research*, 41, 6 (2004) pp. 659–76.

Bowen, J.R., 'The myth of global ethnic conflict', *Journal of Democracy*, 7, 4 (1996) pp. 3–14.

Brewer, J., B. Lockhart and P. Rodgers, 'Informal social control and crime management in Belfast', *British Journal of Sociology*, 49, 4 (1998) pp. 570–85.

Brubaker R. and D.D. Laitin, 'Ethnic and nationalist violence', *Annual Review of Sociology* 24 (1998) pp. 423–54.

Chambers, R., 'The origins and practice of Participatory Rural Appraisal', *World Development*, 22, 7 (1994a) pp. 953–69.

Chambers, R., 'Participatory Rural Appraisal (PRA): analysis of experience', *World Development*, 22, 9 (1994b) pp. 1253–68.

Cox, M., 'Rethinking the end of the Cold War', *Review of International Studies*, 20 (1994) pp. 187–200.

Crawford, G., 'Foreign aid and political conditionality: issues of effectiveness and consistency', *Democratization*, 4, 3 (1997) pp. 69–108.

Der Derain, J., 'Virtuous war/virtual theory', *International Affairs*, 76, 4 (2000) pp. 771–88.

DeRouen, K. and S. Goldfinch, 'Putting the numbers to work: implications for violence prevention', *Journal of Peace Research*, 41, 1 (2005) pp. 27–45.

Dinnen, S., 'Winners and losers: politics and disorder in the Solomon Islands 2000–2002', *Journal of Pacific History*, 37, 3 (2002) pp. 285–98.

Doyle, M., 'Liberalism and world politics', *American Political Science Review*, 80, 4 (1980) pp. 1151–69.

Eriksson, M., P. Wallenstein and M. Sollenberg, 'Armed conflict, 1989–2002', *Journal of Peace Research*, 40, 5 (2003) pp. 593–607.

Falk, R., 'State of siege: will globalization win out?', *International Affairs*, 73, 1 (1997) pp. 123–36.

Fukuyama, F., 'The end of history?', *The National Interest* (Summer 1989) pp. 3–18; Garber, L. and K. Kumar, 'What have we learned about post-conflict elections?', *New England Journal of Public Policy*, 14, 1 (1998) pp. 25–43.

Gleditsch, N.P., P. Wallenstein, M. Eriksson, M. Sollenberg and H. Strand, 'Armed conflict 1946–2001: a new dataset', *Journal of Peace Research*, 39, 5 (2002) pp. 615–37.

Gould, R., 'Collective violence and group solidarity: evidence from a feuding society', *American Sociological Review*, 64 (1999) pp. 356–80.

Gunasekara, T., 'Insurrectionary violence in Sri Lanka: the Janatha Vimukthi Peramuna insurgencies of 1971 and 1987–1989', *Ethnic Studies Report*, 17, 1 (1999) pp. 66–88.

Gurr, T., 'Ethnic warfare on the wane', *Foreign Affairs*, 79, 3 (May/June 2000) pp. 52–64.

Hunter, N., 'Rethinking pacifism: the Quakers' dilemma in a time of war', *The American Prospect*, 12, 21 (2001) pp. 14–17.

Huntington, S., 'The clash of civilizations?', *Foreign Affairs*, 72 (1993) pp. 22–49.

Ikenberry, G.J., 'American power and the empire of capitalist democracy', *Review of International Studies*, 27, (2001), pp. 191–212.

Kaldor, M. 'American Power: from "compellance" to cosmopolitanism', *International Affairs*, 79, 1 (2003) pp. 1–22.

Kaplan, R., 'The coming anarchy', *Elmwood Quarterly* (1994) pp. 11–24.

Knight M. and A. Özerdem, 'Guns, camps and cash: disarmament, demobilization and reinsertion of former combatants in transitions from war to peace', *Journal of Peace Research*, 41, 4 (2004) pp. 499–516.

Lawler, P., 'The "good war" after September 11', *Government and Opposition*, 37, 2 (2002) pp. 151–72.

Le Billon, P., 'Buying peace or fuelling war: the role of corruption in armed conflict', *Journal of International Development*, 15 (2003) pp. 413–26.

Lemke, D., 'African lessons for international relations research', *World Politics*, 56 (October 2003) pp. 114–38.

Mac Ginty, R., 'Constitutional referendums and ethnonational conflict: the case of Northern Ireland', *Nationalism and Ethnic Politics*, 9, 2 (2003a) pp. 1–22.

Mac Ginty, R., 'The pre-war reconstruction of post-war Iraq', *Third World Quarterly*, 24, 4 (2003b) pp. 601–17.

Mac Ginty, R., 'Looting in the context of violent conflict: a conceptualisation and typology', *Third World Quarterly*, 25, 5 (2004a) pp. 857–70.

Mac Ginty, R., 'Unionist political attitudes after the Belfast Agreement', *Irish Political Studies*, 19, 1 (2004b) pp. 87–99.

Mack, A., 'Civil war: academic research and the policy community', *Journal of Peace Research*, 39, 5 (2002) pp. 515–25.

Mack, A., 'Plus ca change …', *Security Dialogue*, 34, 3 (2003) pp. 363–7.

Macrae, J., M. Bradbury, S. Jaspers, D. Johnson and M. Duffield, 'Conflict, the continuum and chronic emergencies: a critical analysis of the scope for linking relief, rehabilitation and development planning in Sudan', *Disasters*, 21, 3 (1997) pp. 223–43.

Masiiwa, M., 'The Fast Track Resettlement Programme in Zimbabwe: disparity between policy design and implementation', *The Round Table: The Commonwealth Journal of International Affairs*, 94, 379 (2005) pp. 217–24.

Matthews, B., 'Sri Lanka in 1989 – peril and good luck', *Asia Survey*, 30, 2 (1990) pp. 144–49.

McGarry, J., ' "Demographic engineering": The state-directed movement of ethnic groups as a technique of conflict regulation', *Ethnic and Racial Studies*, 21, 4 (1998) pp. 613–38.

Muggah, R., 'No magic bullet: a critical perspective on disarmament, demobilization and reintegration (DDR) and weapons reduction in post-conflict contexts', *The Round Table: The Commonwealth Journal of International Affairs*, 94, 379 (2005) pp. 239–52.

O'Connor, R.G., 'Victory in modern war', *Journal of Peace Research*, 6, 4 (1969) pp. 367–84.

Özerdem, A., 'Vocational training of former Kosovo Liberation Army combatants: for what purpose and end?' *Conflict, Security and Development*, 3, 3 (2003) pp. 383–405.

Reilly, B., 'Electoral systems for divided societies', *Journal of Democracy*, 13, 2 (2002) pp. 156–70.

Reno, W., 'War, markets, and the reconfiguration of West Africa's weak states', *Comparative Politics*, 29, 4 (1997a) pp. 493–510.

Reno, W., 'African weak states and commercial alliances', *African Affairs*, 96 (1997b) pp. 165–85.

Sartori, G., 'Concept misinformation in comparative politics', *American Political Science Review*, 64, 4 (1970) pp. 1033–53.

Schirmer, J., 'The Guatemalan Politico-Military Project: legacies of the violent peace', *Latin American Perspectives*, 26, 2 (1999) pp. 92–107.

Schmid, H., 'Peace research and politics', *Journal of Peace Research*, 5, 3 (1968) pp. 217–32.

Singer, M., 'Sri Lanka in 1990 – the ethnic strife continues', *Asia Survey*, 31, 2 (1991) pp. 140–5.

Skinner, Q., 'Meaning and understanding in the history of ideas', *History and Theory: Studies in the Philosophy of History*, 8, 1 (1969) pp. 3–53.

Slim, H., 'The continuing metamorphosis of the humanitarian practitioner: some new colours for an endangered chameleon', *Disasters*, 19, 2 (1995) pp. 110–26.

Slim, H., 'Why protect civilians? Innocence, immunity and enmity in war', *International Affairs*, 79, 3 (2003) pp. 481–501.

Smith, R.P., 'Quantitative methods in peace research', *Journal of Peace Research*, 35, 4 (1998) pp. 418–27.

Spiegel, P.B., M. Sheik, B.A. Woodruff and G. Burnham, 'The accuracy of mortality reporting in displaced persons camps during the post-emergency phase', *Disasters*, 25, 2 (2001) pp. 172–80.

Stedman, S.J., 'Spoiler problems in peace processes', *International Security*, 22, 2 (Fall 1997) pp. 5–53.

Steenkamp, C. 'The legacy of war: conceptualizing a "culture of violence" to explain violence after peace accords', *The Round Table: The Commonwealth Journal of International Affairs*, 94, 379 (2005) pp. 253–67.

Thomas, N.H, 'Land reform in Zimbabwe', *Third World Quarterly*, 24, 4 (2003) pp. 691–712 at p. 700.

Walter, B.F., 'The critical barrier to civil war settlement', *International Organization*, 51, 3 (1997) pp. 335–64.

Walter, B.F., 'Designing transitions from civil war: demobilization, democratization and commitments to peace', *International Security*, 24, 1 (Summer 1999) pp. 127–55.

Books and chapters in books

Acheson, D., *Present at the Creation: My Years in the State Department* (New York: W.W. Norton & Company, 1969).

Adamson, F.B., 'International Democracy Assistance in Uzbekistan and Kyrgyzstan', in S.E. Mendelson and J.K. Glenn (eds), *The Power and Limits of NGOs: A Critical Look at Building Democracy in Eastern Europe and Eurasia* (New York: Columbia University Press, 2002) pp. 177–206.

Addison T. and A. Roe (eds) *Fiscal Policy for Development, Poverty, Reconstruction and Growth* (Basingstoke: Palgrave Macmillan, 2004).

Addison, T., A.R. Chowdhury and S.M. Murshed, 'The Fiscal Dimensions of Conflict and Reconstruction', in T. Addison and A. Roe (eds) *Fiscal Policy for Development, Poverty, Reconstruction and Growth* (Basingstoke: Palgrave Macmillan, 2004) pp. 260–73.

Aldrich, R.J. (ed.) *Witness to War: Diaries of the Second World War in Europe and the Middle East* (London: Corgi, 2005).

Appleby, R.S., *The Ambivalence of the Sacred: Religion, Violence and Reconciliation* (Lanham, MD: Rowman & Littlefield, 2000).

Azar, E.E., *The Management of Protracted Social Conflict: Theory and Cases* (Aldershot: Dartmouth Publishing, 1990).

Bailey, S., *Peace is a Process* (London: Quaker Home Service, 1993).

Ball, N., 'The Challenge of Rebuilding War-torn Societies', in C.A. Crocker, F.O. Hampson and P. Aall (eds) *Turbulent Peace: The Challenges of Managing International Conflict* (Washington, DC: United States Institute of Peace Press, 2001) pp. 719–36.

Bastian, S. and R. Luckham (eds) *Can Democracy be Designed? The Politics of Institutional Choice in Conflict-torn Societies* (London: Zed Books, 2003a).

Bastian, S. and Luckham, R., 'Introduction: Can Democracy be Designed?', in S. Bastian and R. Luckham (eds) *Can Democracy be Designed? The Politics of Institutional Choice in Conflict-Torn Societies* (London: Zed Books, 2003b) pp. 1–13.

Baudrillard, J., *The Gulf War Did Not Take Place* (Indianapolis, IN: Indiana University Press, 1995).

Bellamy, A., P. Williams and S. Griffin, *Understanding Peacekeeping* (Cambridge: Polity, 2004).

Birn, D., *The League of Nations Union, 1918–1945* (Oxford: Clarendon, 1981).

Bose, S., *Bosnia after Dayton: Nationalist Partition and International Intervention* (London: Hurst, 2002a).

Bose, S., 'Flawed Mediation, Chaotic Implementation: The 1987 Indo-Sri Lanka Peace Agreement', in S.J. Stedman, D. Rothchild and E. Cousens (eds) *Ending Civil Wars: The Implementation of Peace Agreements* (Boulder, CO: Lynne Rienner, 2002b) pp. 631–59.

Boulding, K., *Stable Peace* (Austin, TX: University of Texas Press, 1978).

Bourdieu, P., *Language and Symbolic Power* (Cambridge: Polity, 1992).

Boutros-Ghali, B., *An Agenda for Peace: Preventive Diplomacy, Peacemaking and Peace-Keeping* (New York: United Nations, 1992).

Boyce, J., *Investing in Peace: Aid and Conditionality After Civil Wars* (Oxford: Oxford University Press and Institute of Strategic Studies, 2002).

Braddon, D., *Exploding the Myth? The Peace Dividend, Regions and Market Adjustment* (Amsterdam: Harwood Academic Publishers, 2000).

Bratton, M., 'Second Elections in Africa', in L. Diamond and M.F. Plattner (eds) *Democratization in Africa* (Baltimore, MD: The Johns Hopkins University Press, 1999) pp. 18–33.

Brauer J. and K. Hartley (eds) *The Economics of Regional Security: NATO: The Mediterranean and Southern Africa* (Amsterdam: Harwood Academic Publishers, 2000).

Brown, M.E., 'The Causes of Internal Conflicts: An Overview', in M.E. Brown, O.R. Coté Jr., S.M. Lynn-Jones and S.E. Miller (eds) *Nationalism and Ethnic Conflict* (Cambridge, MA: MIT Press, 1997) pp. 3–25.

Brown, M.E., O.R. Coté, S.M. Lynne Jones and S.E. Miller (eds) *Debating the Democratic Peace* (Cambridge, MA: MIT Press, 1996).

Brück, T., 'The Economics of Civil War in Mozambique', in J. Brauer and K. Hartley (eds) *The Economics of Regional Security: NATO: The Mediterranean and Southern Africa* (Amsterdam: Harwood Academic Publishers, 2000) pp. 191–215.

Brynen, R., 'Palestinian-Lebanese Relations: A Political Analysis', in D. Collings (eds), *Peace for Lebanon? From War to Reconstruction* (Boulder, CO: Lynne Rienner, 1994) pp. 83–96.

Brynen, R., *A Very Political Economy: Peacebuilding and Foreign Aid in the West Bank and Gaza* (Washington, DC: United States Institute of Peace Press, 2000).

Burnell, P. (ed.) *Democracy Assistance: International Cooperation for Democratization* (London: Frank Cass, 2000).

Burton, J., *Violence Explained* (Manchester: Manchester University Press, 1997).

Callinicos, A., *Against the Third Way* (Cambridge: Polity, 2001).

Carment, D. and P. James, 'Ethnic Conflict at the International Level: An Appraisal of Theories and Evidence', in D. Carment and P. James (eds) *Wars in the Midst of Peace: The International Politics of Ethnic Conflict* (Pittsburgh, PA: University of Pittsburgh Press, 1997a) pp. 252–63.

Carment, D. and P. James (eds) *Wars in the Midst of Peace: The International Politics of Ethnic Conflict* (Pittsburgh, PA: University of Pittsburgh Press, 1997b).

Chadda, M., *Building Democracy in South Asia: India, Nepal, Pakistan* (Boulder, CO: Lynne Rienner, 2000).

Chandler, D., *Bosnia: Faking Democracy after Dayton* (London: Pluto, 1999).

Chua, A., *World on Fire: How Exporting Free Market Democracy Breeds Ethnic Hatred and Global Instability* (London: Heinemann, 2004).

Colletta, N.J. and M.L. Cullen, *Violent Conflict and the Transformation of Social Capital: Lessons from Cambodia, Rwanda, Guatemala and Somalia* (Washington, DC: World Bank, 2000).

Collier, P., *Breaking the Conflict Trap: Civil War and Development Policy* (Washington, DC and New York: World Bank and Oxford University Press, 2003).

Connor, W., *Ethnonationalism: The Quest for Understanding* (Princeton, NJ: Princeton University Press, 1994).

Conteh-Morgan, E., *Collective Political Violence: An Introduction to the Theories and Cases of Violent Conflicts* (New York: Routledge, 2004).

Cooke, W. and U. Kothari (eds) *Participation: The New Tyranny* (London: Zed Books, 2002).

Cooper, R. and M. Berdal, 'Outside Intervention in Ethnic Conflict', in M. Brown (ed.) *Ethnic Conflict and International Security* (Princeton, NJ: Princeton University Press, 1993) pp. 181–205.

Cousens, E.M., 'From Missed Opportunities to Over-compensation: Implementing the Dayton Agreement in Bosnia', in S.J. Stedman, D. Rothchild and E.M. Cousens (eds) *Ending Civil Wars: The Implementation of Peace Agreements* (Boulder, CO: Lynne Rienner, 2002) pp. 531–66.

Cox, M., G.J. Ikenberry and T. Inoguchi (eds) *American Democracy Promotion: Impulses, Strategies and Impacts* (New York: Oxford University Press, 2000).

Cracknell, B.E., *Evaluating Development Aid: Issues, Problems and Solutions* (Thousand Oaks, CA: Sage, 2000).

Crocker, C.A., F.O. Hampson and P. Aall (eds) *Turbulent Peace: The Challenges of Managing International Conflict* (Washington, DC: United States Institute of Peace Press, 2001).

Darby, J., *The Effects of Violence on Peace Processes* (Washington, DC: United States Institute of Peace Press, 2001).

Darby, J. 'Borrowing and Lending In Peace Processes', in J. Darby and R. Mac Ginty (eds) *Contemporary Peacemaking: Conflict, Violence and Peace Processes* (Basingstoke: Palgrave Macmillan, 2003) pp. 245–55.

Darby, J. and R. Mac Ginty (eds) *Contemporary Peacemaking: Conflict, Violence and Peace Processes* (Basingstoke: Palgrave Macmillan, 2003).

Debiel, T. and A. Klein, *Fragile Peace: State Failure, Violence and Development in Crisis Regions* (New York: Zed Books, 2002).

Dillon, E.J., *The Inside Story of the Peace Conference* (New York: Harper, 1920).

Dixit, J., 'Indian Involvement in Sri Lanka and the Indo-Sri Lanka Agreement of 1987: A Retrospective Evaluation', in K. Rupesinghe (ed.) *Negotiating Peace in Sri Lanka: Efforts, Failures and Lessons* (London: International Alert, 1998) pp. 31–45.

Dunlop, J.B., *Russia Confronts Chechnya: Roots of a Separatist Conflict* (Cambridge: Cambridge University Press, 1998).

Du Toit, P., *South Africa's Brittle Peace: The Problem of Post-settlement Violence* (Basingstoke: Palgrave Macmillan, 2001).

Dyson, R.W., *Aquinas: Political Writings* (Cambridge: Cambridge University Press, 2002).

Early, G. (ed.) *The Muhammad Ali Reader* (New York: Rob Weisbach Books, 1998).

Egeland, J., 'The Oslo Accord: Multiparty Facilitation through the Norwegian Channel', in C.A. Crocker, F.O. Hampson and P. Aall (eds) *Herding Cats: Multiparty Mediation in a Complex World* (Washington, DC: United States Institute of Peace Press, 1999) pp. 529–46.

Elsthtain, J.B. (ed.) *Just War Theory* (Oxford: Blackwell, 1992).

Evans, J. (ed.) *Elsdon Best: Notes on the Art of War* (Auckland: Reed, 2001).

Evans, M. (ed.) *Just War Theory: A Reappraisal* (Edinburgh: Edinburgh University Press, 2005).

Falk, R., 'Global Civil Society and the Democratic Prospect', in B. Holden (ed.), *Global Democracy: Key Debates* (London: Routledge, 2000) pp. 162–78.

Farer, T., 'Introduction', in T. Farer (ed.) *Transnational Crime in the Americas* (New York: Routledge, 1999) pp. xiii–xvi.

Farer, T. (ed.) *Transnational Crime in the Americas* (New York: Routledge, 1999).

Flintan, F. and I. Tamrat, 'Spilling Blood over Water? The Case of Ethiopia', in J. Lind and K. Sturman (eds) *Scarcity and Surfeit: The Ecology of Africa's Conflicts* (Pretoria: Institute for Security Studies, 2002) pp. 243–319.

Gaddis, J.L., *The United States and the End of the Cold War: Implications, Reconsiderations, Provocations* (Oxford: Oxford University Press, 1992).

German, T., *Russia's Chechen War* (London: RoutledgeCurzon, 2003).

Glaeser, E., *An Overview of Crime and Punishment* (Washington, DC: World Bank, 1999).

Glenny, M., *The Fall of Yugoslavia* (London: Penguin, 1996).

Goldsmith, P., L. Abura and J. Switzer, 'Oil and Water in Sudan', in J. Lind and K. Sturman (eds) *Scarcity and Surfeit: The Ecology of Africa's Conflicts* (Pretoria: Institute for Security Studies, 2002) pp. 187–241.

Good, K., *The Liberal Model and Africa* (Basingstoke: Palgrave, 2002).

Gopin, M., 'What Do I Need to Know about Religion and Conflict?', in J.P. Lederach and J.M. Jenner (eds) *A Handbook of International Peacebuilding* (San Francisco, CA: Jossey Bass, 2002), pp. 107–13.

Gordenker, L. and T. Weiss, 'Devolving Responsibilities: A Framework for Analysing NGOs and Services', in T. Weiss (ed.) *Beyond UN Subcontracting: Task-sharing with Regional Security Arrangements and Service-providing NGOs* (Basingstoke: Macmillan, 1998) pp. 30–45.

Guelke, A. 'The Politics of Imitation: The Role of Comparison in Peace Processes', in A. Guelke (ed.) *Democracy and Ethnic Conflict: Advancing Peace in a Deeply Divided Society* (Basingstoke: Palgrave Macmillan, 2004) pp. 168–84.

Gurr, T., *People Versus States: Minorities at Risk in the New Century* (Washington, DC: United States Institute of Peace Press, 2000).

Gurr, T. and B. Harff, *Ethnic Conflict in World Politics* (Boulder, CO: Westview, 1994).

Haskell, J., *Direct Democracy or Representative Government? Dispelling the Populist Myth* (Boulder, CO: Westview, 2001).

Haynes, J., *Democracy in the Developing World: Africa, Asia, Latin America and the Middle East* (Cambridge: Polity, 2001).

Henderson, E.A., *Democracy and War: The End of an Illusion?* (Boulder, CO: Lynne Rienner, 2002).

Heyn, U., *Peacemaking in Medieval Europe: A Historical and Bibliographical Guide* (Claremont, CA: Regina Books, 1997).

Hogan, M., *The Marshall Plan: America, Britain, and the Reconstruction of Western Europe, 1947–1952* (Cambridge: Cambridge University Press, 1987).

Hopkinson, M., *Green against Green: The Irish Civil War* (Dublin: Gill & Macmillan, 2004).

Horowitz, D.L., *Ethnic Groups in Conflict* (Berkeley, CA: University of California Press, 1983).

Horowitz, I.L., *War and Peace in Contemporary Social and Philosophical Theory*, 2nd edn (London: Souvenir Press, 1973).

Howard, M., *War in European History* (Oxford: Oxford University Press, 1976).

Howard, M., *War and the Liberal Conscience* (London: Temple Smith, 1978).

Howard, M., *The Invention of Peace: Reflections on War and International Order* (New Haven, CT: Yale University Press, 2000).

Hill, S. and S. Malik, *Peacekeeping and the United Nations* (Aldershot: Dartmouth, 1996).

Hutt, M. (ed.) *Himalayan 'People's War': Nepal's Maoist Rebellion* (London: Hurst, 2004).

Ignatieff, M., *Empire Lite: Nation-building in Bosnia, Kosovo and Afghanistan* (London: Vintage, 2003).

Ikenberry, G.J. (ed.) *America Unrivalled: The Future of the Balance of Power* (Ithaca, NY: Cornell University Press, 2002).

Ikenberry, G.J.,'Democracy, Institutions, and American Restraint', in G.J. Ikenberry (ed.) *America Unrivalled: The Future of the Balance of Power* (Ithaca, NY: Cornell University Press, 2002) pp. 213–38.

Jinadu, L.A. (ed.), *The Political Economy of Peace and Security in Africa* (Harare: ANPS Books, 2000).

Judah, T., *Kosovo: War and Revenge* (New Haven, CT and London: Yale University Press, 2000).

Junne G. and W. Verkoren (eds) *Postconflict Development: Meeting New Challenges* (Boulder, CO: Lynne Reinner, 2005).

Kagan, R., *Paradise and Power: America and Europe in the New World Order* (London: Atlantic Books, 2003).

Kaldor, M., *New and Old Wars: Organized Violence in a Global Era* (Cambridge: Polity Press, 1999).

Kamphuis, B., 'Economic Policy for Building Peace', in G. Junne and W. Verkoren (eds) *Postconflict Development: Meeting New Challenges* (Boulder, CO: Lynne Reinner, 2005) pp. 185–210.

Kant, I., *Perpetual Peace* (New York: Macmillan, 1957).

Kaufman, S., *Modern Hatreds: The Symbolic Politics of Ethnic War* (Ithaca, NY: Cornell University Press, 2001).

Keesing, R.M., *Custom and Confrontation: The Kwaio Struggle for Cultural Autonomy* (Chicago, IL: University of Chicago Press, 1992).

Kemp, G. and D. Fry (eds) *Keeping the Peace: Conflict Resolution and Peaceful Societies around the World* (New York: Routledge, 2004).

Kennan, G.F., *Memoirs 1925–1950* (London: Hutchinson, 1968).

Kennedy, P., *The Rise and Fall of the Great Powers: Economic Change and Military Conflict from 1500 to 2000* (London: Fontana, 1989).

Kertzer, D. and D. Ariel (eds) *Census and Identity: The Politics of Race, Ethnicity and Language in National Censuses* (Cambridge: Cambridge University Press, 2002).

Khaldi, R., *Resurrecting Empire: Western Footprints and America's Perilous Path in the Middle East* (London: IB Tauris, 2004).

Kissinger, H., *Diplomacy* (New York: Simon & Schuster, 1994).

Kline, H., *State Building and Conflict Resolution in Colombia, 1986–1994* (Tuscaloosa, AL: University of Alabama Press, 2001).

Kymlicka, W., *Multicultural Citizenship* (Oxford: Clarendon Press, 1995).

Leader N. and J. Macrae (eds) *Terms of Engagement: Conditions and Conditionality in Humanitarian Action* (London: Overseas Development Institute, 2000).

Lee, R. and E. Stank (eds) *Researching Violence: Essays on Methodology and Measurement* (London: Routledge, 2001).

Licklider, R., 'Obstacles to Peace Settlements', in C.A. Crocker, F.O. Hampson and P. Aall (eds) *Herding Cats: Multiparty Mediation in a Complex World* (Washington, DC: United States Institute of Peace Press, 1999), pp. 697–718.

Lieven, A., *Chechnya: Tombstone of Russian Power* (New Haven, CT and London: Yale University Press, 1999).

Lind, J. and K. Sturman (eds) *Scarcity and Surfeit: The Ecology of Africa's Conflicts* (Pretoria: Institute for Security Studies, 2002).

Luttwak, E., 'The curse of inconclusive intervention', in C.A. Crocker, F.O. Hampson and P. Aall (eds) *Turbulent Peace: The Challenges of Managing*

International Conflict (Washington, DC: United States Institute of Peace Press, 2001) pp. 265–72.

Lynne Jones, S.M., 'Preface', in M.E. Brown, O.R. Coté, S.M. Lynne Jones and S.E. Miller (eds) *Debating the Democratic Peace* (Cambridge, MA: MIT Press, 1996) pp. ix–xxxiii.

Mac Ginty, R., 'Crime after Peace Accords', in J. Darby (ed.), *Violence and Reconstruction* (South Bend, IN: University of Notre Dame Press, 2006).

MacMillan, J., *On Liberal Peace: Democracy, War and the International Order* (London: I.B. Taurus, 1998).

Makdisi, S., *The Lessons of Lebanon: The Economics of War and Development* (London: I.B. Tauris, 2004).

Mandelbaum, M., *The Ideas that Conquered the World: Peace, Democracy and Free Markets in the Twenty-first Century* (New York: PublicAffairs, 2002)

Marks, S., *The Illusion of Peace: International Relations in Europe 1918–1933* (London: Macmillan, 1976).

Maslow, A.H., *Motivation and Personality*, 3rd edn (New York: Harper Collins, 1987).

Matveeva, A., 'Chechnya: Drive for Independence or Hotbed for Islamic Terrorism?', in P. van Tongeren, H. van de Veen and J. Verhoeven (eds) *Searching for Peace in Europe and Eurasia: An Overview of Conflict Prevention and Peacebuilding Activities* (Boulder, CO: Lynne Rienner, 2002) pp. 354–73.

McKeogh, C., *Innocent Civilians: The Morality of Killing in War* (Basingstoke: Palgrave Macmillan, 2002).

McKittrick, D., *The Nervous Peace* (Belfast: Blackstaff, 1996).

Melzer, Y., *Concepts of Just War* (Leyden: A.W. Sijthoff, 1975).

Miall, H., O. Ramsbotham and T. Woodhouse, *Contemporary Conflict Resolution: The Prevention, Management and Transformation of Deadly Conflicts* (Cambridge: Polity, 2000).

Milward, A., *The European Rescue of the Nation-State* (London: Routledge, 1992).

Mitchell, C., 'Necessitous Man and Conflict Resolution: More Basic Questions about Basic Human Needs Theory', in J. Burton (ed.) *Conflict: Human Needs Theory* (Basingstoke: Macmillan, 1990) pp. 149–76.

Mitchell, C., 'Mennonite Approaches to Peace and Conflict Resolution', in C. Sampson and J.P. Lederach (eds) *From the Ground Up: Mennonite Contributions to International Peacebuilding* (Oxford: Oxford University Press, 2000) pp. 218–32.

Mitchell, C., 'Mediation and Ending Conflicts', in J. Darby and R. Mac Ginty (eds) *Contemporary Peacemaking: Conflict, Violence and Peace Processes* (Houndmills: Palgrave Macmillan, 2003) pp. 77–86.

Moeller, S., *Compassion Fatigue: How the Media Sells Disease, Famine, War and Death* (New York: Routledge, 1999).

Moser C. and C. McIlwaine, *Violence in a Post-conflict Context: Urban Poor Perceptions from Guatemala* (Washington, DC: World Bank, 2001).

Moynihan, D.P., *Pandaemonium: Ethnicity in International Politics* (New York: Oxford University Press, 1993).

Moyroud, C., and J. Katunga, 'Coltan Exploitation in the Eastern Democratic Republic of Congo', in J. Lind and K. Sturman (eds) *Scarcity and Surfeit: The Ecology of Africa's Conflicts* (Pretoria: Institute for Security Studies, 2002) pp. 159–85.

Natsios, A., 'An NGO Perspective', in I. Zartman and J. Rasmussen (eds) *Peacemaking in International Conflict: Methods and Techniques* (Washington, DC: United States Institute of Peace Press, 1997) pp. 337–61.

Nicolson, H., *Peacemaking 1919* (London: Constable, 1944).

Nordstrom, C., *Shadows of War: Violence, Power, and International Profiteering in the Twenty-first Century* (Berkeley, CA: University of California Press, 2004).

Nüsse, A., *Muslim Palestine: The Ideology of Hamas* (Amsterdam: Harwood Academic Publishers, 1998).

Obi, C., 'Economic Adjustment and the Deepening Environmental Conflict in Africa', in L.A. Jinadu (ed.) *The Political Economy of Peace and Security in Africa* (Harare: ANPS Books, 2000) pp. 131–47.

Olsen, G., 'Neo-medievalism in Africa: Whither Government-to-government Relations between Africa and the European Union?', in N. Winn (ed.) *Neo-medievalism and Civil Wars* (London: Frank Cass, 2004) pp. 94–120.

O'Neill, W., *Kosovo: An Unfinished Peace* (Boulder, CO: Lynne Rienner, 2002).

Owen, J.M., 'How Liberalism Produces Democratic Peace', in M.E. Brown, O.R. Coté, S.M. Lynne Jones and S.E. Miller (eds) *Debating the Democratic Peace* (Cambridge, MA: MIT Press, 1996) pp. 116–54.

Paris, R., 'Wilson's Ghost: The Faulty Assumptions of Postconflict Peacebuilding', in C.A. Crocker, F.O. Hampson and P. Aall (eds) *Turbulent Peace: The Challenges of Managing International Conflict* (Washington, DC: United States Institute of Peace Press, 2001) pp. 765–84.

Petkov, K., *The Kiss of Peace: Ritual, Self, and Society in the High and Late Medieval West* (Leiden: Brill, 2003).

Prunier, G., *From Genocide to Continental War: The Congo Conflict and the Crisis of Contemporary Africa* (London: Hurst, 2005).

Rapport, D. and L. Weinberg (eds) *The Democratic Experience and Political Violence* (London: Frank Cass, 2001).

Rasmussen, J., 'Peacemaking in the Twenty-first Century: New Rules, New Roles and New Actors', in Zartman and Rasmussen (eds) *Peacemaking in International Conflict*, pp. 23–50.

Rawls, J., *The Law of Peoples* (Cambridge, MA: Harvard University Press, 1999).

Reilly, B., 'Democratic Validation', in Darby and Mac Ginty (eds) *Contemporary Peacemaking: Conflict, Violence and Peace Processes* (Basingstoke: Palgrave Macmillan, 2003) pp. 174–83.

Richani, N., *Systems of Violence: The Political Economy of War and Peace in Colombia* (Albany, NY: State University of New York Press, 2002).

Richards, P., *Fighting for the Rain Forest: War, Youth and Resources in Sierra Leone* (London and Oxford: The International African Institute and James Currey, 2002).

Richmond, O.P., *The Transformation of Peace: Peace as Governance in Contemporary Conflict Endings* (Basingstoke: Palgrave, 2006).

Roche, C., *Impact Assessment for Development Agencies: Learning to Value Change* (Oxford: Oxfam, 1999).

Rowan, B., *The Armed Peace: Life and Death after the Ceasefires* (Edinburgh: Mainstream Publishing, 2004).

Ryan, S., *The United Nations and International Politics* (New York: St. Martin's Press, 2000).

Said, E., *The End of the Peace Process: Oslo and After*, 2nd edn (London: Granta, 2002).

Salih, M.A.M. *African Democracies and African Politics* (London: Pluto, 2001).

Sandbrook, R., *Closing the Circle: Democratization and Development in Africa* (London: Zed Books, 2000).

Scott, D., *Ask that Mountain: The Story of Parihaka* (Auckland: Reed/Southern Cross, 1994).

Sisk, T.D. 'Elections – Conflict Management in Africa: Conclusions and Recommendations', in T.D. Sisk and A. Reynolds, *Elections and Conflict Management in Africa* (Washington, DC: United States Institute of Peace Press, 1998) p. 147.

Sisk, T.D. and A. Reynolds, *Elections and Conflict Management in Africa* (Washington, DC: United States Institute of Peace Press, 1998).

Sites, P., 'Legitimacy and Human Needs', in J. Burton and F. Dukes (eds) *Conflict: Readings in Management and Resolution* (Basingstoke: Macmillan, 1990) pp. 117–44.

Smith, A.D., 'Interpretations of National Identity', in A. Dieckhoff and N. Gutiérrez (eds) *Modern Roots: Studies of National Identity* (Aldershot: Ashgate, 2001) pp. 21–43.

Smith, R., 'The Unfinished Tasks of Liberalism', in B. Yack (ed.) *Liberalism without Illusions: Essays on Liberal Theory and the Political Vision of Judith N. Shklar* (Chicago, IL: Chicago University Press, 1996) pp. 241–62.

Smyth, M. and G. Robinson (eds) *Researching Violently Divided Societies: Ethical and Methodological Issues* (London and Tokyo: Pluto and United Nations University Press, 2001).

Sollenberg M (ed.) *States in Armed Conflict 1996* (Uppsala: Department of Peace and Conflict Research, Uppsala University, 1997).

Soros, G., *The Bubble of American Supremacy: Correcting the Misuses of American Power* (London: Weidenfeld & Nicolson, 2004).

Stedman, S.J., 'Policy Implications', in S.J. Stedman, D. Rothchild and E. Cousens (eds) *Ending Civil Wars: The Implementation of Peace Agreements* (Boulder, CO: Lynne Rienner, 2002) pp. 633–71.

Stedman, S.J., 'Peace Processes and the Challenges of Violence', in J. Darby and R. Mac Ginty (eds) *Contemporary Peacemaking: Conflict, Violence and Peace Processes* (Basingstoke: Palgrave Macmillan, 2003) pp. 103–13.

Stephanopoulos, G., *All Too Human: A Political Education* (London: Hutchinson, 1999).

Tajfel, H. (ed.) *Differentiation between Social Groups: Studies in the Social Psychology of Intergroup Relations* (London: Academic Press, 1978a).

Tajfel, H., 'Social Categorization, Social Identity and Social Comparison', in H. Tajfel (ed.) *Differentiation between Social Groups: Studies in the Social Psychology of Intergroup Relations* (London: Academic Press, 1978b) pp. 61–76.

Tilly, C., 'Violent and Non-violent Trajectories in Contentious Politics', in K. Worcester, S. Bermanzohn and M. Ungar (eds) *Violence and Politics: Globalization's Paradox* (New York: Routledge, 2002) pp. 13–31.

Trefon, T. (ed.) *Reinventing Order in the Congo: How People Respond to State Failure in Kinshasa* (London: Zed Books, 2004).

Turner, J.C., M. Hogg, P. Oakes, S. Reicher and M. Wetherell, *Rediscovering the Social Group: A Self-categorization Theory* (Oxford: Blackwell, 1987).

Usher, U., *Dispatches from Palestine: The Rise and Fall of the Oslo Peace Process* (London: Pluto, 1999).

Vaněček, V., *The Universal Peace Organization of King George of Bohemia: A Fifteenth Century Plan for World Peace 1462–1464* (Prague: Publishing House of the Czechoslovak Academy of Sciences, 1964).

Vayada, A.P., *Maori Warfare* (Wellington: Reed, 1960).

Vayada, A.P., *War in Ecological Perspective: Persistence, Change and Adaptive Processes in Three Oceanian Societies* (New York: Plenum Press, 1976).

Verkoren, W., 'Bringing It All Together: A Case Study of Cambodia', in Junne and Verkoren (eds) *Postconflict Development: Meeting New Challenges* pp. 289–306.

Wallenstein, P. and Sollenberg, M., 'Armed Conflicts, Conflict Termination and Peace Agreements, 1989–96', in M. Sollenberg (ed.)., *States in Armed Conflict 1996* (Uppsala: Department of Peace and Conflict Research, Uppsala University, 1997) pp. 7–12.

Walzer, M. *Just and Unjust Wars: A Moral Argument with Historical Illustrations* (New York: Basic Books, 1992).

Watson, G.R., *The Oslo Accords: International Law and the Israeli-Palestinian Peace Agreements* (Oxford: Oxford University Press, 2000).

Weiss T. (ed.) *Beyond UN Subcontracting: Task-sharing with Regional Security Arrangements and Service-providing NGOs* (Basingstoke: Macmillan, 1998).

Wells, L. and G. Marwell, *Self-esteem: Its Conceptualisation and Measurement* (London: Sage, 1976).

White, N.D., *Keeping the Peace: The United Nations and the Maintenance of International Peace and Security* (Manchester: Manchester University Press, 1993).

Williams, A., *Failed Imagination? New World Orders of the Twentieth Century* (Manchester: Manchester University Press, 1998).

Winn, N. (ed.) *Neo-medievalism and Civil Wars* (London: Frank Cass, 2004).

Woodward, S.L., 'Economic Priorities for Successful Peace Implementation', in S.J. Stedman, D. Rothchild and E.M. Cousens (eds) *Ending Civil Wars: The Implementation of Peace Agreements*, pp. 183–214.

Yoder, J.H. *When War is Unjust: Being Honest in Just War Thinking* (New York: Orbis, 1996).

Young, C., 'Explaining the Conflict Potential of Ethnicity', in J. Darby and R. Mac Ginty (eds.) *Contemporary Peacemaking: Conflict, Violence and Peace Processes* (Basingstoke: Palgrave Macmillan, 2003) pp. 9–18.

Zahar, M.J., 'Peace by Unconventional Means: Lebanon's Taif Agreement', in S.J. Stedman, D. Rothchild and E.M. Cousens (eds) *Ending Civil Wars: The Implementation of Peace Agreements* (Boulder, CO: Lynne Rienner, 2002) pp. 567–97 at p. 567.

Zahar, M.J., 'Reframing the Spoiler Debate in Peace Processes', in J. Darby and R. Mac Ginty (eds) *Contemporary Peacemaking: Conflict, Violence and Peace Processes* (Basingstoke: Palgrave Macmillan, 2003) pp. 114–24.

Zartman I. and J. Rasmussen (eds) *Peacemaking in International Conflict: Methods and Techniques* (Washington, DC: United States Institute of Peace Press, 1997).

Index